I0117593

Is Secession Treason?

Is Secession Treason?

Albert Bledsoe
Edited by Paul Dennis Sporer

QUANTERNESS PRESS

ANZA PUBLISHING, Chester, NY 10918
Quanterness Press is an imprint of Anza Publishing
Copyright © 2005 by Anza Publishing

This is a new, unabridged edition of *Is Davis a traitor; or, Was secession a constitutional right previous to the war of 1861?* by Albert Taylor Bledsoe (1809-1877), originally published by the author in 1866.

Library of Congress Cataloguing-in-Publication Data
Bledsoe, Albert Taylor, 1809-1877.
   [Is Davis a traitor?]
   Is secession treason? / Albert Bledsoe;
   edited by Paul Dennis Sporer.
     p.   cm.
   "This is a new, unabridged edition of Is Davis a traitor; or, Was secession a constitutional right previous to the war of 1861? by Albert Taylor Bledsoe, 1809-1877, originally published by the author in 1866."
   Includes index.
   ISBN 1-932490-19-1 (hardcover : alk. paper)
   1. Secession—Southern States.
   2. Davis, Jefferson, 1808-1889.
   3. Confederate States of America—Politics and government.
   4. United States—History—Civil War, 1861-1865.
   5. United States—Politics and government—1861-1865.
   6. Constitutional history—United States.
I. Sporer, Paul D. II. Title.
E459.B65 2005
973.7'13--dc22   2005021075

All rights reserved. No part of this publication may be reproduced, stored in a retrieval system, or transmitted, in any form or by any means, electronic, mechanical, photocopying, recording or otherwise, without the prior permission of the copyright holder.

Visit AnzaPublishing.com for more information on outstanding authors and titles. Please support our efforts to restore great literature to a place of prominence in our culture.

∞ This book is printed on acid-free paper.
ISBN: 1-932490-19-1 (hardcover)
ISBN: 1-932490-80-9 (softcover)

CONTENTS

Editor's Preface   *i*

I Opinions about Secession   1

II The Issue or Point in Controversy   5

III The Idea That the States "Acceded" to the Constitution   9

IV The First Resolution Passed by the Convention of 1787   14

V The Constitution of 1787 a Compact, Part 1   17

VI The Constitution of 1787 a Compact, Part 2   23

VII The Constitution of 1787 a Compact, Part 3   30

VIII The Constitution of 1787 a Compact, Part 4   36

IX The Constitution of 1787 a Compact, Part 5   44

X The Constitution of 1787 a Compact, Part 6   50

XI The Constitution of 1787 a Compact, Part 7   56

XII The Constitution of 1787 a Compact, Part 8   69

XIII Mr. Webster Versus Mr. Webster   72

XIV The Will of the People in the Making of the Constitution   79

XV Do the People of America Form One Nation?   82
    The Attempt of Mr. Curtis to Show That the People of America
      Formed one nation, or political community   *87*
    The Use of the Term People   *91*

XVI Arguments in Favor of the Right of Secession   96
    Argument in Favor of Secession from the Doctrine of
       Reserved Rights   96
    Argument from the Sovereignty of the States   99
    Argument from the Silence of the Constitution   105
    Argument from the Fundamental Principle of the Union   108
    Argument from the Right of Self-government   109
    Argument from the Opinion of Well-informed and
       Intelligent Foreigners   119
    Argument from the Virginia Ordinance of Ratification   121

XVII Arguments Against the Right of Secession   125
    Argument from "The Very Words" of the Constitution   125
    Argument from the Wisdom of the Fathers   128
    Argument from the Opinion of Mr. Madison   132
    Argument from the Opinion of Hamilton   136
    Argument from the Very Idea of a Nation   138
    Argument from the Purchase of Louisiana, Florida, &c.   139
    Argument from Analogy   139

XVIII Is Secession Treason?   143
    Massachusetts and the Hartford Convention   146
    Did the South Condemn Secession in 1815?   154
    Thomas Jefferson on the Right of Secession   156
    The Political Creed of the State-rights Party   161
    The Decline of the Doctrine of the Sovereignty of the
       States, and its Causes   162

XIX The Causes of Secession   166
    The Balance of Power   166
    The Relative Decline of the South in the New Union   184
    The Formation of a Faction   189
    Summary of Other Causes of Secession   196

XX The Legislators of 1787 as Political Prophets   198

    Notes   203

    Index   213

Editor's Preface

This remarkable book represents not only the pinnacle of Albert Bledsoe's achievements, but is a landmark in American political literature. After the Southern States seceded from the Union, Confederate leaders directed Bledsoe to write a comprehensive legal justification of their brazenly divisive act. He certainly did not fail his patrons. With power and eloquence, Bledsoe discusses the complex issues surrounding Secession, and argues that its result, the Confederacy, was not in violation of Constitutional law; he further states that the Federal government acted with greedy self-interest by invading the "new nation".

Bledsoe was a man of tremendous capability and knowledge. He utilized these attributes in the service of a remarkably rich career, at times being a soldier, professor of mathematics, lawyer, and church minister. Highly respected by his peers, Bledsoe developed the reputation of a fighter, someone who was willing to gamble everything on promoting and defending what he believed were fundamental ethical principles. The greatest compliment, however, might have come from the lawyers representing Jefferson Davis, President of the Southern Confederacy: they used the present work as a key source of material in defense of their client from charges of treason.

Bledsoe's peregrinations fortuitously brought him into contact with many persons who were to become major figures in American history. Thus, his work must be considered important, not only on account of his careful scholarship, but also because it reveals, one might say, the worldview of the Southern leadership in the Civil War period.

This edition is based on Bledsoe's self-published 1866 book. In order to preserve the author's intellectual and emotional vigor, we have kept alterations to a minimum. For the sake of consistency, we have modified several of the chapter titles. We have corrected a fair number of errors, such as incorrect punctuation, missing quotation marks, and footnotes in the wrong place. We have converted the original footnotes to more convenient endnotes, and have added a detailed index.

PAUL DENNIS SPORER

Chapter I

Opinions about Secession

The final judgment of history in relation to the war of 1861 will, in no small degree, depend on its verdict with respect to the right of secession. If, when this right was practically asserted by the South, it had been conceded by the North, there would not have been even a pretext for the tremendous conflict which followed. Is it not wonderful, then, that a question of such magnitude and importance should have been so little considered, or discussed? Perhaps no other question of political philosophy, or of international law, pregnant with such unutterable calamities, has ever been so partially and so superficially examined as the right of secession from the Federal Union of the United States. From first to last, it seems to have been decided by passion, and not by reason. The voice of reason, enlightened by the study of the facts of history and the principles of political philosophy, yet remains to be heard on the subject of secession.

No one, at present, denies that the States had a right to secede from the Union formed by the old Articles of Confederation. Indeed, this right was claimed and exercised by the States, when they withdrew from that Confederation in order to form "a more perfect Union." Yet, while that Union was standing and in favor with the people, the right of secession therefrom was vehemently denied. The reason of this is well stated by Mr. Madison in "The Federalist." Having explained and vindicated the right of the States, or any portion of them, to secede from the existing Union, he adds: "The time has been when it was incumbent on all of us to veil the ideas which this paragraph exhibits. The scene has now changed, and with it the part which the same motives dictate."[1] That is to say, the time has been when it became all Americans, as patriots and worshippers of the existing Union, to veil the right of secession; but now is the time to unveil this sacred right, and let the truth be seen! Accordingly, the Convention of 1787 unveiled this right, and the States, one after another, seceded from the Union;

though the Articles by which it was formed expressly declared that it should be "perpetual," or last forever.

The same thing happened, in a still greater degree, under the new and "more perfect Union." This, unlike the one for which it had been substituted, did not pronounce itself immortal. Still it was deemed incumbent on all men by Mr. Madison, and especially upon himself, to veil the right of secession from the new Union; which he, more than any other man, had labored to establish and preserve. But having exercised the right of secession from one compact between the States, how could he veil that right under another compact between the same parties? Having, for the benefit of his age, revealed the truth, how could he hope to hide it from all future ages? Having laid down the right of secession from one Federal Union, as the great fundamental law to which the new Union owed its very existence, how could he hope to cover it up again, and make the new compact forever binding on posterity? There is not, it is believed, in the whole range of literature, a sophism more ineffably weak and flimsy than the one employed by Mr. Madison to veil the right of secession from the new Union.

The first compact, says he, was made by the Legislatures of the States, and the second by the people themselves of the States. Hence, although the States had seceded from the first compact or Union, he supposed, or hoped, they would have no right to secede from the second.[2] The first compact was, it is true, originally adopted by the Legislatures of the States; but then it was approved by the people themselves, who lived under it as the Constitution and government of their choice. Were not the States, then, just as much bound by this compact, as if it had been originally made by the people themselves? What would be thought of an individual, who should approve and adopt as his own a contract made by his agent, and, having derived all the advantages of it, should seek to repudiate it on the ground that it was not originally entered into by himself? He would be deemed infamous. Yet, precisely such is the distinction and the logic of Mr. Madison, in his attempt to justify the act of secession from the first Union, and to deny the right of secession from the second Union between the same parties! The two compacts are construed differently; because the one was originally made by agents and afterwards ratified by the principals, and the other was originally made by the principals themselves Could any sophism be more weak or flimsy? Is it not, indeed, in the eye of reason, as thin as gossamer, as transparent as the air itself? Hopeless, indeed, must be the attempt to find a difference between the two cases, which shall establish the right of secession in the one and not in the other; since James Madison himself, with all his unsurpassed powers of logic and acute discrimination, was compelled to rely on so futile a distinction.

But the majority needed no veil, not even one as thin as that employed by Mr. Madison, to conceal the right of secession from their eyes. The mists raised by its own passions were amply sufficient for that purpose. The doctrine of secession was regarded, by the reigning majority, as simply equivalent to the destruction of "the best Government the world had ever seen," or was ever likely to see. Hence, before the dread tribunal of the sovereign majority, the touch of secession was political death. The public men of the country, and all aspirants after office, shrank front it as from plague, pestilence, and famine. As to whether secession was a Constitutional right or otherwise, the multitude knew nothing, and cared less; but still, in their passionate zeal, they denounced it as rebellion, treason, and every other crime in the dark catalogue of political offences. Their leaders, having studied the subject as little as themselves, were no less ignorant respecting the merits of the question, and even more fierce in denouncing secession as the sum of all villainies, treasons, and rebellions. Thus, what the logic of Mr. Madison failed to accomplish, was achieved by the rhetoric of angry politicians and the passions of an infuriated majority; that is, the right of secession was veiled. The object of this book is simply to appeal from the mad forum of passion to the calm tribunal of reason.

But why, it may be asked, appeal to reason? Has not the war of secession been waged, and the South subjugated? Can reason, however victorious, bind up the broken heart, or call the dead to life? Can reason cause the desolate, dark, waste places of the South to smile again, or the hearts of her downcast and dejected people to rejoice? Can reason strike the fetters from the limbs of the downtrodden white population of the South? True, alas! reason can do none of these things; but still she has a high office and duty to perform. For, however sore her calamities, all is not yet lost to our bleeding and beloved South. She still retains that which, to every true man, is infinitely dearer than property or life. She still retains her moral wealth, — the glory of her Jacksons, her Sidney Johnsons, her Lees, her Davises, and of all who have nobly died or suffered in her cause. These are her imperishable jewels; and, since little else is left to her, these shall be cherished with the greater love, with the more enthusiastic and undying devotion.

Let no one ask, then, except a dead soul, why argue the question of secession? For, it is precisely as this question is decided, that the Jacksons, the Johnsons, the Lees, and the Davises of the South, will be pronounced rebels and traitors, or heroes and martyrs; that the South itself will be disgraced, or honored, in the estimation of mankind. History is, at this moment, busy in making up her verdict on this momentous question; which is to determine so much that is most dear to every true son of the South. Shall Ave, then, remain idle spectators, mere passive lookers-on, while the North is flooding the world with volumes against the justice of our cause? Shall we stand, like the dumb brutes around us, having no word to utter in the great cause of truth, justice and humanity, which is now pending at the bar of History? Or shall we, on the contrary, contribute our mite toward the just decision of that glorious cause? The radicals themselves might, perhaps, derive some little benefit from our humble labors. For, if duly weighed and considered by them, these labors might serve to mitigate their wrath, and turn their thoughts from schemes of vengeance to the administration of justice, from persecution and ruin to peace and prosperity. Be this as it may, however, I shall proceed to argue the right of secession; because this is the great issue on which the whole Southern people, the dead as well as the living, is about to be tried in the person of their illustrious chief, Jefferson Davis.

Chapter II

The Issue or Point in Controversy

It is conceded, both by Webster and Story, that if the Constitution is a compact to which the States are the parties, then the States have a right to secede from the Union at pleasure. Thus, says Webster, in stating the consequences of Mr. Calhoun's doctrine: "if a league between sovereign powers have no limitation as to the time of duration, and contain nothing making it perpetual, it subsists only during the good pleasure of the parties, although no violation be complained of. If, in the opinion of either party, it be violated, such party may say he will no longer fulfil his obligations on his part, but will consider the whole league or compact at an end, although it might be one of its stipulations that it should be perpetual." In like manner Mr. Justice Story says: "The obvious deductions which may be, and, indeed, have been, drawn from considering the Constitution a compact between States, are that it operates as a mere treaty or convention between them, and has an obligatory force no longer than suits its pleasure or its consent continues,"[3] &c. Thus the great controversy is narrowed down to the single question: Is the Constitution a compact between the States? If so, then the right of secession is conceded, even by its most powerful and determined opponents; by the great jurist, as well as by "the great expounder" of the North.

The denial that the Constitution was a compact, is presented in every possible form, or variety of expression. We are told, that it was not made by the States, nor by the people of the States, but "by the people of the whole United States in the aggregate."[4] The States, we are assured, did not accede to the Constitution; it was ordained by the sovereign people of America as one nation. Echoing the bold assertion of Webster, Mr. Motley says, that "The States never acceded to the Constitution, and have no power to secede from it. It was 'ordained and established' over the States by a power superior to the States, by the people of the whole land in their aggregate capacity."[5] It was not made by the States, and it was not ratified by the States. It was, on the contrary, made and ordained by the people of America as one nation, and is, therefore, the constitution of a national government. Such is the doctrine which, in every mode of expression, is inculcated by the Storys, the Websters, and the Motleys of the North.

When we consider, in the simple light of history, the manner in which the Constitution of the United States was made, or framed, and afterwards ratified, such assertions seem exceedingly wonderful, not to say inexplicable on the supposition that their authors were honest men. But who can measure the mysterious depths of party spirit, or the force of political passions in a democracy? I know something of that force; for, during the greater part of my life, I followed, with implicit confidence, those blind leaders of the blind, Mr. Justice Story and Daniel Webster. History will yet open the eyes of the world to the strange audacity of their assertions.

Ever since the Declaration of Independence, there have been two great political parties in the United States; the one, regarding the American people as one nation, has labored to consolidate the Federal Union, while the other, attaching itself to the reserved rights of the States, has zealously resisted this tendency to consolidation in the central power. Even under the old Articles of Confederation, or before the new Constitution was formed, these political opinions and parties existed. For, however strange it may seem, there were those who, even under those Articles, considered "the States as Districts of people composing one political society,"[6] or the "American people as forming one nation."[7] Indeed, in the great Convention of 1787, by which the Constitution was formed, it was boldly asserted by a leading member, "that we never were independent States, were not such now, and never could be, even on the principles of the Confederation. The States, and the advocates of them, were intoxicated with the idea of their sovereignty."[8] Now, if any aberration of the mind under the influence of political passions could seem strange to the student of history, it would be truly wonderful, that such an assertion, could have been put forth under the Articles of Confederation which expressly declared that "each State" of the Union formed by them "retains its sovereignty, freedom, and independence."[9] The author of that assertion did not interpret, he flatly contradicted, the fundamental law of the government under which he lived and acted.

The above opinion or view of the old Articles of Confederation passed away with the passions to what it owed its birth. No one, at the present day, supposes that the old Articles moulded the States into "one political society," or "nation," leaving them merely "districts of people." For since those Articles have passed away, and the struggle for power under them has ceased, all can clearly see what they so plainly announced that "each state" of the confederation established by them retained "its sovereignty, freedom, and independence."

But the natures of men were not changed by changing the objects to which their political passions might attach themselves. Hence, the same opposite tendencies arose under the new "Articles of Union," as the Constitution of 1787 is habitually called by its authors, and produced the same conflicting parties. Each party had, of course, its extreme wing.

There were those who, unduly depressing the States, identified their relations to the central power with that of so many counties to a state, or of individuals to an ordinary political community. On the other hand, there were those who, from an extreme jealousy of the central authority, resolved the States into their original independence, or into their condition under the Articles of Confederation. The watch-word of one party was the sovereignty of the Federal Union; and the watch-word of the other, was the sovereignty of the States.

It was in the Senate of the United States, in 1833, that these two theories of the Constitution stood face to face in the persons of those two intellectual giants—Webster and Calhoun—then engaged in the most memorable debate of the New World. It was then predicted, and events have since verified the prediction, that the destinies of America would hinge and turn on the principles of that great debate. The war of words then waged between the giants has since become a war of deeds and blood between the sections which they represented. Now the question is, on which side, was right, truth, justice?

This is precisely the question which, in 1833, the great combatants submitted to the decision of after ages. As he drew toward the close of his speech, Mr. Calhoun reminded his great antagonist "that the principles he might advance would be subjected to the revision of posterity." "I do not decline its judgment," said Mr. Webster, in rising to reply, "nor withhold myself from its scrutiny." Mr. Webster's speech on this occasion is pronounced by his learned biographer[10] the greatest intellectual effort of his life, and is represented as having annihilated every position assumed by Mr. Calhoun. But the combatants did not submit the controversy to the judgment of Mr. Everett; they submitted it to "the revision of posterity." History is the great tribunal to which they appealed; and history will settle the great issue between them, and between the two hostile sections of the Union.

It was in 1833, for the first time in the history of the country, that it was solemnly asserted and argued, that the Constitution of the United States was not a compact between the States. This *new doctrine* was simultaneously put forth, by Mr. Justice Story in his "Commentaries on the Constitution of the United States," and by Mr. Daniel Webster in "the greatest intellectual effort of his life," that is, in his great speech in the Senate of the 16th of February, 1833. In order to show that the Constitution is not a compact between the States, the position is assumed, that it is not a compact at all. If it be a compact, say they, then the States had a right to secede. But it is not a compact; and hence secession is treason and rebellion. The great fundamental questions, then, on which the whole controversy hinges, are, first, Is the Constitution a compact? and, secondly, Is it a compact between the States? These are the questions which shall and ought to be subjected to "the revision of posterity."

Chapter III

The Idea That the States "Acceded" to the Constitution

Mr. Webster was supposed to have studied the Constitution, and its history, more carefully and more profoundly than any other man. He habitually spoke, indeed, as if he had every particle of its meaning, and of its history, at his finger's end. Hence he acquired, at least among his political friends, the lofty title of "The great expounder." His utterances were listened to as oracles. If, indeed, his great mind had been guided by a knowledge of facts, or a supreme love of truth; the irresistible force of his logic, and the commanding powers of his eloquence, would have justified those who delighted to call him "the god-like Daniel." But, unfortunately, no part of his god-likeness consisted in a scrupulous regard for truth, or the accuracy of his assertions. He was, however, so great a master of words, that he stood in little need of facts, in order to produce a grand impression by the rolling thunders of his eloquence. I only wonder, that he was not also called, "The thunderer." No one better understood, either in theory or in practice, the wonderful magic of words than Daniel Webster.

"Was it Mirabeau," says he, "or some other master of the human passions, who has told us that words are things? They are indeed things, and things of mighty influence, not only in addresses to the passions and high-wrought feelings of mankind, but in the discussion of legal and political questions also; because a just conclusion is often avoided, or a false one reached, by the adroit substitution of one phrase, or one word, for another." Nothing can be more just than this general reflection; and nothing, as we shall presently see, can be more unjust than the application made of it by Mr. Webster.

He finds an example of this adroit use of language in the first resolution of Mr. Calhoun. "The first resolution," says he, "declares that the people of the several States *'acceded'* to the Constitution." As "the natural converse of *accession* is *secession*," so Mr. Webster supposes that Calhoun has adroitly, and "not without a well-considered purpose," shaped his premises to a foregone conclusion. "When it is stated," says he, "that the people of the State *acceded* to the Union, it may be more plausibly argued that they may secede from it. If; in adopting the Constitution, nothing was done but *acceding* to a compact, nothing would seem necessary, in order to break it up, but to *secede* from the same compact."

But "this term *accede*," maintains Mr. Webster, "is wholly out of place . . . There is more importance than may, at first sight, appear in the introduction of this new word by the honorable mover of the resolutions . . . " "The people of the United States," he continues, "used no such form of expression in establishing the present Government." . . . It is "unconstitutional language." Such are a few of the bold, sweeping, and confident assertions of "the great expounder of the Constitution." But how stands the fact? Is this really "a new word," or is it as old as the Constitution itself, and rendered almost obsolete at the North by the progress of new ideas and new forms of speech? Was it not, in fact, as familiar to the very fathers and framers of the Constitution of the United States as it afterwards become foreign and strange to the ears of its Northern expounders? This is the question and, fortunately, the answer is free from all metaphysical refinement, from all logical subtlety, from all curious speculation. For there lies the open record, with this very word *accede,* and this very application of the word, spread all over its ample pages in the most abundant profusion. No mode of expression is, indeed, more common with the fathers and the framers of the Constitution, while speaking of the act of its adoption, than this very phrase, "the accession of the States." No household word ever fell more frequently or more familiarly from their lips.

Thus in the Convention of 1787, Mr. James Wilson, to whose great influence the historian of the Constitution ascribes its adoption by the State of Pennsylvania,[11] preferred "a partial union" of the States, "with a door open for the *accession* of the rest," rather than to see their disposition "to confederate anew on better principles" entirely defeated.[12] "But will the small States," asks another member of the same Convention, "in that case, *accede to* it" (the Constitution) Mr. Gerry, a delegate from Massachusetts, was opposed to "a partial confederacy, leaving other States to *accede* or not to *accede,* as had been intimated."[13] Even Mr. Madison, "the father of the Constitution," as by way of eminence he has long been called, used the expression "*to accede*" in the Convention of 1787, in order to denote the act of adopting "the new form of government by the States."[14]

In like manner Governor Randolph, who was also a member of the Convention of 1787, and who had just reported the form of ratification to be used by the State of Virginia, said, "That the *accession of* eight States reduced our deliberations to the single question of Union or no Union." "If it (the Constitution)," says Patrick Henry, "be amended, every State will *accede* to it."[15] "Does she (Virginia) gain anything from her central position," asks Mr. Grayson, "by *acceding* to that paper," the Constitution?[16] "I came hither," says Mr. Innes, "under the persuasion that the felicity of our country required that we should *accede* to this system,"[17] (the new Constitution.) "Our new Constitution," says Franklin, who next to Washington was the most illustrious member of the Convention of 1787, "is now established with eleven States, and the *accession* of a twelfth is soon expected."[18] And, finally, George Washington himself, who, watching the States as one after another adopted the new Constitution, says: "If these, with the States eastward and northward of us, should *accede* to the Federal Government," &c[19] Thus, while the transaction was passing before their eyes, the fathers of the Constitution of the United States, with the great father of his country at their head, described the act by which the new Union was formed as "the *accession* of the States," using the very expression which, in the resolution of Mr. Calhoun, is so vehemently condemned as "unconstitutional language," as "a new word," invented by the advocates of secession for the vile purpose of disunion.

To these high authorities, may be added that of Chief Justice Marshall; who, in his Life of Washington, notes the fact, that "North Carolina *accedes* to the Union."[20] This was many months after the new Government had gone into operation. Mr. Justice Story, is, in spite of his artificial theory of Constitution, a witness to the same fact. "The Constitution," says he, "has been ratified by all the States . . . Rhode Island did not *accede* to it, until more than a year after it had been in operation," just as if he had completely forgotten his own theory of the Constitution.[21]

If it were necessary, this list of authorities for the use of the word in question, and for the precise application made of it by Mr. Calhoun, might be greatly extended. But surely we have seen enough to show how very ill-informed was "the great expounder" with respect to the language of the fathers. Not only John C. Calhoun, but Washington, Franklin, Wilson, King, Morris, Randolph, Madison, and all the celebrated names of the great Convention of 1787, came under the denunciation of this modern "expounder of the Constitution."

There is, as Mr. Webster says, more importance to be attached to the word in question than may at first sight appear. For if "the States acceded" to the Constitution, each acting for itself alone, then was it a voluntary association of States, from which, according to his own admission, any member might secede at pleasure. Accordingly this position of the great oracle of the North is echoed and re-echoed by all who, since the war began, have written against the right of secession. Thus, says one of the most faithful of these echoes, Mr. Motley — "The States never acceded to the Constitution, and have no power to secede from it." It was "ordained and established" over the States by a power superior to the States, by the people of the whole land in their aggregate capacity.[22] If, with the fathers of the Constitution, in opposition to its modern expounder and perverter, he had seen that the new Union was formed by an accession of the States, then he would have been compelled, on his own principle, to recognise the right of secession. For he has truly said, what no one ever denied, that "the same power which established the Constitution may justly destroy it."[23] Hence, if the Constitution was established by the accession or consent of the States, then may the Union be dissolved by a secession of the States. This conclusion is, as we have seen, expressly admitted by Mr. Webster and Mr. Justice Story.

Mr. Webster has well said that a true conclusion may be avoided, or a false one reached, by the substitution of one word or one phrase for another. This offence, however, has been committed, not by Mr. Calhoun, but by "the great expounder" himself. The one has not reached a false, but the other has shunned a true conclusion by "the adroit use of language." Instead of saying and believing with the authors of the Constitution, that the new Union was formed by as an "accession of the States," he repudiates both the language and the idea, preferring the monstrous heresy that it was ordained and established by "the whole people of the United States in their aggregate capacity"[24] or as one nation — a heresy which may, with the records of the country, be dashed into ten thousand stones.

I agree with Mr. Webster, that "words are things, and things of mighty influence." It is, no doubt, chiefly owing to the influence of language, in connection with the passions of men in a numerical majority, that the words and views of the fathers became so offensive to the Northern expanders of the Constitution. "Words," says the philosopher of Malmesbury, "are the counters of wise men, but the money of fools." To which I may add, if this last phrase be true, as most unquestionably it is, then is there scarcely a man on earth without some touch of folly; for all are, more or less, under the influence of words. A far greater than either Mirabeau or Hobbes has said that we are often led captive by the influence of words, even when we think ourselves the most complete masters of them. Mr. Webster was himself, as we shall frequently have occasion to see, a conspicuous instance and illustration of the truth of the profound aphorism of Bacon. Of all the dupes of his own eloquence, of all the spell-bound captives of his own enchantments, he was himself, perhaps, at times, the most deluded and the most unsuspecting victim.

When, from his high position in the Senate, Mr. Webster assured the people of the United States, that it is "unconstitutional language" to say "the States acceded to the Constitution," he was no doubt religiously believed by the great majority of his readers and hearers. He was supposed to know all about the subject; and was, therefore, followed as the great guide of the people. But, as we have seen, he was profoundly ignorant of the facts of the case, about which he delivered himself with so much confidence. The "new word," as he called it, was precisely *the* word of the fathers of the Constitution. Hence, if this word lays the foundation of secession, as Mr. Webster contended it does, that foundation was laid, not by Calhoun, but by the fathers of the Constitution itself, with "the father of his country" at their head.

So much for the first link in "the great expounder's" argument against the right of secession. His principles are right, but his facts are wrong. It is, indeed, his habit to make his own facts, and leave those of history to take care of themselves. He just puts forth assertions without knowing, and apparently without caring, whether they are true or otherwise. We shall frequently have occasion to notice this utter, this reckless unveracity in "the great expounder."

Chapter IV

The First Resolution Passed by the Convention of 1787

Mr. Webster lays great stress on the fact, that the first resolution passed by the Convention of 1787 declared, "That a *national* government ought to be established, consisting of a supreme legislative, judiciary, and executive." But the fact only shows that the Convention, when it first met, had the desire to establish "*a national* government," rather than a federal one. This resolution was passed before the Convention was fully assembled, and by the vote of only six States, a minority of the whole number. After the members had arrived, and the Convention was full, the resolution in question was reconsidered and rescinded. The Convention, when filled up, changed the name of their offspring, calling it "the government of the United States."[25] A fraction of the Convention named it, as Mr. Webster says; but the whole Convention refused to baptise it with that name, and gave it another. Why then resuscitate that discarded name, and place it before the reader, as Mr. Webster does, in capital letters? Is it because "words are things; and things of mighty influence"? or why persist, as Mr. Webster always does, in calling "the government of the United States" a *national* one? If the Convention had called it a *national* government, this name would have been so continually rung in our oars that we could neither have listened to the Constitution itself, or to its history, whenever these proclaimed its federal character. No, although the Convention positively refused to name it a national government, on the avowed ground that it did not express their views, yet has this name been eternally rung in our ears by the Northern School of politicians, and declaimers; just as if it had been adopted, instead of having been repudiated and *rejected,* as it was, by the authors of the Constitution.

In like manner Mr. Justice Story, in his "Commentaries on the Constitution," builds an argument on the name given to the new government "in the first resolution adopted by the convention," without the slightest allusion to the fact that this resolution was afterwards reconsidered, and the name changed to that of *"the government of the United States."* Is this to reason, or merely to deceive? Is this to build on facts, or merely on exploded names? Is this to follow the Convention in its deliberation, or is it to falsify its decision?

The Convention, by a vote of six States, decided that "a national government ought to be established." But when this resolution was reconsidered, Mr. Ellsworth "objected to the term *national government,*"[26] and it was rejected. The record says: "The first resolution 'that a national government ought to be established,' being taken up" . . . "Mr. Ellsworth, seconded by Mr. Gorham, moves to alter it, so as to run that *the government of the United States* ought to consist, &c . . ." This alteration, he said, would drop the word *national,* and retain the proper title "the United States."[27] This motion was unanimously adopted by the Convention.[28] That is, they unanimously rejected "the term national government," and yet both Story and Webster build an argument on this term just as it had been retained by them!

The Madison Papers were not published, it is true, when the first edition of Story's Commentaries made their appearance; but they were published long before subsequent editions of that work. Why, then, was not this gross error corrected? Why has it been repeated in every edition of the Commentaries in question? Indeed, if Mr. Justice Story had desired to ascertain the truth in regard to the first resolution of the Convention, he might very easily have learned it from "Yates' Minutes," which were published before the first edition of his Commentaries. For, in those Minutes, we find the passage: "Ellsworth. I propose, and therefore move, to expunge the word 'national,' in the first resolve, and to place in the room of it, government of the United States, which was agreed to *nem con.*"[29] Yet, directly in the face of this, Mr. Justice Story builds an argument on the word *national* used in the first resolution passed by the Convention! and, in order to give the greater effect to the same argument, Mr. Webster prints that rescinded resolution in capital letters!

"The name 'United States of America'," says the younger Story, "is in unfortunate one, and has, doubtless, led many minds into error. For it may be said, if the States do not form a confederacy, why are they called 'United States'"?[30] This name is, indeed, a most unfortunate one for the purpose of his argument, and for that of the whole school of politicians to which he belongs. But then, as we learn from the journal of the convention of 1787, it was deliberately chosen by them as the most suitable name for the work of their own hands; and that too in preference to the very name which the whole Northern school clings to with such astonishing pertinacity. From the same journal, as well as from the other records of the country, I shall hereafter produce many other things which are equally unfortunate for the grand argument of the Storys, the Websters, and the Motleys, of the North.

Chapter V

The Constitution of 1787 a Compact, Part I

Was the constitution a compact? Was it a compact between the States, or to which the States were the parties? Was it a compact from which any State might recede at pleasure? These three questions are perfectly distinct, and all the rules of clear thinking require that they should be so held in our minds, instead of being mixed up and confounded in our discussions. Yet Mr. Justice Story, in his long chapter on the "Nature of the Constitution," discusses these questions, not separately and distinctly, but all in one confused mass, to the no little perplexity and distraction of his own mind. He carries them all along together, and in the darkness and confusion occasioned by this mode of proceeding, he is frequently enabled to elude the force of his adversaries' logic.

Thus, for instance, he sets out with the flat denial of the doctrine that the Constitution is a compact; and yet, when the evidences become too strong for resistance, or a cloud of witnesses rise up to confound him, he turns around, and instead of fairly admitting that the Constitution is a compact, asserts that if it is a compact it is not one between the States. When too hardly pressed on this position, replies, well, if it is a compact between the States it is not such a compact that it may be revoked at the pleasure of the parties. Thus, when he is driven from one position he falls back upon another, and finally rallies to a second, a third, and a fourth denial of the main proposition that the Constitution is a compact. Now, I intend to discuss each one of these questions distinctly and by itself; holding Mr. Justice Story to one and the same precise point, until it is either made good or else demolished. I hope, in this way, to dispel the mists and fogs he has thrown around the subject, and to bring out the truth into a clear and unmistakable light.

The same confusion of thought, and arising from the same source, pervades Mr. Webster's celebrated speech of Feb. 16, 1833; though it must be admitted, not to the same extent that it prevails in the

"Commentaries" of Mr. Justice Story. Mr. Calhoun *very* justly complains of this want of clearness and precision in the positions of his great antagonist. "After a careful examination," says he, "of the notes which I took of what the Senator said, I am now at a loss to know whether, in the opinion of the Senator, our Constitution is a compact or not, though the almost entire argument of the Senator was directed to that point. At one time he would seem to deny directly and positively that it was a compact, while at another he would appear, in language not less strong, to admit that it was."[31]

Mr. Webster emphatically and repeatedly denies both that a Constitution is a compact and also that a compact is a Constitution; or, in other words, he conceives that the natures of the two things are utterly incompatible with each other.

He is very bold, and asserts that it is new language to call "the Constitution a compact."

"This is the reason," says he, "which makes it necessary to abandon the use of Constitutional language for a new vocabulary, and to substitute, in place of plain historical facts, a series of assumptions. This is the reason why it is necessary, to give new names to things, to speak of the Constitution, not as a Constitution, but as a compact, and if the ratifications of the people not as ratifications, but as acts of accession."[32] Again, he complains of Mr. Calhoun, that "he introduces a new word of his own, viz., 'compact,' as importing the principal idea, and designed to play the principal part, and degrades Constitution into an insignificant idle epithet attached to compact. The whole then stands a Constitutional compact!" He is then particularly severe and eloquent upon the supposed outrage perpetrated on "our American political grammar," in thus degrading "CONSTITUTION" (the capitals are his own) from its rightful rank "as a noun substantive." But, after all, the plain, simple fact is, that this "new word," as Mr. Webster calls it, was as familiar to the ears of the authors of the Constitution as any other in the vocabulary of the great Convention of 1787. The terms Constitution and compact are, indeed, twin words, and convertible in the language of the fathers.

Though "the term Constitutional affixes to the word compact no definite idea," says Mr. Webster, and in such connection "is void of all meaning," "yet it is easy, quite easy, to see why the gentleman uses it in these resolutions." Now, what is the reason, the deep design, that induces Mr. Calhoun to use an epithet "so void of all meaning"? "He cannot open the book" says Mr. Webster, "and look upon our written frame of government without seeing that it is called a Constitution. This may well be appalling to him." We cannot possibly imagine that Mr. Calhoun should, for one moment, have been disturbed or alarmed by such a discovery or revelation. It is certain that he nowhere betrays the least symptom of dismay at "the appalling" consideration that the Constitution is really a Constitution. That "noun substantive" seems to have inspired him with no sort of terror whatever. On the contrary, it appears to sit as easily on his political faith and to flow as familiarly from his lips as any other word in the language.

We can imagine, however, why the Northern States should wish to get rid of both the idea of a compact and of the word; why the powerful should wish to obliterate and erase from the tablets of their memory every recollection and vestige of the solemn compact or bargain into which they had entered with the weak, but which they have never observed in good faith.

It is perfectly certain that Mr. Webster's horror of the term compact, as applied to the Constitution, is of comparatively recent origin. It was wholly unknown to the fathers of the Constitution themselves. Mr. Gouverneur Morris, it is well known, was one of the most celebrated advocates for a strong national government in the Convention of 1787; and yet, in that assembly, he used the words: "He came here to form a compact for the good of America. He was ready to do so with all the States. He hoped and believed that all would enter into such a compact. If they would not, he would be ready to join with any States that would. But as the compact was to be voluntary, it is in vain for the Eastern States to insist on what the Southern States will never agree to."[33] Thus, this celebrated representative of the State of Pennsylvania, and staunch advocate of a strong national government, did not hesitate to call the Constitution a compact into which the States were to enter. Indeed, no one, at that early day, either before the Constitution was adopted or afterwards, hesitated to call it a compact.

Mr. Gerry, the representative of Massachusetts, says, "If nine out of thirteen (States) can dissolve the compact, six out of nine will be just as able to dissolve the new one hereafter." Here again the new Constitution is called a compact.

"In the case of a union of people under one Constitution," says Mr.

Madison, while contending for the ratification of the new Constitution by the people, "the nature of the pact has always been understood to exclude such an interpretation."[34] Thus, in the Convention of 1787, Mr. Madison called the Constitution a compact; a word which he continued to apply to it during the whole course of his life.

In the celebrated resolutions of Virginia, in 1798, Mr. Madison used these words, "That this assembly does explicitly and peremptorily declare, that it views the powers of the Federal Government as resulting from the compact, to which the States are parties." Again, in his almost equally celebrated letter to Mr. Everett, in 1830, he calls "the Constitution" "a compact among the States in their highest sovereign capacity." In the same letter Mr. Madison speaks of the States as "the parties to the Constitutional compact," using the very expression which is so offensive to Mr. Webster's new "political grammar." No, it was only three years before, in the great debate on Foot's resolutions, that Mr. Webster himself had, like everyone else, spoken of the Constitution as a compact, as a bargain which was obligatory on the parties to it. "It is the original bargain," says he, in that debate; "the compact—let it stand; let the advantage of it be fully enjoyed. The Union itself is too full of benefits to be hazarded in propositions for changing its original basis. I go for the Constitution as it is, and for the Union as it is." Nor is this all. He there indignantly repels, both for "himself and for the North," "accusations which impute to us a disposition to evade the Constitutional compact." Yet, in the course of three short years, he discovers that there is no compact to be evaded and no bargain to be violated! All such trammels are given to the winds, and Behemoth is free! How sudden and how wonderful this revolution in the views and in the vocabulary of the great orator of New England![35]

This language, in which the Constitution is called a compact, is not confined to Morris, and Gerry, and Madison, and the Webster of 1830. Mr. Chief Justice Jay, of the Supreme Court of the Union, in the case of "Chisholm vs. State of Georgia," expressly declares that "the Constitution of the United States is a compact."[36] "Our Constitution of the United States," says John Quincy Adams, the sixth President of the Republic, "and all our State Constitutions, have been voluntary compacts, deriving all their authority from the free consent of the parties to them." The Virginia Resolutions of 1798, already referred to as expressing the opinion of Mr. Madison, assert that "Virginia views the powers of the Federal Government as resulting from the compact to which the States are parties." Again, in the Virginia Report of 1800, it is said, "The States being parties to the Constitutional compact," &c. Edmund Pendleton, President of the ratifying Convention of Virginia, in 1788, in the course of his argument in favor of the new Constitution, says, "This is the only Government founded in real compact."[37] Judge Tucker, in his commentaries on Blackstone, repeatedly calls the Constitution in question "a compact between the States" of the Union. The third President of the United States, as well as the sixth, Thomas Jefferson as well as John Quincy Adams, considered the Constitution "a compact." "The States," says Jefferson, "entered into a compact, which is called the Constitution of the United States."[38] The Convention of Massachusetts, which was called to ratify the Constitution of the United States, was, if possible, still more emphatic and decided in the expression of the same opinion. "Having impartially discussed, and fully considered," say they, "the Constitution of the United States of America," we acknowledge, "with grateful hearts, the goodness of the Supreme Ruler of the Universe in affording the people of the United States an opportunity, deliberately and peaceably, without fraud and surprise, of entering into an explicit and solemn compact with each other, by assenting to and ratifying a new Constitution," &c. Yet, in the face of all these high authorities, and of a hundred more that might be easily adduced, running from James Madison in the Convention of 1787 to Daniel Webster in the great debate of 1830, and embracing the lights of all sections and of all parties, it is asserted by this celebrated statesman, though certainly not as a statesman, that the term compact, as applied to the Constitution, is "a new word," is a part and parcel of "the unconstitutional language," of the "new vocabulary," which has been invented to obscure the fundamental principles of the Government of the United States, and to justify secession! Can posterity admire such an exhibition of his powers!

So far, indeed, is this from being a new mode of speech, that it is one of the most familiar words known to the fathers of the Constitution itself, or to its more early expounders. Even the *Federalist,* in submitting the Constitution to the people, sets it before them as "the compact."[39] "The man," says Mr. Webster, "is almost untrue to his country who calls the Constitution a compact." It were, indeed, much nearer the truth to say that the man is not only almost but altogether untrue to himself, as well as to the most solemn records of his country, who can assert that the term compact, as applied to the Constitution, is "a new word," or the exponent of a new idea. The arguments of Mr. Webster to prove that the Constitution is not a compact, are, if possible, as unfortunate as his assertions. If words be not things in reality, as well as in effect, then it will be found that his arguments possess an exceedingly small value. There are two words, in particular, in the use of which he displays far more of rhetorical legerdemain than of rigid logic. These are the two words "compact" and "Constitution."

No one pretends, for a moment, that every compact is a Constitution. There are compacts about soap and candles, about pepper and calicoes, or some such trifling thing, which no one would call a Constitution. It is only when a compact has for its object the institution or organization of a political society, or a civil government, that it is properly denominated a Constitution. Hence, in the ordinary acceptation of the words, compact falls far below the high-sounding noun substantive Constitution; a circumstance of which any rhetorician may, if he choose, very easily avail himself. Mr. Webster has done so, and that, too, with no little popular effect. "We know no more of a Constitutional compact between sovereign powers," says he, "than we do of a Constitutional indenture of partnership, a Constitutional deed of conveyance, or a Constitutional bill of exchange. But we know what the Constitution is," &c. Perhaps we do, and perhaps we do not; that is the very point in dispute. But certain it is, that if we do know what the Constitution is we need not seek to illustrate its nature or to exhibit its history by any such deceptive use of words. Akin to this sort of reasoning, or rhetoric, is all that is said by Mr. Webster and Mr. Justice Story about lowering the Constitution by considering it as a "mere compact," or as "nothing but a compact." It is, indeed, something more than a compact, something more high, and holy, and honorable. Though in its nature it is a mere compact, yet in its object, which is no less than to institute or organize a political society, it is the most solemn and sacred of all earthly transactions. Such compacts should not be despised, nor should they be explained away, or trampled under foot by the powerful; they involve the destiny of millions.

Chapter VI

The Constitution of 1787 a Compact, Part 2

"A Constitution," says Mr. Webster, "is certainly not a league, compact, or confederation, but a fundamental law ... Do we need to be inform-ed in this country what a Constitution is? Is it not an idea perfectly familiar, definite, and well settled? We are at no loss to understand what is meant by the Constitution of one of the States; and the Consti-tution of the United States speaks of itself as being an instrument of the same nature." Now it is a very remarkable fact that Alexander Hamilton was just as clearly and decidedly of opinion that the Constitu-tion of a State is a compact, as Mr. Webster was of the opposite notion. Thus, says he, in relation to the Constitution of New York, "The Consti-tution is the compact made between the society at large and each individual. The society, therefore, cannot, without breach of faith and injustice, refuse to any individual a single advantage which he derives under the compact, no more than one man can refuse to perform an agreement with another. If the community have good reason for abro-gating the old compact and establishing a new one it undoubtedly has a right to do it; but until the compact is dissolved with the same solem-nity and certainty with which it was made, the society, as well as individuals, are bound by it."[40] Indeed, this idea, that the Constitution of an American State is a compact, made and entered into, was far more familiar to Alexander Hamilton and to his age—the age of the Constitution itself—than the contrary notion was to Mr. Webster and to his school.

The Constitution of Massachusetts not only calls itself a compact, but the people therein acknowledge, with grateful hearts, that Providence has afforded them an opportunity of entering into this "original, ex-plicit, and solemn compact." The same State, as we have seen, in her ordinance of ratification, makes the same acknowledgment of the goodness of the Supreme Ruler of the Universe for affording the people of the United States an opportunity of entering into "an explicit and

solemn compact by assenting to, and ratifying a new Constitution."
Now, both Story and Webster lay great stress on the fact that the Constitution off the United States does not call itself a compact. But here
they have a Constitution, and it is that of their own State, which calls
itself an explicit and solemn compact—and how do they receive this
language? There is not, perhaps in all literature an attempt more awkward, or a failure more signal, to explain away the clear and unequivocal language of a written instrument, than is here exhibited by these
two great sophists. It deserves a most especial notice.

Mr. Justice Story first gets away from the plain language of the
instrument, and then calls around him the darkness of one of the very
darkest metaphysical theories of Europe, which he introduces to our
notice, however, by a very just remark. "Mr. Justice Blackstone," says
he, "has very justly observed that the theory of an original contract
upon the first formation of society is a visionary notion." Granted; but
what has this to do with the Constitution of Massachusetts? Every Constitution we admit is not a compact, any more than every compact is
a Constitution. Most Constitutions have indeed grown, and only a few
in these later ages of the world have been made. It has been the boast
of America, and of Virginia especially, that she was the first in the history of mankind to make a complete Constitution, to reduce it to writ-
ing, and, in the name of the people in Convention assembled, to adopt
and sign it for the government of themselves and their posterity. By
those authors, such as Blackstone, and Paley, and Hume, who reject
the theory of an original contract as "a visionary notion," as having no
foundation in history or in fact, it is not denied, but expressly admitted,
that a people might, if they chose, enter into such a compact. Paley,
in spite of his opposition to the theory of the social compact, admits
that something of the kind has been entered into in America. "The
present age has," says he, "been witness to a transaction which bears
the nearest resemblance to this political idea (that of an original compact) of any of which history has preserved the account or memory.
I refer to the establishment of the United States of North America. We
saw the people assembled to elect deputies for the avowed purpose of
framing the Constitution of a new empire. We saw this deputation of
the people deliberating and resolving upon a form of government,
erecting a permanent legislature, distributing the functions of sovereignty, establishing and promulgating a code of fundamental ordi-

nances which were to be considered by succeeding generations, not merely as acts and laws of the State, but as the very terms and conditions of the Confederation." Indeed, Paley does not doubt that it was a compact; he only seems to question whether it may be called original, since "much was pre-supposed." For, "in settling the Constitution," says he, "many important parts were presumed to be already settled. The qualifications of the constituents who were admitted to vote in the election of members of Congress, as well as the modes of electing the representatives, were taken from the old forms of government." It is true that, in framing the Constitution of the Federal Union, these things were adopted from the State Governments; but if this prevented the compact from being original it certainly did not keep it from being a compact. In fact, these words of Paley refer to the old Articles of Confederation, and not to the new Constitution, for they were written and published in 1785[41], two years before the Convention met to frame this new instrument or plan of government. Both Webster and Story, like all others, admit that the old Articles of Confederation were "a compact between the States."

The question is, whether the Constitution of Massachusetts is an instrument of the same nature, or, in other words, whether it is a compact? The more than doubtful metaphysical theories of Europe have nothing to do with this question. The darkness of those theories is not permitted either by Webster or Story to obliterate or obscure the fact that the Articles of Confederation, or the Constitution to which Paley refers, was a compact. Why, then, is it brought to bear on the Constitution of Massachusetts? Is the political history of this country, so widely and so amazingly different from that of all others, to be read and interpreted in the light, or rather in the darkness, of those vague and visionary theories respecting the origin of the governments of the Old World which have not the least semblance nor shadow of a foundation in their respective histories? The Constitution of Great Britain, for example, has grown; the Constitution of Massachusetts was made. The one is the slow but mighty product of the labor of ages; the other is the creation of yesterday. The one is written; the other is traditional. The most important and beneficent elements of the one resulted from the Norman Conquest, and the gradual rise of the lower orders in cultivation, in wealth, and in importance. Every provision of the other, without a single exception, was framed and adopted by the people of

Massachusetts in Convention assembled. Hence the more than doubtful theories respecting the origin and the nature of the one have nothing to do with the interpretation of the plain and unquestionable facts of the other. These facts should be allowed to speak for themselves, and not to be discredited or obscured by involving them in the fate of any doubtful or false hypothesis whatever.

Nor is this all. As there is not the slightest foundation in history for the theory of an original contract in relation to the governments of Europe, so theorists have been forced to adopt the hypothesis of an "implied compact" as constituting at once the origin, the basis, and the binding authority of civil society. Mr. Justice Story finds this idea of an "implied" contract, or consent, in Blackstone;[42] and he does not hesitate to assert that it is in this sense that the Constitution of Massachusetts calls itself a compact. According to this hypothesis the consent of every subject is implied, and this implication is forced upon the unwilling. It is an implied consent, even in spite of an actual dissent. Did the people of Massachusetts then acknowledge, with grateful hearts, that Providence had given them an opportunity of entering into an "implied" compact? Did they thus pour forth in their Constitution devout thanks for a privilege which they could not possibly have avoided, and which has been fully enjoyed by every subject of every despotic government in the world? Did they thank the Supreme Ruler of the Universe for an opportunity of entering into a forced implication, and yet ignorant of their bonds, most foolishly style it an "original, explicit, and solemn compact"?

If we may believe Mr. Justice Story, such was precisely the absurd and ridiculous farce enacted by the people of Massachusetts.

Mr. Webster treads in the footsteps of Mr. Justice Story. "The Convention," says the Massachusetts formula of ratification, "having impartially examined and fully considered the Constitution of the United States of America . . . submitted to us . . . and acknowledging with grateful hearts the goodness of the Supreme Ruler of the Universe in affording the people of the United States, in the course of His providence, an opportunity, deliberately and peaceably, without fraud or surprise, of entering into an explicit and solemn compact with each other, by assenting to and ratifying a new Constitution," &c. Now is this the language of an implied or of an explicit and deliberate compact? Yet in the face of this language Mr. Webster asserts that the

Convention of Massachusetts and New Hampshire merely speak of compact in the sense of "European writers!" Now, the European writers here referred to mean either an explicit or an implied consent. But the idea of an explicit consent or compact is rejected by Mr. Justice Story and Mr. Webster, as "a visionary notion," as well as by Blackstone, Hume, Paley, and a host of others. Hence Mr. Webster must be understood to refer to those European writers who maintain the hypothesis of an implied compact. Hence the people of Massachusetts are represented by him as being exceedingly grateful for the opportunity of freely and deliberately entering into an "implied compact," which, however, they blindly call "an explicit and solemn" one! They are represented as voluntarily entering into an implied compact, a thing which is never made or entered into at all, but is only an implication or fiction of law, from which there is no escape!

The Constitution, says Mr. Webster, is "certainly not a compact." He lays great stress on the fact that it does not call itself a compact. Nor do the old Articles of Confederation call themselves a compact; and yet Mr. Webster admits that they were "a compact between the States." They call themselves, it is true, "a league of friendship," but then a league of friendship is not, *ex vi termini, a* social compact or a political union. "We speak of ordaining Constitutions," says Mr. Webster; "but we do not speak of ordaining leagues and compacts." True, because our language is determined by the ordinary and more frequent transactions of society. Hence we naturally speak of making or entering into leagues and compacts in conformity with the everyday use of language. But when compacts relate to the institution of a new government, and when all their terms and articles and stipulations are agreed upon, then we enter into them by ordaining them as Constitutions. Is not this so?

Every compact is not a Constitution. But the Articles of Confederation, which are admitted to be a compact, were a Constitution. This is clear from Mr. Webster's own definition. "What is a Constitution?" says he; and he replies, it is "a fundamental law."

Now, most assuredly the articles in question constituted the "fundamental law" of the old Union. They are, as we have already seen, very properly called by Dr. Paley "a code of fundamental ordinances, which were to be considered by succeeding generations not merely as laws and acts" . . . "but as limitations of power, which were to control and regulate the future legislation." This is, indeed, the definition of a Constitution; and hence Dr. Paley calls those "terms and conditions of the Confederation" a "Constitution."

But on this point there is much higher authority than that of Dr. Paley. The "Address of the Annapolis Convention," penned, as is well known, by Alexander Hamilton, recommends commissioners to meet at Philadelphia, "to take into consideration the condition of the United States, and to devise such further provisions as shall appear to them necessary to render the *Constitution* of the Federal government adequate to the exigencies of the Union."[43] Again, he says, in the ratifying convention of New York, "The Confederation was framed amidst the agitation and tumult of society. It was composed of unsound materials put together in haste. Men of intelligence discovered the feebleness of the structure in the first stages of its existence; but the great body of the people, too much engrossed with their distresses to contemplate any but the immediate causes of them, were ignorant of the defects of their *constitution.*"[44] Mr. Madison also speaks of "the Federal Constitution" under the old Confederation.[45]

"The Constitution," says Mr. Webster, "speaks of that political system which is established as 'the government of the United States.' Is it not doing strange violence to language to call a league or compact between sovereign powers a government?" Is it not, I reply, requiring too much of a compact to be both the Constitution and the government? No one pretends that either a compact or the Constitution is the government of the United States. Mr. Webster himself makes the distinction in the two next sentences. "The government of a state," says he, "is that organization in which the political power resides. It is the political being created by the Constitution or fundamental law." Thus, the government is created by the Constitution; and if a compact were both Constitution and government, then the creature would be its own creator. All I contend for is, that in this particular case the compact is a Constitution, and the Constitution is a compact. Neither the one nor the other is the government. The Constitution is neither the executive, nor the legislature, nor the judiciary, nor any other conceivable functionary of the government of which it is the supreme law.

But the design of Mr. Webster's argument is to prove that no government was actually established by the old articles of Union, or under the compact of the Confederation. In designating those powers which he deems essential to the very existence of a government, he specifies those which did not belong to the legislature of the Confederacy, or which he supposes did not belong to it; and then he adds, "when it ceases to possess this power it is no longer a government," and consequently it is doing strange violence to language to call it one.

We have already seen that Alexander Hamilton, in speaking of the Confederacy, calls it the "Federal government." "We saw the deputation of the people," says Dr. Paley, "deliberating and resolving upon a form of government, erecting a public legislature, distributing the functions of sovereignty, establishing and promulgating a code of fundamental ordinances." We cannot open "Curtis's History of the Constitution," and turn to the appropriate heads, without seeing that he discusses the "Nature of the government established by the Confederation,"[46] or the "form of the government established by it,"[47] or without perceiving that the same thing is habitually and familiarly called a government. Nor can we look into the commentaries of Mr. Justice Story, and cast our eyes over the pages in which he treats of the first Confederation, without discovering that he frequently speaks of the "general government,"[48] or the "national government"[49] established by it. In the very first sentence of "The Federalist," as well as in various other sentences of the same work, "the existing Federal government" is spoken of just as if no one entertained a doubt as to its real nature or its name.

Chapter VII

The Constitution of 1787 a Compact, Part 3

Mr. Webster admits that the Constitution is "founded on consent or agreement, or on compact," meaning no more by that word than "voluntary consent or agreement." But he denies that it is itself a compact. "The Constitution is not a contract," says he, "but the result of a contract; meaning no more by contract than assent. Founded on consent it is a government proper." Now, Mr. Webster himself being the judge, the Constitution is not a government at all; for a government is, says he, "the political being created by the Constitution or fundamental law." But "founded on consent," not on implied or necessitated, but on "voluntary consent," it is a compact proper. Mr. Webster is compelled to call the Constitution a government, in direct violation of his own definitions and principles, in order to keep from calling it a compact.

In what manner the Constitution is founded on consent, on a deliberate and voluntary consent, Mr. Webster has himself told us, only a few pages in advance of the above admission. "It is to be remarked," says he, "that the Constitution began to speak only after its adoption. Until it was ratified by nine States it was but a proposal, the mere draft of an instrument. It was like a deed drawn but not executed." This is most exactly and perfectly true. The Constitution was a dead letter, a powerless and inoperative thing, until the ratification or solemn "voluntary assent" of nine States breathed into it the breath of life. It was from this consent, from this compact of nine States, that "the Constitution resulted" as a living or an authoritative document. But when the nine States assented to that "proposal or mere draft of an instrument," and ratified the same by signing it, then each and every article therein specified and written became an article of agreement between the parties to it. "It was like a deed drawn but not executed." But when executed or ratified it was then like a deed signed by the parties; and all the written articles thereof became articles of agreement between the parties. Thus the Constitution not only resulted from the compact of the nine States, but became itself the compact; or, in other words, the written expression of the terms, the conditions, and the articles of the compact. This is what we mean by calling the Constitution a compact between the States. And is not this the language of truth?

Now, on what conditions, or in what cases, does such voluntary consent become a compact proper? Each of the nine States, as it assented to and ratified the Constitution, agreed to all its terms and articles. It agreed to forego the exercise of various powers, and to assume various important liabilities, in consideration that eight other States would do precisely the same thing. And it also agreed that the powers thus delegated by the nine States, or conferred on the general government to be erected for the common good, should be distributed, exercised, limited, and controlled, according to the terms and articles of the Constitution. Is not this a compact proper? Have we not here mutual *promises*, each State parting with what it possessed, and, in consideration thereof, seeking to derive some benefit from the others? If so, then is not this a compact in the proper sense of the word?

The same idea is perfectly expressed by Mr. Webster, in the speech before us. "On entering into the Union," says he, "the people of each State gave up a part of their own power to make laws for themselves, in consideration that, as to common objects, they should have a part in making laws for other States." Here is the voluntary relinquishment on the one part, and the valuable consideration on the other. Is not this a contract proper? If not, then have Blackstone, and Kent, and Pothier, and Domat, and Story written in vain on the nature and law of contracts. If not, then indeed may we despair of ever arriving at the meaning of any one word in any one language under the sun.

It possesses every conceivable attribute of a valid contract. 1. There were "the parties capable of contracting"—the States. 2. It is admitted to have been "voluntary." 3. There was "the sufficient consideration" — the powers surrendered, and the liabilities incurred. Thus it fully answers to every condition laid down by Judge Story himself,[50] as the tests or criteria of a contract proper. It bears no resemblance to those imaginary transactions which certain European writers have invented to explain the origin of their governments, and to give stability to their political theories by fastening them, as with anchors, to past ages. On the contrary, it is historical and real. The time and the manner, the substance and the form, and all the stipulations, are written down and known. It was deliberately and solemnly entered into yesterday; and it is as deliberately and solemnly denied today. Such is the incurable sophistry of power!

The constitution of England is not a compact. There is not, in all the history of England, the least intimation of the people's having assembled, either by themselves or by their representatives, to establish the institution of King, or Lords, or Commons. Yet these three powers constitute the main features in the government of Great Britain. Each power holding the balance between the other two, so as to prevent either from gaining the ascendancy, is what forms the stable equilibrium of the constitution of England. But yet certain parts of the British constitution are compacts, and are so called by writers who reject the theory of a compact as to the whole. According to De Lolme and other authors, Great Britain owes her admirable constitution to the Norman conquest rather than to compact. "It is to the era of the conquest," says he, "that we are to look for the real foundation of the English constitution." Yet changes and improvements in that constitution which, instead of growing, were made by competent parties, he calls compacts. Thus, says he, in reference to the accession of William III. to the throne, "care was taken to repair the breaches which had been made in the constitution, as well as to prevent new ones, and advantage was taken of the rare opportunity of entering into an original and express compact between king and people."[51] Then, after having specified some of the improvements made in the constitution by this compact, he adds, "Lastly, the keystone was put to the arch by the final establishment of the liberty of the press. The Revolution of 1689 is, therefore, the third grand era in the history of the constitution of England." Again, he says, "Without mentioning the compacts which were made with the first Kings of the Norman line, let us only cast our eyes on Magna Charta, which is still the foundation of English liberty,[52] being the great compact by which the Kings, the barons, and the people[53] entered into certain mutual stipulations respecting the prerogatives of the Crown and the rights of the subject."

Thus, the English revolution, like our own, was followed by a compact; and the only difference was that the compact of 1688 was in addition to an old constitution, whereas the compact of 1788 was a constitution in *toto caelo*.

Locke, the great popular champion of the theory of the social compact, was then in the ascendant in the United States, as he was with the Whigs in England. That theory, though exploded now, was then almost universally received in America. That is to say, exploded by showing that there is no historical evidence of any such compact at the origin of the governments of the Old World, and that the alleged transaction was fictitious.[54] But the fiction, which had been only partially realized at the end of revolutions, and not at the beginning of societies, became a fact in the hands of American legislators. In the language of Gouverneur Morris, they came to the convention of 1787 "to make a compact," and they made one. But this draft of a compact, we are told, calls itself a constitution, and not a compact at all. Very well. Suppose it had called itself a compact, even an "original, explicit, and solemn compact," would it not have been just as easy for Mr. Justice Story to affirm that this only meant an "implied contract," as it was for him to do the same thing in regard to the Constitution of Massachusetts? But although the convention of 1787 did not, on the very face of the Constitution, call itself a compact, yet in the letter which, by their "unanimous order," was dispatched with that instrument to the President of Congress, they use the same language in describing the nature of the transaction, that is employed by Sidney, and Locke, and Rousseau. to define "the social contract," as we shall hereafter see.

Although Mr. Justice Story endeavors to bring discredit on the "explicit and solemn" compacts of the New World, by identifying them with the vague and visionary theories of the Old, yet he is perfectly aware of the difference between the fact in the one case and the hypothesis in the other, whenever it suits his purpose to use such knowledge. Thus, he says, in relation to his own Pilgrim Fathers: "Before their landing they drew up and signed a voluntary compact of government, forming, if not the first, at least the best authenticated case of an original social contract for the establishment of a nation, which is to be found in the annals of the world. Philosophers and jurists have perpetually resorted to the theory of such a compact, by which to measure the rights and duties of governments and subjects; but for the most part it has been treated as an effort of imagination, unsustained by the history or practice of nations, and furnishing little of solid instruction for the actual concerns of life. It was little dreamed of, that America should furnish an example of it in primitive and almost patriarchal simplicity."[55] Thus Massachusetts has taken the lead of all the States in the world in the making of social compacts and also in the breaking of them. This last point will, hereafter, be most fully illustrated and proved.

The original draft of the Constitution of Massachusetts was drawn up by John Adams, the second President of the United States, and he certainly entertained no doubt that he was drawing up an "explicit and solemn compact," or reducing the theory of European writers to practice. "It is," says he, "Locke, Sidney, Rousseau, and DeMably reduced to practice."[56] All these celebrated authors on the "social contract" reduced to practice! But it is all in vain. For if the fiction is reduced to fact it is only that the fact may be again reduced to fiction. Massachusetts keep her bargains! Even her most gifted sons, her Storys and her Websters, exert all their genius and exhaust the stores of their erudition to explain away and reduce to a mere nullity her most solemn social compacts, both State and Federal! The theory becomes a fact, and this fact calls itself "an original, explicit, and solemn compact." But then, as interest or power dictates, the fact is explained away, and there ends all the solemn farce.

"Majorities, in a democracy, do not rely on Constitutions, do not care for Constitutions. They rely on numbers and the strong arm." They spurn, with more than imperial scorn, the limitations and restraints which written Constitutions or judicial decisions would impose on their sovereign will and pleasure. They respect such paper checks, such dictates of reason and justice, just about as much as the raging billows of the ocean respected the line which Canute drew upon its shores. In the strong language of De Tocqueville, nothing can restrain them from crushing whatever lies in their path. This has been most emphatically and pre-eminently true of the Northern majority in every instance in which it has gained the ascendency in the grand Democratic Republic of the New World. Cruel as death, and inexorable as the grave, it has moved right on to its object, regardless of the outcries and "complaints of those whom it crushes upon its path."[57] Like every other despotic power, it must, of course, have its sophists, its sycophants, and flatterers, to persuade it that it can never violate its compacts, because it has never made any compact to be violated.

Its character is most perfectly described by a great Northern politician; by one who, indeed, as a distinguished member of the Convention of 1787, helped to frame the Constitution of the United States. What, then, is it in his view? Is it the wild beast of Plato? Is it "the armed rhinoceros or the Hyrcan tiger?" In more respectful language he simply calls it "the legislative lion," but yet, seeming to know its nature, as Falstaff knew the true Prince, by instinct, he paints it beforehand with the pencil of a master. "But, after all," says he, "what does it signify that men should have a written Constitution, containing unequivocal provisions and limitations? The legislative lion will not be entangled in the meshes of a logical net. Legislation will always make the power which it wishes to exercise, unless it be so arranged as to contain within itself the sufficient check. Attempts to restrain it from outrage, by other means, will only render it the more outrageous. The idea of binding legislators by oaths is puerile. Having sworn to exercise the powers granted, according to their true intent and meaning, they will, when they feel a desire to go further, avoid the shame, if not the guilt of perjury, by swearing the true intent and meaning to be, according to their comprehension, that which suits their purpose."[58] Here, in one sentence, we have the whole history of the Northern power in advance; with all its hypocrisy, violation of oaths, and sovereign contempt of its most solemn compacts and engagements. Is it any wonder, then, that the writer should have looked forward, with such sad foreboding, "to the catastrophe of the tragico-comical drama,"[59] in the earliest stages of which he himself had acted so conspicuous a part?

Chapter VIII

The Constitution of 1787 a Compact, Part 4

In discussing the question of the preceding chapters, whether the Constitution was a compact, I introduced much matter which incidentally showed that it was a compact between the States. In like manner, I shall, in proving that the States are the parties to the Constitution, produce much additional evidence that it is a compact. In order to show that the States are the parties to the constitutional compact, let us consider—1. The facts of the case; 2. The language of the Constitution itself; and 3. The views of Hamilton, Madison, Morris, and other framers of the Constitution; and 4. The absurdities flowing from the doctrine that the Constitution is not a compact between the States, but was ordained by the people of America as one nation.

1. *The facts of the case.* "It appears to me," says Mr. Webster, "that the plainest account of the establishment of this government presents the most just and philosophical view of its foundation." True, very true. There is, indeed, no proposition in the celebrated speech of Mr. Webster, nor in any other speech, more true than this; and besides, it goes directly to the point. For the great question which Mr. Webster has undertaken to discuss relates not so much to the superstructure of the government as to "its foundation."

This is the question: How was the Constitution made or ordained, and on what does it rest? Bearing this in mind, let us proceed to consider, first, his plain account of the establishment of the government of the United States, and then the arguments in favor of his position.

First, let us consider, item by item, his plain account. "The people of the several States," says he, "had their separate governments, and between the States there also existed a Confederation." True. "With this condition of things the people were not satisfied, as the Confederation had been found not to fulfil its intended objects. It was proposed, therefore, to erect a new common government, which should possess certain definite powers, such as regarded the property of the people of all the States, and to be formed upon the general model of American Constitutions." This is not so plain. It seems partly true and partly false. We are told that the people had discovered the defects of the Confederation, and were consequently not satisfied with it. Alexander Hamilton, a contemporary witness, tells a very different story. "Men of intelligence," says he, "discovered the feebleness of the structure" of the Confederation; "but the great body of the people, too much engrossed with their distresses to contemplate any but the immediate causes of them, were ignorant of the defects of their Constitution."[60] It was only "when the dangers of the war were removed," and the "men of intelligence" could be heard, that the people saw "what they had suffered, and what they had yet to suffer from a feeble form of government."[61]

"There was no need of discerning men," as Hamilton truly said, "to convince the people of their unhappy condition." But they did need to be instructed respecting the causes of their misery. So far was the great body of the people from having discerned for themselves the causes of their troubles, that Mr. Madison ascribes his ability to make this discovery to his peculiar situation. "Having served as a member of Congress," says he, "through the period between March, 1780, and the arrival of peace, in 1783, I had become intimately acquainted with the public distresses, and the *causes* of them." Thus enlightened, and, under the dreadful aspect of affairs, "sympathizing in the alarm of the friends of free government at the threatened danger of an abortive result to the great, and perhaps last, experiment in its favor," Mr. Madison could not be "insensible to the obligation to aid as far as he could in averting the calamity."[62] Hence he acceded to the desire of his fellow-citizens of the county, and became a member of the legislature of Virginia, "hoping," as he declared, "that he might there best contribute to inculcate the critical posture to which the revolutionary cause was reduced, and the merit of a leading agency of the state in bringing about a rescue of the Union, and the blessings of liberty staked on it, from an impending catastrophe."

It thus appears that the first step which, in the end, led to a change of the Federal Government, was not a popular movement; it did not originate with the people, but sprang from the brain of James Madison, and manifested itself in the action of the legislature of Virginia. But what was this action? Was it to change the form of the Federal Government? Far from it. The resolution of the Virginia legislature, drawn up

by Mr. Madison, and introduced by Mr. Tyler,[63] merely appoints commissioners to meet such commissioners as may be appointed by the
other States, "to take into consideration the trade of the United States,"
and "to consider how far a uniform system in their commercial regulations may be necessary to their common interest and permanent harmony." It suggests no change whatever in the Federal government,
except insofar as this may be implied in a uniform system of commercial regulations.

This resolution, as everyone knows, led to the Annapolis Convention,
which took the next great step towards the formation of the new Constitution. Nor was this a popular movement. It originated in the brain
of Alexander Hamilton. In the address of that convention, he says "That
the express terms of the power to your commissioners supposing a deputation from all the States, and having for its object the trade and commerce of the United States, your commissioners did not conceive it
advisable to proceed on the business of their mission under the circumstances of so partial and defective a representation." The address then
proceeds to recommend "a general meeting of the States in a future
Convention," with powers extending to "other objects than those of
commerce." "They are the more naturally led to this conclusion," say
the Convention, "as in their reflections on the subject they have been
induced to think that the power of regulation, trade is of such comprehensive extent, and will enter so far into the grand system of the Federal government, that to give it efficacy, and to obviate questions and
doubts concerning its precise nature and limits, may require a correspondent adjustment in other parts of the Federal system."

"That there are important defects in the system of the Federal Government," continues the address, "is acknowledged by the acts of those
States which have concurred in the present meeting. That the defects,
upon a close. examination, may be found greater and more numerous
than even these acts imply, is at least so far probable from the embar-
rassment which characterizes the present state of our national affairs,
foreign and domestic, as may reasonably be supposed to merit a deliberate and candid discussion, in some mode which will unite the sentiments and counsels of all the States."

In compliance with this recommendation of "a general meeting of
the States in a future convention," twelve States met at Philadelphia
on the 14th of May, 1787, with instructions to join "in devising and

discussing all such alterations and further provisions as may be necessary to render the Federal Constitution adequate to the exigencies of the Union."[64] "The recommendation was received by the legislature of Virginia," says Mr. Madison, "which happened to be the first that acted on it, and the example of her compliance was made as conciliatory and impressive as possible."[65] Thus it was Alexander Hamilton, as the master spirit of the Annapolis Convention, who first conceived the idea of a general convention to revise and amend the Federal Government, and it was James Madison, as the great ruling genius of the legislature of Virginia, who gave the first and most powerful impulse to that conception. The great mass of the people had very little to do with the movement.

"A resort to a general convention," says Mr. Madison, "to re-model the Confederacy, was not a new idea."[66] He then mentions five persons by whom this idea had been entertained; namely, Pelatiah Webster, Colonel Hamilton, R. H. Lee, James Madison, and Noah Webster. None of these, however, go beyond the idea of Hamilton, "to strengthen the Federal Constitution," or of Madison, to supply its defects.[67] But if this had been a popular movement, Mr. Madison could easily have found, during the period of three years, more than five candidates for the once hotly-contested honor of having conceived the first idea of a Convention to re-model the Confederacy or to amend the Federal Constitution.

The plain truth is, that it was Alexander Hamilton, and not the people who, grappling with the vast and complicated idea of a regular commercial system, saw the changes which such a system must introduce into the Federal Government. Hence, it was Alexander Hamilton, and not the people, who became dissatisfied with the Confederation as it was, and sought to have its Constitution re-modeled. "He was the first," as the historian of the Constitution has truly said, "to perceive and develop the idea of a real union of the people of the United States."[68]

It was not proposed then, as Mr. Webster alleges, and no one ever proposed, to set aside the Confederation in order to establish a government. The Confederation was itself a government. This contrast between the Confederation and a government, as things essentially different in kind, which pervades the whole of Mr. Webster's speech, and which is even interwoven with his "plain account of the establishment of the government" of the United States, is purely a hypothesis of his own. Hamilton and the Convention of Annapolis repeatedly speak, as we have seen, of "the Federal Constitution" and "the Federal Government." Madison and the legislature of Virginia use precisely the same language in reference to the same objects. Even Pelatiah Webster, in this respect, far less original than his great namesake, speaks of the "Constitution" of the Federal Government. The Convention of 1787, also call the old Confederation "the Federal Government."[69]

But we must proceed to the next item of Mr. Webster's plain account. "This proposal," says he, "was assented to, and an instrument was presented to the people of the several States for their consideration. They approved it, and agreed to adopt it, as a Constitution." True, as far as it goes. But when Mr. Webster asks, "Is not this the truth of the whole matter?" we are bound to answer that this is either not the truth of the whole matter, or it is not the whole truth of the matter. On the contrary, it omits precisely those great truths which shed the most light on the foundation of the government of the United States. One might well suppose, from the above statement, that the people of the several States had jointly approved the Constitution, and jointly ordained it as a Constitution. But however essential this view may be to the theory of Mr. Webster—and his theory is as baseless as the fabric of a vision without it—it has not the shadow of a foundation in the facts of history.

The plain and unquestionable fact is, that each State adopted or rejected the Constitution for itself, and for itself alone. No twelve States could by their united action lay the bonds of the new Constitution on the thirteenth State. This was universally conceded. The little State of Rhode Island stood aloof; and though her conduct was reprobated, no one denied her right. Neither all the other States combined, nor all the people of America, had the shadow of an authority to constrain her action, or to control her own free choice. No power on earth could touch the priceless pearl of her sovereignty in the affair. No one presumed to question her right to decide for herself. This right was then as clear as the sun, and all eyes recognized it. And this was true, not only in relation to Rhode Island, but also to each State in the Confederacy. For in the act of re-union each State was perfectly free and independent, uncontrolled and uncontrollable by any power upon earth.

But this fact, which is far too recent and too well authenticated to be denied by anyone, goes to the very foundation of the government of the United States, and shows that its Constitution rested on a federal, and not on a national act. It shows that it was a union of States, effected by the several act of each State, and not the union of all the individuals in America, acting as one political community.

All this was known to Mr. Webster. No man with the least political information or reading could have remained ignorant of it. But still he glossed it over, or kept it in the far distant background, as unsuited to his hypothesis and to the logic of the Northern power, that the Constitution was ordained by "the people of the United States in the aggregate," and not by the people of the United States in the segregate. And yet, after he has given his one-sided, superficial, and unfair statement, he calls it "a plain account," and asks, "Now, sir, is not this the truth of the whole matter? And is not all that we have heard of a compact between Sovereign States the mere effect of a theoretical and artificial mode of reasoning upon the subject? — a mode of reasoning which disregards plain facts for the sake of hypothesis?" Comment here is unnecessary.

Mr. Webster's "plain account" is, in fact, a gross falsification of history. If possible, however, it is surpassed by Mr. Motley. This most unscrupulous writer asserts "The Constitution was not drawn up by the States, it was not promulgated in the name of the States, it was not ratified by the States."[70] Now each and every one of these assertions is diametrically opposed to the truth. Strike out the little syllable "not" from every clause of the above sentence, and it will then express the exact truth. For, in the first place, as the record shows, it is a plain and incontrovertible fact, that the Constitution was drawn up or framed by the States.

It was drawn up or framed, as everyone knows, by the Convention of 1787, in which the States, and the States alone, were represented. Every iota of the Constitution was decided upon, and found a place in that written instrument, by a vote of the States; each State having one vote; the little State of Delaware, for example, having an equal vote with New York, Pennsylvania, or Virginia. No fact should be more perfectly notorious, or well-known, than this; for it stands out everywhere on the very face of the proceedings of the Convention, which framed the Constitution. Thus, for example, "On the question for a single Executive; it was agreed to, Massachusetts, Connecticut, Pennsylvania,

Virginia, North Carolina, South Carolina, Georgia, aye—7; New York, Delaware, Maryland, no—3."[71] In like manner, every other item of the Constitution was decided upon, and the whole instrument formed, by a vote of the States; acting as separate, independent, and equal bodies. How, in the face of such a fact, could Mr. Motley so boldly assert, that the Constitution was not drawn up, or framed, by the States? By whom, then, was it framed? Was it framed by "the people of the United States in the aggregate," acting as one nation? Nothing is farther from the truth. There is not even the shadow of a foundation for any such assertion or insinuation. Will it be said, that the Constitution was drawn up, not by the States, but by those who proposed its various articles? If so, such a subterfuge would be nothing to the purpose, and very far from deserving a moment's notice.

The second assertion of Mr. Motley, that the Constitution "was not promulgated in the name of the States," is equally unfortunate. For, as everyone knows, it was promulgated by the Congress of the Confederation in which the States alone were represented, and in which all the States were perfectly equal. The "Articles of Confederation" says: "In determining questions in the United States, in Congress assembled, *each State shall have one vote.*"[72] It was thus as equals that the States voted in determining to promulgate the new Constitution; and it was in consequence of that action of the States, that the Constitution was promulgated and laid before the people of the several States for their adoption. here, again, in direct opposition to the unblushing assertion of Mr. Motley, the Constitution was promulgated by the States in Congress assembled. If Mr. Motley had only deigned to glance at the history of the transaction about which he speaks so confidently, he could not have failed to perceive, that the Constitution was first submitted, by the Convention of 1787, "to the United States in Congress assembled,"[73] and that it was afterwards, in conformity with the opinion of the Convention, promulgated by the States "in Congress assembled." But Mr. Motley's theory of the Constitution takes leave of history; and has little to do with facts, except to contradict them.

"The Constitution was not ratified by the States," says Motley. In the Resolutions just quoted, and which were unanimously adopted by the Convention of 1787, we find this clause: *"Resolved,* That in the opinion of this Convention that as soon as the Convention of nine States shall have ratified this Constitution, the United States in Congress assembled should fix a day on which electors should be appointed by *the States which shall have ratified the same,*" &c. Not one of the fathers of the Constitution ever imagined that it was not ratified by the States. But in this instance, as well as in many others, their most familiar idea is repudiated, and their most explicit language is contradicted, by Mr. Motley.

In the sentence next to the one above quoted from Motley, he says: *"The States never acceded to it* [the Constitution,] and possess no power to secede from it."[74] This peremptory and flat contradiction of the language of the fathers of the Constitution deserves no further notice; since it has already been sufficiently exposed.

Chapter IX

The Constitution of 1787 a Compact, Part 5

2. The Language of the Constitution. "We, the people of the United States, in order to for in a more perfect union . . . do ordain and establish this Constitution for the United States of America." The first clause of this preamble to the Constitution, wholly detached from its history and from every other portion of the same instrument, as well as from all the contemporary and subsequent expositions of its authors, is made the very cornerstone of the Northern theory of the general government of the United States. That tremendous theory, or scheme of power, has been erected on this naked, isolated, and, as we expect to show, grossly misinterpreted clause.

From the bare words of this clause it is concluded, both by Story and Webster, that the Constitution was established or ratified, not by a federal but by a national act; or, in other terms, that it was not ratified by the States, but by a power superior to the States, that is, by the sovereign will of "the whole people of the United States in the aggregate," acting as one nation or political community. With Puritanical zeal they stick to "the very words of the Constitution," while the meaning of the words is unheeded by them, either because it is unknown, or because it does not suit their purpose. But words are not the money, they are merely the counters, of wise men. The meaning of the Constitution is the Constitution.

In arriving at the meaning of these words, of the very clause in question, I shall not do the least violence to any law of language, or to any rule of interpretation. I shall, on the contrary, show that we are not "obliged to depart from the words of the instrument,"[75] as Mr. Justice Story alleges, in order to sustain our interpretation of any portion of it. I shall show that the Southern interpretation of the clause in question is, in reality, the only fair, legitimate and reasonable sense of the preamble itself. Nor shall I, for this purpose, repeat the arguments which are usually employed by the friends of the South in this controversy. Those arguments are amply sufficient to refute the interpretation of Story and Webster. But they are so well put by others, by John Taylor, of Caroline; by Judge Upshur, of Virginia; by John C. Calhoun, of South Carolina; and especially by Mr. Spence, of Liverpool, that I need not repeat them here. Everyone may find access to them in the admirable work of Mr. Spence.[76] Hence, passing by those arguments, I shall, by an appeal to the records of the Convention of 1787, make my position good, and annihilate the great cornerstone of the Northern theory of the Constitution of the United States.

"We, the people of the United States." The history of these words is curious and instructive. Only a portion of that history has, as yet, been laid before the public of England or of the United States. In the light of that history the great cornerstone in question will be found to crumble into dust and ashes; and the only wonder will be, that considerations so clear and so conclusive should have been so long locked up, as a profound secret, in the records of the very Convention that formed the Constitution of the United States.

It is well known that in the original draft of the Constitution, its preamble, instead of saying, "We, the people of the United States," specified each State by name, as the previous Articles of Confederation had done. If it had remained thus, then the States would have appeared, on the very face of the preamble itself, as the parties to the Constitution. But the preamble, as is well known, was afterwards changed, by omitting to mention the States by name. There are, however, some most important facts connected with the change and the origin of the words in question, which seem to be wholly unknown on both sides of the Atlantic. They have, certainly, attracted no notice whatever from any of the writers on the great controversy between the North and the South.

The first of these facts relates to the person by whom, and the manner in which, the change in question was effected; or, the words, "We, the people of the United States," were substituted for an enumeration of the States by name. During all the great discussions of the Convention, the preamble to the Constitution retained its original form; nor was there, from the beginning to the end of their deliberations, a single whisper of dissatisfaction with it in that form. Every member of the Convention appeared perfectly satisfied that the States should stand, on the very front of the Constitution, as the parties to the compact into which they were about to enter. It was only after the provisions of the Constitution were agreed upon, and its language was referred to "a committee on style," that the names of the States were silently omitted, and the clause, "We, the people of the United States," substituted in their place. Now, it will not be denied, that if this change had not been made by the "committee on style," then the States would have bean the parties to the new Constitution just as they had been to the old Articles of Confederation. Hence, if the interpretation of Story and Webster be the true one, then it must be admitted that the "committee on style," appointed merely to express the views of the Convention, really transformed the nature of the Constitution of the United States! Then it must be admitted, that the "committee on style," by a single turn of its pen, changed the course of history and the meaning of its facts; causing the supreme power of the Federal Government to emanate, not from the States, but from the people of America as one political community! Did the "committee on style" do all this? And is it on legislation like this that a sovereign State is to be deemed guilty of treason and rebellion against the sublime authority of the people of America, and visited with the utmost vengeance of that malign power? The sublime authority of the people of America, the one grand nation, erected and established solely by the pen of the "committee on style"!

This clause, "We, the people of the United States," introduced by the "committee on style," and passed over in perfect silence by the whole Convention, is the great stronghold, if it has one, of the Northern theory of the Constitution. The argument from these words appears in every speech, book, pamphlet, and discussion by every advocate of the North. It was wielded by Mr. Webster in his great debate with Mr. Calhoun, in 1833, and still more fully in his still more eloquent speech on Foot's resolutions in 1830. "The Constitution itself," says he, "in its very front, declares that it was ordained and established by the people of the United States in the aggregate." The fact is not so. The Constitution neither declares that it was established by the people of the United States in the aggregate, nor by the people of the United States in the segregate. But if we look into the history of the transaction, we shall find that it was established by them in the latter character, and not in the former. We shall find that each State acted separately, and for itself alone; and that no one pretended, or imagined, that the whole aggregate vote of any twelve States could bind the thirteenth State, without its own individual consent and ratification. In order to make out his interpretation, Mr. Webster interpolates the legislation of the "committee on style" with words of his own.

The change in the preamble to the Constitution was effected by the pen of Gouverneur Morris, one of the most zealous advocates in the Convention of 1787, for a strong national Government. He certainly wished all power to emanate from the people of America, and to have them regarded as one great nation. But did he accomplish his wish? In the Convention, says the record, "Gouverneur Morris moved that the reference of the plan (i e., of their Constitution) be made to one General Convention, chosen and authorized by the people, to consider, amend, and establish the same."[77] This motion, if adopted, would indeed have caused the Constitution to be ratified by "the people of the United States in the aggregate," or as one nation. This would, in fact, have made it a Government emanating from the people of America in one General Convention assembled and not from the States. But how was this motion received by the Convention? Was it approved and passed in the affirmative by that body? It did not even find a second in the Convention of 1787. So says the record, and this is a most significant fact. So completely was such a mode of ratification deemed out of the question that it found not the symptom or shadow of support from the authors of the Constitution of the United States.

Now was the very object, which Gouverneur Morris so signally failed to accomplish directly and openly by his motion, indirectly and covertly effected by his style? And if so, did he design to effect such a change in the fundamental law of the United States of America? It is certain that precisely the same effect is given to his words, to his style, as would have resulted from the passage of his motion by the Convention. Did Gouverneur Morris then intend that his words should have such force and effect? In supposing him capable of such a fraud on the Convention of 1787, I certainly do him no injustice, since we have his own confession that he actually perpetrated several such frauds on that assembly of Constitution-makers. "That instrument," says he in reference to the Constitution, "was written by the fingers which writes this letter. Having rejected redundant terms, I believed it to be as clear as language would permit; excepting, nevertheless, a part of what relates to the judiciary. On that subject conflicting opinions had been maintained with so much professional astuteness, that it became necessary to select phrases, which expressing my own notions would not alarm others, nor shock their self-love; and to the best of my recollection this was the only part which passed without cavil."[78] How adroitly, then, how cunningly, he cheats the Convention into the unconscious sanction of his "own notions," and this great legislator of the North, even in the purer days of the infant republic, was proud of the fraud!

Nor is this the only instance in which, according to his own confession and boast, Gouverneur Morris tricked the Convention into the adoption of his own private views. "I always thought," says he, in another letter, "that when we should acquire Canada and Louisiana, it would be proper to govern them as provinces, and allow them no voice in our councils. In wording the third section of the fourth article I went as far as circumstances would permit to establish the exclusion. Candor obliges me to add my belief that, had it been more pointedly expressed, a strong opposition would have been made."[79] Thus, as the penman of the committee on style, he abused his high position, not only to mould the judiciary system of the United States to suit his "own notions," but also to determine the fate of two vast empires! Is not such legislation truly wonderful? Instead of weighing every word with the utmost care, and then depositing it in the Constitution asunder the solemn sanction of an oath, the Convention trusts the style of the instrument to a fine writer, who cunningly gives expression to his own views in opposition to those of the assembly! "In a play, or a moral," says Jeremy Bentham, "an improper word is but a word; and the impropriety, whether noted or not, is attended with no consequences. In a body of laws—especially of laws given as Constitutional ones—an improper word would be a national calamity, and civil war may be the consequences of it. Out of one foolish word may start a thousand daggers." How true, and how fearfully has this truth been illustrated by the history of the United States!

But although Gouverneur Morris was capable of such a fraud on the Convention, we have no good reason to believe he intended one, by the substitution of the words, "We, the people of the United States," for the enumeration of all the States by name. He has nowhere confessed to any such thing; and besides he did not understand his own words as they are so confidently understood by Story and Webster. Every rational inquirer after truth should, it seems to me, be curious to know what sense Gouverneur Morris attached to the words in ques-

tion, since it was by his pen that they were introduced into the preamble of the Constitution. Nor will such curiosity be diminished, but
rather increased, by the fact that he did, in some cases, aim to foist his
own private views into the Constitution of his country. How, then, did
Gouverneur Morris understand the words, "We, the people of the
United States"? Did he infer from these words that the Constitution
was not a compact between States, or that it was established by the
people of America, and not by the States? I answer this question in the
words of Gouverneur Morris himself. "The Constitution," says he, "was
a compact, not between individuals, but between political societies, the
people, not of America, but of the United States, each enjoying sovereign power and of course equal rights."[80] Language could not possibly
be more explicit. Nor could it be more evident than it is, that Gouverneur Morris, the very author of the words in question, entertained
precisely the same view of their meaning as that maintained by Mr.
Calhoun and his school. This point was, indeed, made far too clear by
the proceedings of the Convention of 1787 for any member of that body
to entertain the shadow of a doubt in relation to it. Nor can anyone
read these proceedings as they deserve to be read, without agreeing
with Gouverneur Morris, that the authors of the Constitution designed
it to be ratified, as in fact it was, by "the people of the United States,"
not as individuals, but as "political societies, each enjoying sovereign
power, and of course equal rights." Or, in other words, without seeing
that "the Constitution was a compact," not between individuals, "but
between political societies," between sovereign States. This, in the next
chapter, I hope and expect to make perfectly clear, by bringing to view
the origin of the words "We, the people," and by showing the sense in
which they were universally understood and used by the members of
the Convention of 1787 in the very act of framing the Constitution of
the United States.

Chapter X

The Constitution of 1787 a Compact, Part 6

The Convention of 1787 did, as we have seen, refuse to call the government a national one, and gave it the name of "the government of the United States." Did they then make it a national one by enacting that it should be ordained by "the whole people of the United States in the aggregate" as one political society? Again, when it was proposed in the Convention to ordain the Constitution by "the people of the United States in the aggregate," in one general Convention assembled, the motion failed, as we have seen, to secure a second. Did Gouverneur Morris, then, the author of that proposal, achieve by his style what he failed to accomplish by his motion? If so, what should we think of the incompetency of the Convention?

Nor was this all. For Madison introduced a motion which required "a concurrence of a majority of both the States and the people"[81] at large to establish the Constitution; and this proposition was rejected by the Convention. All these motions, designed to connect the new government with a national origin, were lost, and the decree went forth that the Constitution should be established by the accession of nine States, each acting for itself alone, and to be bound only by its own voluntary act. Now, the question is, was all this action of the Convention overruled and defeated by the committee on style, or rather by its penman, Gouverneur Morris? If he formed such design, then it must be admitted that the Northern theory of the Constitution was conceived in fraud and brought forth in iniquity; and every honest man at the North ought to be ashamed both of its origin and its existence. But, as we have already seen, Gouverneur Morris did not understand his own words, "We, the people," as they are understood by the more modern expounders of the Constitution at the North. Hence we have no reason to believe that he intended, in this case at least, a fraud on the design and will of the Convention.

Was the whole thing done then, and the nature of the Constitution transformed, by a slip of the pen, or by accident? After all their opposition both to the name and to the thing did the Convention, by sheer oversight, blunder into the construction of a purely national government, by permitting it to be established by the people of America as one grand political community? If Mr. Justice Story's view of the words, "We, the people of the United States," be correct, how did it happen that the opponents of such a mode of ratification said absolutely nothing? The whole instrument, as amended by the committee on style, was read in the hearing of the Convention, beginning with the preamble, and yet the words, "We, the people of the United States," now deemed so formidable to the advocates of State sovereignty, did not raise a single whisper of opposition. How could this have happened if the words in question were supposed to mean the people of America, or the whole people of the United States as one political society? Were Mason, and Martin, and Paterson, and Ellsworth, all too dull to perceive that meaning, which is so perfectly obvious to Mr. Justice Story, and which he imagines that nothing but the most purblind obstinacy can resist? Were all the friends of the States, as independent sovereignties, asleep on their posts while Gouverneur Morris thus transformed the nature of the Constitution, without knowing it himself, by causing it to emanate, not from the States, but from the people of America as one nation? No. Not one of these suppositions is the true one. The whole mystery is explained in the proceedings of the Convention of 1787, as exhibited in "The Madison Papers," an explanation which, however, has hitherto been most unaccountably overlooked. We may there find the real meaning of the words in question, and see why they gave no alarm to the advocates of State sovereignty.

If we cast our eyes all along the subject of "the mode of ratification," ranging from page 735 to page 1632 of "The Madison Papers," we shall perceive that the question, whether the Constitution should be ratified by the people of "the United States in the aggregate," or by the several States, was not considered by the Convention at all. No such question was before the Convention. It was neither mooted nor considered by them. The error of Story and Webster is, that they construe the first clause of the Constitution as if it referred to one question; whereas, in fact, it referred to quite another and a far different question—that is, they construed this clause in profound darkness as to the origin of its words, as well as to their use and application in the Convention of

1787. If they had understood them as actually and uniformly used or applied by the framers of the Constitution, then they could neither have deceived. themselves nor the people of the North. If, indeed, they had been members of that Convention, or had only examined its proceedings, they would have seen why the staunch advocates of State sovereignty raised not even the slightest whisper of opposition to the words, "We, the people." Or, if Patrick Henry had been a member of that assembly, then he could not have exclaimed, as he did, "Why say We, the people, and not We, the States?"—an exclamation so often-quoted by Story, Webster, and the whole Northern school of politicians as a conclusive authority—for then he would have seen that "We, the people," in the language of the framers of the Constitution, meant precisely the same thing as "We, the States," and neither more nor less.

The question before the Convention was, whether the Constitution should be ratified by the legislatures or by the sovereign peoples of the several States. No one doubted that it was to be ratified by the States. This, as we shall see, was on all hands regarded as a settled point. The only question was, whether it should be ratified by the States, acting through their legislatures, or through Conventions elected to represent the people for that special purpose. In the discussion of this question, most of the members insisted that the Constitution should be ratified by the people, by the States in their sovereign capacity, or by their Conventions These several modes of expression were, in the vocabulary of the Convention, used as convertible terms, as perfectly synonymous with each other. Hence the phrase, "the people of the United States," as used and understood by them, meant the people of the several States as contradistinguished from their legislatures, and not the people of America as contradistinguished from the distinct and separate sovereign peoples off the different States. This application of the words is the invention of theorists merely. It was unknown to the Convention of 1787, and has had no existence except in the imaginations of those by whom their labors have been systematically misconstrued and perverted from their original design.

Some few members of the Convention were in favor of leaving "the States to choose their own mode of ratification," but the great majority of them insisted that the Constitution should be referred to the States for ratification, either through their legislatures or through their people in Conventions assembled. It was in regard to these two methods that the Convention was divided. All agreed that it should be done by "the States," and the only question was as to how "the States" should do it. The idea that it was designed to be done, or that it was done, by the people of America as one nation, is the dream of a later day, and, as we shall see, is nothing but a dream.

Some insisted that it should be ratified by the States in their corporate capacity—that is, by their legislatures; and others that it should be ratified by the States in their sovereign political capacity—that is, by their Conventions assembled for that express purpose. In other words, some contended that it ought to be ratified by their general agents, the legislatures; and others that it ought to be ratified by their special agents, the Conventions elected and assembled to perform that act of sovereign power. In both cases, it was to be ratified by the States, but the opposite parties preferred different modes of ratification by them.

In debating this question, as to the mode of ratification by the States (the only one before the Convention), some of the most inflexible advocates of State sovereignty insisted that it should be ratified by "the people of the United States." But then they understood this language, and every member of the Convention understood it to mean the peoples of the several States, as distinguished from their legislatures. If, for one moment, they had imagined that their language could have been construed to mean a ratification of the Constitution by the collective will of the whole people of America, they would have shrunk from its use with horror; for they dreaded nothing more than the idea of such an immense consolidated democracy. On the contrary, they clung to the States, and to their rights, as the only anchor of safety against the overwhelming and all-devouring floods of such a national union of mere numbers or individuals. George Mason, no less than Patrick Henry, would have exclaimed against the words, "We, the people," if, as a member of the Convention of 1787, he had not learned that they only meant "We, the States."

In discussing the question as to the mode of ratification by "the States," Mr. Mason said "he considered a reference of the plan to the authority of the people as one of the most important and essential of the resolutions. The legislatures have no power to ratify it . . . Another strong reason (said he) was that admitting the legislatures to have a competent authority it would be wrong to refer the plan to them, because succeeding legislatures, having equal authority, could undo the acts of their predecessors."[82] This argument was repeatedly urged by other members; and it was insisted that if the Constitution should be ratified by the legislatures of the States, instead of by the people of the States, it would rest upon a weak and tottering foundation, since the legislatures which had established might claim the power to repeal.

In like manner Mr. Madison said, "For these reasons, as well as for others, he thought it indispensable that the new Constitution should be ratified in the unexceptionable form, and by the supreme authority of the people themselves"[83]—that is, as the context shows, by the supreme authority of the people of the several States in opposition to their "legislative sanction only." Not one word was ever said during the whole of the debate about referring the Constitution to the people of the whole country in the aggregate for ratification. This idea had not then risen above the horizon of the political world, though it afterwards became the political sun of the Northern section of the Union.

Those who advocated the mode of ratification by the people, or by the Conventions of the States elected for that purpose, prevailed over those who had urged the ratification by the legislatures. The majority favored the mode of ratification by the people or the Conventions. Accordingly, when the committee of detail reported a draft of the Constitution, we find these words—"Article XXI. The ratifications of the Conventions of States shall be sufficient for the organization of this Constitution."[84] Thus it came to be perfectly understood that it should be ratified by the Conventions or the peoples of the several States, and not by their legislatures.

But here the question arose, if the blank for the number of States should be filled with "seven," "eight," or "nine." The Constitution, as it stood, might, in the opinion of Mr. Madison, be put in force over "the whole body of the people, though less than a majority of them should ratify it." But, in the opinion of Mr. Wilson, "As the Constitution stands, the States only which ratify can be bound."[85] In order to remove this difficulty, and settle the question, Mr. King moved to add, at the end of Article XXI, the words "between the said States, so as to confine the operation of the government to the States ratifying the same."[86] Thus it was Rufus King, at first one of the most strenuous advocates in the Convention of 1787 for a strong national government, who introduced the words by which the Constitution was made binding "between the

States so ratifying the same." These words proved acceptable to Madison and Wilson, though both were among the most zealous advocates of a strong general government in the Convention of 1787, and they became a part of the new Constitution. Thus it was universally understood by the Convention, and so expressed, that the new Constitution was to be established "by the ratification of the Conventions of States," and to be binding only "between the States so ratifying the same."

During all this time the name of each State still retained its place in the preamble to the Constitution, in which the committee of detail made no change; and if the party, with Gerry and Hamilton at their head, who wished to fill the blank with the whole thirteen States, had prevailed, we have no reason to believe that any alteration would in this respect have been made in the preamble to the Constitution. But when, after debate, the blank was filled with "nine," it became impossible to specify the States between whom the new Constitution might be established or the new government organized. Hence it became proper, if not necessary, to drop the specification of the States by name —a change which, as we have seen, was first introduced by the committee on style, and read to the Convention without raising the slightest objection or murmur.

We are now prepared to see, as in the clear light of noon-day, why the words, "We, the people of the United States," which have since made so much noise in the political world, did not make any whatever in the Convention of 1787. Why should George Mason, or any other adherent of State sovereignty, object to the words introduced by the committee on style? They merely expressed the very thing for which he had contended, and which had been fully expressed in the seventh Article of the new Constitution. For when it was determined that the Constitution should be ratified by "the Conventions of the States," and not by the legislatures, this was exactly equivalent, in the uniform language of the Convention of 1787, to saying that it shall be ratified by "the people of the States." Hence, the most ardent friend of State rights, or State sovereignty, saw no reason why he should object to the words, "We, the people of the United States," because he knew they were only intended to express the mode of ratification by the States for which he had contended—that is, by the States in their sovereign capacity, as so many political societies or peoples, as distinguished from their legislatures.

Chapter XI

The Constitution of 1787 a Compact, Part 7

The views of Hamilton, Madison, Morris, and other Framers of the Constitution. This subject has already been anticipated, but by no means exhausted. Considering the unparalleled boldness of Northern assertion, it is necessary to lay bare a few more of its hidden mysteries. "Indeed," says Mr. Webster, "if we look into all contemporary history; to the numbers of *The Federalist;* to the debates in the Convention; to the publication of friends and foes, they all agree, that a change had been made from a confederacy of States to a different system; they all agree, that the Convention had formed a Constitution for a national government. With this result some were satisfied, and some were dissatisfied; but all admitted that the thing had been done. In none of the various productions and publications, did anyone intimate that the new Constitution was but another compact between States in their sovereign capacity. I do not find such an opinion advanced in a single instance."[87]

Now this is certainly as bold and sweeping an assertion as could well be made in human language. It is certainly as full, round, and complete an untruth as was ever uttered. It will, upon examination, be found that, to use the mildest possible terms, it is fitly characterized by the two words—*high-sounding and hollow.* It would, perhaps, be difficult for any man, except Mr. Webster and his successor in the Senate of the United States, to produce a bold and sweeping an assertion, which, like the above, is at every point diametrically opposed to the truth. I shall proceed to prove, and to establish beyond the shadow of a doubt, this heavy accusation against "the great expounder," by extracts from the records and publications to which he so solemnly, and yet so unscrupulously, appeals.

I shall begin with the Convention that formed the Constitution itself. It will not be necessary to reproduce the language of Gouverneur Morris, one of the most celebrated men of that Convention, and one of the warmest advocates of a strong national government. We have already seen,[88] that he pronounced the Constitution *"a compact . . . between the United States, each enjoying sovereign power."* Indeed, in the Convention of 1787, he expressly declared, that the object was to form a "compact with other States," and he afterwards declared, that "the thing had been done." Again, James Madison himself, "the father of the Constitution," and the most laborious member of the Convention of 1787, called it, as we have seen, "a pact" between the States in that Convention; and from that day to the end of his life, Mr. Madison continued to pronounce the new Constitution "a compact to which the States are the parties." In the Virginia ratifying Convention of 1788, in "the numbers of the *Federalist,"* in the Virginia Resolutions of 1798 and 1799, in the Virginia Report of 1800, in his celebrated letter to Mr. Everett of 1830; in one and all of these well-known public documents, as well as in others from his pen, this illustrious architect of the Constitution most emphatically pronounced it "a compact to which the States are the parties." In the Virginia Resolutions, a political formula which the American people, of all parties and all sections, had sworn by for more than thirty years, Mr. Madison wrote for the legislature of his State: "This Assembly does explicitly and peremptorily declare, *that it views the powers of the Federal Government, as resulting from the compact, to which the States are parties."* How completely, then, was the very existence of Mr. Madison, and of all the great transactions in which he had borne so conspicuous a part, ignored by Mr. Webster in the bold and astounding assertion, that neither friend nor foe had ever considered the new Constitution as a "compact between the States." The venerable old man must, indeed, have felt, as he read the speech of Mr. Webster, that he was fast sinking into oblivion, and that all the great transactions of his life were fast being forgotten amid the blaze of new ideas.

Accordingly, in a letter to Mr. Webster, called forth by the very speech in question, Mr. Madison once more raised his voice in favor of the one invariable doctrine of his life. "It is fortunate," says he, "in the letter referred to," when disputed theories can be decided by undisputed facts; and here the undisputed fact is, *"that the Constitution was made by the people, but as embodied into the several States, who were parties to it."* Again, in the same letter, he says: "The Constitution of the United States, being established by a competent authority, *by that of the sovereign people of the several States, who were parties to it.* " Most fortunate is it, indeed, when disputed theories may be tested by undisputed facts; but how infinitely unfortunate is it, when new and disputed theories begin to pass for everything, and indisputable facts for nothing! No, when those who cling to hitherto undisputed facts are accounted traitors, and visited with a merciless and a measureless vengeance, by those who, having nothing better than disputed theories to stand on, are nevertheless backed by the possession of brute force sufficient to crush their opponents, and silence the voice of truth!

All agree, says Mr. Webster, *"The Federalist,"* "the debates in the Conventions," "the publications of friends and foes"—all agree, *"that a change had been made from a confederacy of States to a different system."* Now, there is James Wilson, inferior only to Madison and Hamilton in the influence he exerted in favor of the new Constitution, who declares, that the only object aimed at by the Convention of 1787, was to enable the States "to confederate anew on better principles," and if no more could be effected, he would agree to "a partial union of the States, with a door left open for the accession of the rest." Accordingly, it was finally agreed by the Convention, that nine States might form the new Union, with a door left open for the accession of the other four. In fact, eleven States confederated on the new principles; and it was more than a year before the remaining two States acceded to the compact of the Constitution, and became members of the Union.

Even Alexander Hamilton, in that great authority, *The Federalist, to* which Mr. Webster so confidently appeals, is directly and flatly opposed to the bold and unscrupulous assertion of "the great expounder." If the new Constitution should be adopted, says he, the Union would "still be, in fact and in theory, an association of States, or a confederacy."[89] Again, in the eightieth number of the work, Hamilton calls the new Union "the CONFEDERACY," putting the word in capital letters, in order that it may not be overlooked by the most superficial reader. If necessary , it might be shown by various other extracts, that Alexander Hamilton, while insisting on the adoption of the new Constitution in *The Federalist,* speaks of the new Union as a confederacy of States. How, then, could Mr. Webster avouch *The Federalist* to support the assertion, that "a change had been made from a confederacy to a different system"? Was this in his character of "the great expounder," or of the great deceiver?

This appeal to the *Federalist* appears, if possible, still more wonderful, when viewed in connection with other numbers of the same work. Indeed, it was objected to the new Constitution by its enemies, that "it would make a change from a confederacy to a different system," and this very objection is met and repelled in the pages of the *Federalist*. "Will it be said," demands the *Federalist*, "that the *fundamental principles* of the confederation were not within the purview of the Convention, and ought not to have been varied? I ask, what are these principles? Do they require, that in the establishment of the Constitution, the States should be regarded as distinct and independent sovereigns? They are so regarded by the Constitution proposed."[90] Now here the position of Mr. Webster, that the new Union was not a confederacy of States, that it was not made by the States "as distinct and independent sovereigns," but was ordained by "the people of the United States in the aggregate" as one nation; is directly and emphatically negatived by the very authority to which he appeals in support of his monstrous heresy.

Nor is this all. In the preceding number of the *Federalist*, it is said, "Each State, in ratifying the Constitution, is considered as a sovereign body, independent of all others, and only to be bound by its own voluntary act." Thus, according to the *Federalist*, the Constitution was ratified by "each State, as a sovereign body, independent of all others." No such thing, says Mr. Webster, it was not ratified by the States at all, it was ordained by a power superior to the States, by the sovereign will of the whole people of the United States; and yet he boldly and unblushingly appeals to the *Federalist* in support of his assertion! Why did he not quote the *Federalist*? No, why did he not read the *Federalist*, before he ventured on such a position?

Mr. Webster has, indeed, quoted one expression from the *Federalist*. "The fabric of American empire," says Hamilton, in the twenty-second number of the *Federalist*, "ought to rest on the solid basis of *the consent of the people*." After quoting these words, Mr. Webster adds, with his usual confidence, "Such is the language, sir, addressed to the people, while they yet had the Constitution under consideration. The powers conferred on the new government were perfectly well understood to be conferred, not by any State, or the people of any State, but by the people of the United States." Now, if Mr. Webster had only paid more attention to the debates of the Convention of 1787, he might have escaped this egregious blunder, this gross perversion of the words of Alexander Hamilton. No, if he had only considered the three sentences which immediately precede the extract made by him, he would have seen that Hamilton was speaking to a very different question from that which had so fully engrossed and occupied his mind. He would have seen, that the language related, not to the question whether the Constitution ought to be ratified by the people of the States, or by the people of America as one nation; but to the question, whether it ought to be ratified by the Legislatures, or by the people, of the several States. This was the question of the Convention of 1787; and this was the question to which its ablest member was speaking, when he said "the fabric of American empire ought to rest on the solid basis of the consent of the people." Read the context, and this will be perfectly plain. "It has not a little contributed," says the context, "to the infirmities of the existing federal system, that it never had a ratification of the PEOPLE. Resting on no better foundation than the consent of the several Legislatures, it has been exposed to frequent and intricate questions concerning the validity of its powers; and has, in some instances, given rise to the enormous doctrine of legislative repeal." Such is the context of Mr. Webster's very partial and one-sided extract. It shows that Hamilton was arguing the advantage of the new system over the old, just as it had been argued in the Convention of 1787; because the old confederation rested on the consent of the Legislatures of the several States, whereas the new confederacy was to rest on the consent of the people of the several States. Hence it would be free from all doubts with respect to the power of "legislative repeal."

Alexander Hamilton certainly knew that the Constitution was merely a proposal, or plan of government, and would so remain until it should be ratified by "the Conventions of nine States," and that then it would be binding only "between the States so ratifying the same." For these are the words of the Constitution itself, as well as of his own formula of ratification in the Convention of 1787. These nine States or more, thus leagued together by a solemn compact entered into by the people of the several States in their highest sovereign capacity, is "the solid basis" to which he refers; and which, like so many massive columns, were to bear up "the fabric of American empire." The consent of the whole people indeed! The majority of the whole voting population of the United States; which may be one thing today and another tomorrow, and which is bound by nothing but its own sovereign will and pleasure! Surely, nothing could be less solid or stable, or less fit to support "the fabric of American empire." Such a system were, indeed, more like Aristophanes' City of the Birds, floating in mid air, and tossed by the winds, than like the scheme of a rational being for the government of men. No conception could be more utterly inconsistent with all the well-known sentiments of Alexander Hamilton.

But if, instead of perverting the high authority of the *Federalist* by wresting one particular passage from its context, Mr. Webster had only read a little further, he would have discovered what was then "perfectly well understood" respecting the nature of the Constitution. He would have discovered, that it was, according to the *Federalist,* established, not by "the people of the United States in the aggregate," or as one nation, but by each of the States acting for itself alone. "The Constitution is to be founded," says the *Federalist,*[91] "on the assent and ratification of the people of America, given by deputies elected for the special purpose." This, too, is the language "addressed to the people, while they yet had the Constitution under consideration." Why, then, is not this language seized upon, and held up as proof positive, that the Constitution rested on the assent, "not of any State, or the people of any State," but on that of "the people of America"? The reason is plain. Though these words, taken by themselves, would have answered Mr. Webster's purpose better than his extract from the *Federalist;* yet are they immediately followed, in the same sentence, by an explanation, which shows their meaning when used in the *Federalist.* "The Constitution is to be founded," says that highest of all authorities "on the assent and ratification of the people of America, given by deputies elected for the special purpose," but, it is added, "this assent and ratification is to be given by the people, *not as individuals comprising one entire nation, but as composing the distinct and independent States to which they respectively belong. It is to be the assent and ratification of the several States, derived from the supreme authority in each State—the authority of the people themselves.* The act, therefore, establishing the Constitution will not be *a national,* but *a federal* act."[92] Not so, says Mr. Webster, the Constitution was established not by a *federal,* but by a *national* act; not by any State, or the people of any State, but by the whole people of the United States as one sovereign body; and yet he appeals to the *Federalist* in support of his doctrine!

"That it will be a federal, and not a national act," continues the *Federalist*, "as these terms are understood by objectors, the act of the people, as forming so many independent states, not as forming one aggregate nation, is obvious from this single consideration, that it is to result neither from the decision of a *majority* of the people of the Union, nor from that of a *majority* of the states. It must result from the *unanimous* assent of the several States that are parties to it, differing no otherwise from their ordinary assent than in its being expressed, not by the legislative authority, but by that of the people themselves. Were the people regarded in this transaction as forming one nation, the will of the majority of the whole people of the United States would bind the minority; in the same manner as the majority in each State must bind the minority; and the will of the majority must be determined either by a comparison of the individual votes, or by considering the will of the majority of the States, as evidences of the will of a majority of the people of the United States. Neither of these has been adopted. Each State, in ratifying the Constitution, is considered as a sovereign body, independent of all others, and only to be bound by its own voluntary act." Could language be more perfectly explicit? Yet, directly in the face of all this, or else in profound ignorance of all this, Mr. Webster appeals to the authority of the *Federalist* in favor of the very position which, as we have seen, it so pointedly condemns. No, in spite of the clear, explicit, and unanswerable words of the *Federalist*, Mr. Webster appeals to that work to show, as a fact then "perfectly well understood," that the powers of the new government were to be conferred, or its Constitution established, not by the States, nor by the people of the States, considered as sovereign bodies, and each acting for itself, but by the whole people of the United States as one sovereign body or nation! To show, in one word, that the Union was formed, not by an accession of the States, but by the one people of the United States acting as a unit! "The great expounder" does not follow, he flatly contradicts, the very work he appeals to as the highest of authorities; and that, too, in regard to the greatest of all the political questions that have agitated the people of America!

There were those, it is true, who regarded the new Constitution as the fundamental, or organic law, of one great consolidated government. But these were its enemies. They represented it as such because they wished it to be rejected, and because they knew no other objection would render it so obnoxious to the people of the States. It is well known, indeed, that the greatest difficulty in the way of the new Union was the jealousy of the central power, which the several States had long entertained.

This jealousy was so great in the States of New York and of Virginia, that when their Conventions met to ratify or to reject the Constitution, it is well understood, and admitted, that they were both opposed to the new grant of powers. The State-Rights men in both Conventions, who, at first, were in favor of rejecting the Constitution, were in a majority, as is well known, and fully conceded. It was only by the herculean labors of Alexander Hamilton, that the Convention of New York were, at last, induced to ratify it by a majority of three votes. In like manner, the labors, the management, and the eloquence of Mr. Madison, succeeded, finally, after a long and desperate struggle, in carrying it in the Convention of Virginia by the small majority of ten votes. The result was long doubtful in both Conventions.

Patrick Henry, in the ratifying Convention of Virginia, put forth all his powers to cause the new Constitution to be rejected. His appeals to the jealousy of the States with respect to the power of the Central Government were tremendous. He dwelt, particularly on the words of the preamble, "We, the people of the United States," to show that his most fatal objection to the new Constitution was well founded; and he added, "States are the characteristic and soul of a confederacy. If the States are not the agents of this compact, it must be one great consolidated government of the people of the United States." He insisted that it would be so. But Patrick Henry, it should be remembered, was not a member of the Convention of 1787, and he was an enemy of the new Constitution. His mind was fertile and overflowing with objections. If he had known the history of the words, "We, the people of the United States," as it appears in the debates of the Convention, which had not then been published, he would have seen, that "We, the people," really meant "We, the States; or We, the Convention, acting in the name and by the authority of the sovereign people of the several States."[93] Or, if he had compared the words in question with the seventh Article of the Constitution, he would have seen, that the new Constitution was to be established by the States, and was to be binding only "between the States so ratifying the same." But as the enemy, and not the advocate, of the new Constitution, he labored to enforce his objection to it, rather than to consider and weigh its words, or explain its real meaning to the Convention.

His objection would, no doubt, have proved fatal to the new Constitution, but for the presence and the power of James Madison, who met the great objection of Patrick Henry, and silenced much of the apprehension which his eloquence had created. He was known to have been the most diligent and active member of the Convention that formed the Constitution; and was supposed, therefore, to understand its real import better than any man in the ratifying Convention of Virginia. His position, and his means of information, certainly gave him a great advantage over his eloquent rival, Patrick Henry. In his reply to Mr. Henry, he explained the words "We, the people," precisely as he had before explained them in the *The Federalist*. He said: "The parties to it were the people, but not the people as composing one great society, but the people as composing *thirteen sovereignties.*" Again: "If it were a consolidated government," said he, "the assent of a majority of the people would be sufficient to establish it. But it was to be binding on the people of a State only *by their own separate consent.*" This argument, founded on a well-known fact, was absolutely unanswerable.

Yet Mr. Justice Story has, two or three times, quoted the words of Patrick Henry in the Virginia Convention, as if they were a most valuable authority, without a single solitary word in relation to the unanswerable reply of Mr. Madison! On this point he is profoundly silent! That is to say, he construes the Constitution, not as it was understood by its framers and its friends, but as it was misrepresented by its enemies, in order to cause its rejection! He holds up the words of the one, as a great authority, and he does not let the reader of his most learned Commentaries know the language of the other in reply! Was that honest?

Nor is this all. He construes the preamble to the Constitution, so as to make it contradict itself. "We, the people of the United States, in order to form a more perfect Union." A Union of what—of individuals, or of States? Does not every man under the sun know, this means a Union of States, and not of individuals? Or why speak of the United States at all? Or why, in the same preamble, say "this Constitution for the United States of America?"

I object to the Massachusetts interpretation of the first clause of the preamble to the Constitution:

1. Because it falsifies the facts of history respecting the mode of its ratification, which was by the several States in Convention assembled, each acting for itself alone, "as a sovereign body, independent of all others, and to be bound only by its own voluntary act," and not by the people of America as one nation. 2. Because it makes these words, "We, the people," contradict the seventh Article of the Constitution; an Article which, historically considered, has precisely the same origin and the same sense with those words themselves. 3. Because it attaches to these words a different sense from that attached to them by the Convention of 1787, as seen in the debates which gave rise to them. 4. Because it contradicts the sense given to these words by Gouverneur Morris, by James Madison, and by other framers of the Constitution of the United States. 5. Because, not satisfied with making this clause contradict everything else, it makes it contradict itself, or at least the very next clause in the same sentence with itself.

But there is another thing which Mr. Webster could not find in "all contemporary history," nor in "the numbers of *The Federalist,*" nor in "the publications of friends or foes." In none of these various productions or publications did anyone intimate that the new Constitution was but another compact between the States in their sovereign capacity. I do not find such an opinion advanced in a single instance. Hence, after so careful, so conscientious, and so laborious a search, he feels perfectly justified in the assertion, that "the Constitution is not a compact between sovereign States." This is, indeed, the very title of his speech in 1833, and the great burden of all his eloquence. Yet, with no very great research, I have found, and exhibited in the preceding pages, a multitude of instances in which "such an opinion is advanced." Nor was it at all necessary to ransack "all contemporary history" for this purpose. *The Federalist* itself, the great political classic of America, has already furnished several such instances. It teaches us, as we have seen, that "each State, in ratifying the Constitution, is considered as a *sovereign body, independent of all others,*"[94] and also that, in the establishment of the Constitution, the States are "regarded as distinct and independent sovereigns."[95]

But this, it may be said, does not use the term *compact*. Very well. The same number of *The Federalist,* which says that the Constitution was to be established by each State, as a sovereign body, independent of all others, calls that Constitution "THE COMPACT." Thus, according to *The Federalist,* the Constitution, THE COMPACT, was established by "distinct and independent sovereigns."

But numbers XXXIX and XL were written by Mr. Madison. Everyone knows, that he always regarded the Constitution as a compact between "distinct and independent sovereigns." That is, everyone at all acquainted with the political history of the United States, except Mr. Justice Story and Mr. Webster during the great struggle of 1833. It must be conceded, then, in spite of the sweeping assertion of Mr. Webster, that Madison held the Constitution to be "a compact between the States in their sovereign capacity," and that, too, in the pages of the *Federalist* as well as elsewhere. A rather conspicuous instance to be overlooked by one, whose search had been so very careful and so very conscientious! Nor does this instance stand alone. Alexander Hamilton is the great writer of the *Federalist.* Out of its existing eighty-five numbers, no less than fifty proceeded from his pen; five from the pen of Jay, and thirty from that of Madison; and, in the opinion of the North, the numbers of Hamilton surpass those of Madison far more in quality than in quantity. In the estimation of the North, indeed, Hamilton is the *one* sublime architect of the Constitution, to whom it owes "every element of its durability and beauty." What, then, does Hamilton say about the nature of the Constitution? Does he call it a compact between States, or does he allege that it was ordained by the people of the United States as one sovereign nation? I do not wish to shock anyone. I am aware, it will be regarded, by many of the followers of Story, as akin to sacrilege to charge Alexander Hamilton with having entertained the treasonable opinion, that the Constitution was a compact between the States. But as we have, at the South, no grand manufactory of opinions to supply "all contemporary history," so we must take the sentiments of Alexander Hamilton just as we find them, not in the traditions of the North, but in his own published productions. The simple truth is, then, that he calls the provisions of the Constitution of 1787, "The *compacts* which are to embrace thirteen distinct States, in a common bond of amity and Union," and adds, these compacts must "necessarily be compromises of as many dissimilar interests and inclinations."[96] Thus, according to Hamilton, the "thirteen distinct States" made compromises with each other, and adopted them as "the compacts" of the new Union!

Nor is this all. On the following page, he says: "The moment an alteration is made in the present plan, it becomes, to the purpose of adoption, a new one, *and must undergo a new decision of each State."*[97] Indeed, even Hamilton, the great consolidationist of his day, never dreamed of any other mode of adopting the new Constitution, than by "a decision of each State." Hence he continues, "To its complete establishment throughout the Union, it will therefore require the concurrence of thirteen States." Again, he says, "Every Constitution for the United States must inevitably consist of a great variety of particulars, in which thirteen INDEPENDENT STATES are to be accommodated in their interests or opinions of interest."[98] . . . "Hence the necessity of moulding and arranging all the particulars which are to compose the whole, in such a manner, as to satisfy all the parties to *the compact."* That is, in such a manner as to satisfy the thirteen independent states, who are "the parties to the compact."[99] Well may the great usurpers of the North exclaim, *"et tu Brute!"*

The whole *Federalist* is in perfect harmony with this key note of the system it recommended to the people. By Hamilton, the States are called "the members of the Union,"[100] the units of which it is composed, and not the fractions into which it is divided. Again, he speaks of "the Union, and of its members,"[101] by which, as appears from the context, he evidently means the States. In like manner, Mr. Madison speaks of the new Union as "Confederated States."[102] Again, he says, "Instead of reporting a plan requiring the confirmation *of all the States,* they reported a plan, which is to be confirmed, and may be carried into effect, by *nine States only."*[103] Indeed, similar testimonies to the fact, that the States entered into the compact of the Constitution, are spread over the pages of the *Federalist,* as well as over "all contemporary history."

I might easily produce a hundred other proofs of the same fact from "the *Federalist,"* from "the publications of friends and foes," from "the debates of the Convention," without the aid of "all contemporary history." But I am tired of dealing with such unbounded and disgusting license of assertion.

The truth is, that Mr. Webster was a mere theorist, no, a mere party sophist. He took an oath to support, but not to study, the Constitution. hence, instead of a close, patient, and honest study of the political history of the country and of the Constitution; he merely looked into the great original fountains of information to furnish himself out with the weapons and the armor of a party champion, or prize fighter. If he ever read any of the documents to which he so confidently appeals, he must have read them with a veil over his eyes; or else, in the heat of debate, he must have forgotten all his first lessons in the political history of his country. From his own generation, he won the proud title of "the great expounder," yet, after his appeal to posterity shall have been decided, he will be pronounced "the great deceiver."

Chapter XII

The Constitution of 1787 a Compact, Part 8

The Convention of 1787, in their letter describing the formation of the new Constitution, use precisely the political formula employed by Sidney, Locke, and other celebrated authors, to define a social compact.

Hobbes was the first to reduce this theory to a scientific form; and it is nowhere more accurately defined than by himself. "Each citizen," says he, "compacting with his fellow, says thus: *I convey my right on this party, upon condition that you pass yours to the same;* by which means, that right which *every* man had before to use his faculties to his own advantage, is now wholly translated on some certain man or council for the common benefit."[104] Precisely the same idea is conveyed by the formula of 1787: "individuals entering into society must give up a share of liberty to preserve the rest; and the great difficulty is, as to what rights should be delegated to the governing agents for the common benefit, and what right should be retained by the individual." This is the social compact as defined by Hobbes himself; and although it was an imaginary transaction in regard to the governments of the Old World, it became a reality in relation to the solemnly enacted Constitutions of America.

But, in the letter of the Convention of 1787, it comes before us in a new relation. In Hobbes, "each citizen compacts with his fellow," as in the formation of our State Constitutions; whereas, in the letter before us, each State compacts with her sister States. "It is obviously impracticable," says the Convention,[105] "in the Federal Government of these States to secure all rights of independent sovereignty to each, and yet provide for the honor and safety of all. Individuals entering into society must give up a share of liberty to preserve the rest.". . ."It is at all times difficult to draw with precision the line between those rights which must be surrendered, and those which may be reserved; and on the present occasion this difficulty was increased by a difference among the several States [the parties about to enter into a new Union] as to their situation, extent, habits, and particular interests."

Yet, in the face of all this, the whole school of Massachusetts politicians, with Story and Webster at their head, assert, that the Federal Government is a union, not of States, but only of individual citizens! Who, before or beside these gross perverters of the most palpable truth, ever applied the term "Union" to a government of individuals? Whoever heard of the Union of Massachusetts, or of New York, or of Virginia? The truth is, that this word is only applicable to a confederation of States; and hence, even Alexander Hamilton, after he had failed to establish a consolidated national government, familiarly called the new Union "a CONFEDERACY."[106] It was reserved for a later day, and for a bolder period in the progress of triumphant error, to scout this as an unconstitutional idea; and to declare, by way of proof, that "there is no language in the Constitution applicable to a confederation of States."[107] Is not the term "Union," applicable to a confederation of States, or is it only applicable to a social combination of individuals? Does not the Constitution speak of "the United States," or the States united? No, does it not expressly declare, that it shall be binding "between the States so ratifying the same?" Or, if the Constitution itself has been silent, does not the letter of 1787, which was struck in the same mint with that solemn compact, declare that *each State,* on entering into the new Union, give up a share of its "rights of independent sovereignty," in order to secure the rest?

I shall now take leave of the proposition, that the Constitution was a compact between the States of the Union; a proposition far too plain for argument, if the clearest facts of history had only been permitted to speak for themselves. "I remember," says Mr. Webster, "to have heard Chief Justice Marshall ask counsel, who was insisting upon the authority of an act of legislation, *if he thought an act of legislation could create or destroy a fact, or change the truth of history?*" "Would it alter the fact," said he, "if a legislature should solemnly enact, that Mr. Hume never wrote the *History of England?*"[108] "A legislature may alter the law," continues Mr. Webster, "but no power can reverse a fact." Hence, if the Convention of 1787 had expressly declared, that the Constitution was ordained by "the people of the United States *in the aggregate,*" or by the people of America as one nation, this would not have destroyed the fact, that it was ratified by each State for itself, and that each State was bound only by "its own voluntary act." If the Convention had been lost to all decency, it might indeed have stamped, such a falsehood on the face of the Constitution; but this would not have "changed the truth of history."

Story and Webster lay great stress, as we have seen,[109] on the fact, that the first resolution passed by the Convention of 1787 declared, that "*a National Government* ought to be established." But, by a gross *suppressio veri,* they conceal the fact, that this resolution was afterward taken up, and the term *national* deliberately dropped by the unanimous decision of the Convention. They also conceal the fact, that after the Constitution was actually formed, the Convention called the work of their hands, not "a National Government," but "The Federal Government on These States." This name was given, not before, but after, the Convention was full; not before the first article of the Constitution was adopted, but after the whole instrument had been completely finished; and it was given, too, by "the unanimous order of the Convention."[110] Yet, in contempt of all this, Story and Webster say, that the Convention made, not a "Federal Government of States," but "a National Government" for the one people of America, and they prove this, by the exploded resolution passed by them! That is, they still insist on the name expressly rejected by the Convention, as if it had received the sanction of their high authority; and that, too, in direct opposition to the name actually given by them! Could any style of reasoning, if reasoning it may be called, be more utterly contemptible?

Chapter XIII

Mr. Webster Versus Mr. Webster

In the preceding chapter, Mr. Webster has been confronted with reason and authority; showing that "the greatest intellectual effort of his life" is merely a thing of words. In this, he shall be confronted with himself for, in truth, he is at war with himself, as well as with all the great founders of the Constitution of the United States. He is, in fact, too much for himself; and the great speech which, in 1833, he reared with so much consummate skill as a rhetorician, he has literally torn to tatters.

"If the States be parties" [to the Constitution], asks Mr. Webster, in that speech, with an air of great confidence, "where are their covenants and stipulations: And where are their rights, covenants, and stipulations expressed? The States engage for nothing, they promise nothing." On reading this passage, one is naturally inclined to ask, did Mr. Webster never hear of "the grand compromises of the Constitution" about which so much has been written? But what is a compromise, if it is not a mutual agreement, founded on the mutual concessions of the parties to some conflict of opinions or interests? Does not the very term *compromise* mean mutual promises or pledges? Look at the large and small States in the Convention of 1787. We see, in that memorable struggle for power, the large States insisting on a large or proportionate representation of themselves in both branches of the federal legislature; and we see the small States, with equal pertinacity, clinging to the idea of an equal representation in both. The struggle is fierce and obstinate. The Convention is on the point of dissolution, and its hopes are almost extinguished. But, a compromise is suggested, considered, argued, and finally adopted; according to which there is to be a proportionate representation of each State in one branch of the federal legislature, and an equal representation in the other. These are the terms, "the covenants," "the stipulations," on which the two classes of States agree to unite; these are their mutual promises.

The same thing is true in regard to all the other "grand compromises of the Constitution." It seems, indeed, that Mr. Webster could not well speak of these compromises, without using some such word as *terms,* or *covenants,* or *promises,* or *stipulations.* Accordingly, if we turn to the general index to his works, in order to see how he would speak of the compromises of the Constitution; we shall be led to make a very curious discovery, and one which is intimately connected with an interesting passage of his political life. It will conduct us to a scene, in which "the beautiful vase," then "well known throughout the country as the Webster Vase," was presented to that celebrated statesman. Several thousand persons "had assembled at the Odeon, in Boston," in order to witness the presentation of that costly memorial, and to hear the reply of the great orator. "The vase," we are told "was placed on a pedestal covered with the American flag, and contained on its side the following inscription:

PRESENTED TO
DANIEL WEBSTER, *The Defender of the Constitution,*
BY THE CITIZENS OF BOSTON. OCTOBER 12, 1835."

Now this beautiful vase, so rich in its material and so exquisite in its workmanship, was presented to Mr. Webster in honor of his great speech of 1833, in which he demonstrated to the entire satisfaction of the New England universe, that it is absurd to call the Constitution "a compact," or to speak of its "stipulations." Now I shall produce one extract from this speech at the Odeon, not only on account of the striking contrast it presents to the doctrine of the speech of 1833, whose glories thousands were there assembled to celebrate, but also on account of the simple, solid, and important truth it contains. "The Constitution," says Mr. Webster, in that speech, "is *founded on compromises,* and the most perfect and absolute good faith, in regard to every stipulation of this kind contained in it is indispensable to its preservation. Every attempt to accomplish even the best purpose, every attempt to grasp that which is regarded as an immediate good, in violation of these stipulations, is full of danger to the whole constitution."[111] Such glaring inconsistencies, and there are many of them in the writings of the great orator, will be flaws and cracks in the vase of his reputation as long as his name is known.

Nor is this the only instance in which Mr. Webster has spoken of the stipulations of the Constitution. "All the *stipulations,*" says he, "contained in the Constitution in *favor of the slave States* ought to be fulfilled."[112] Here, then, are stipulations in favor of States, and made by States. "Slavery," says he, "as it exists in the States, is beyond the reach of Congress. It is a concern of the States themselves; *they have never submitted it to Congress, and Congress has no rightful power over it.*"[113] Nor has the Federal Government the rightful power over anything in relation to the States; unless this power was granted by *the States,* and so became one of the stipulations in the new "Articles of Union," as the Constitution is called throughout the debates in the Convention of 1787.[114]

The power of the Federal Government over commerce has been very justly called "the cornerstone of the whole system." The Constitution originated, as we have seen, in the desire to establish a uniform and permanent system of commercial regulations, by which the hostile legislation of Europe might be resisted, and the havoc of the international legislation of the States repaired. Whence did this great power, or rather this great system of powers, emanate? *"The States,"* says Mr. Webster, *"delegated their whole authority over imports to the general government."*[115] In like manner, every other power of the vast superstructure reared upon that corner stone, was delegated or conferred on the Federal Government by the States in the "Articles of Union."

Mr. Webster and Mr. Justice Story say the Constitution speaks the language of authority to the States, saying you shall do this, or you shall not do that, and eschews the verbal forms of a compact. Very great stress is laid on this point. The Constitution, say they, is not "a compact between States," it is "the supreme law," as if the two things were utterly incompatible. But it is a rather unfortunate circumstance for this argument, that precisely the same language of authority is used in the old Articles of Confederation, which is universally admitted to have been a compact. "No State shall," is the style of the old Articles of Union,[116] as well as of the new; in this respect, they are perfectly parallel.

But here, again, we may appeal from Philip drunk to Philip sober, from Webster intoxicated with the fumes of a false theory of power to Webster under the influence of a simple view of truth. After having read the terms on which Texas was admitted into the Union, Mr. Webster asks, "Now what is here *stipulated, enacted,* secured?", thus admitting that the *stipulations* were *enactments,* or that the contract was a law. Nor is this all. For, having specified the stipulations in this case, he proceeds to say, "I know no form of *legislation* which can strengthen this. I know no mode of recognition that can add a tittle to the weight of it. I listened respectfully to the resolutions of my friend from Tennessee. He proposed to recognize that *stipulation* with Texas. But any additional recognition would weaken the force of it; *because it stands here on the ground of a contract, a thing done for a consideration.* It is a law founded on a contract with Texas." There is, then, after all, no incompatibility between a contract and a law! On the contrary, the very highest form of legislation may be that of a compact between sovereign States. It was thus, that Texas came into the Union; and, in consideration of certain things promised to her, agreed to accept the Constitution of the United States as the supreme law of the land. It was thus also, that the original thirteen States, in view of certain advantages expected by them, and held out to them, conferred various powers on the Federal Government to be exercised for the common good. Each State, as it adopted the Constitution, virtually said to every other, I will abstain from the exercise of certain powers, and grant or delegate certain powers, according to all the stipulations of this instrument, provided you will do the same thing. I will neither coin money, nor emit bills of credit, nor enact laws impairing the obligation of contracts, nor do any other thing, which, in the view of the authors of the Constitution, has proved so injurious to the best interests of the country, provided you will abstain from the exercise of the same powers. And I will, on the other hand, consent that the General Government may regulate commerce, levy taxes, borrow money on the common credit, wage war, conclude peace, and do all acts and things as stipulated in the new "Articles of Union," provided you will delegate the same powers. Such was "the contract, the thing done for a consideration." The great stipulation of all was, that the Constitution should be the supreme law of the land; for that became the supreme law only by the mutual agreement of the States. But why argue a point so plain? How any man can look the Constitution in the face, or read its history, and then ask, "Where are its stipulations?" is more than I can conceive. It does seem to me, that he might almost as well look into the broad blaze of noon, and then ask, If the sun really shines, where are its rays?

But if the Constitution is not a compact for the North, it is at least held to be binding, as such, on the South. The free States, said Mr. Webster in 1850, "complain that, instead of slavery being regarded as an evil, as it was then, it is now regarded by the South as an institution to be cherished, and preserved, and extended."[117] "The North finds itself," be continues, "in regard to the relative influence of the South and the North, of the free States and the slave States, where it did not expect to find itself, when they agreed to the compact of the Constitution."[118] Thus, after all, the States agreed to the compact of the constitution, Mr. Webster himself being the judge.

Again, in 1851, Mr. Webster says: "When the Constitution was framed, its framers, and the people who adopted it, came to a clear, express, unquestionable stipulation and compact."[119] In the same speech, he says: "These States passed acts defeating the law of Congress, as far as it was in their power to defeat it. Those of them to whom I refer, not all, but several, nullified the law of 1793. They said, in effect, 'we will not execute it. No runaway slave shall be restored.' Thus the law became a dead letter. But here was the *Constitution and compact* still binding; here was the stipulation, as solemn as words could form it, and which every member of Congress, every officer of the general government, every officer of the State government, from governors down to constables, is sworn to support."[120] Thus, in 1850 and 1851, it appears that Mr. Webster had as completely forgotten "the greatest intellectual effort of his life," as in 1833 he had forgotten all the great intellectual efforts of Mr. Madison's life. The truth is, that Mr. Webster had became alarmed at the condition of the country; because the North, which he had taught to deny that the Constitution is a compact, seemed resolved to reduce his theory to practice and give all its stipulations to the winds, provided they only stood in the way of their passions. Many of his former friends had, indeed, deserted and denounced him, because he would not go all lengths with them in disregarding the most solemn compact of the Constitution, which all had sworn to support. Hence, he wished to retrace his steps; but he could not lay the mighty spirit of insubordination and rebellion which he had helped to arouse in the North. He could only plead, expostulate, and denounce in return.

Accordingly, in the speech just quoted, he says: "It has been said in the States of Now York, Massachusetts, and Ohio, over and over again, that the law shall not be executed. That was the language of Conventions in Worcester, Massachusetts; in Syracuse, New York; and elsewhere. And for this they pledged their lives, their fortunes, and their sacred honors. Now, gentlemen, these proceedings, I say it upon my professional reputation, are distinctly treasonable. Resolutions passed in Ohio, certain resolutions in New York, and in Conventions held in Boston, are distinctly treasonable. And the act of taking away Shadrick from the public authorities in Boston, and sending him off, was an act of clear treason."[121]

The spirit of the resolutions which are here so emphatically denounced by Mr. Webster, afterward seized whole States, and controlled their legislation. In fourteen of the Northern States, indeed, laws were enacted to prevent the execution of the law of Congress. These laws, as Mr. Webster himself, if living, would have said, were "distinctly treasonable." They came directly into conflict with the law of Congress, and nullified the compact of the Constitution relative to fugitive slaves. What shall we say then? Was secession, under such circumstances, treason? Was it rebellion? Mr. Webster has, in one of his speeches, laid down a principle which never has been, and never can be, controverted. He says: "I do not hesitate to say and repeat, that if the Northern States refuse wilfully and deliberately to carry into effect that part of the Constitution which respects the restoration of fugitive slaves, the South would be no longer bound to keep the compact. A bargain broken on one side is broken on all sides." I have said, that this is a principle of truth and justice, which never has been, and never can be denied. It was, indeed, precisely the principle which governed the Convention of 1787 in withdrawing from the first compact between the States. I do not mean to say, however, that this great principle of truth and justice may not be practically denied. In fact, the Northern power has not only claimed, but exercised, the right to trample the compact of the Constitution under foot; and, at the same time, to visit with fire, sword, desolation, and ruin, those who merely wished to withdraw from the broken thing, and let it alone.

According to the doctrine laid down by Story and Webster, if a compact between States assign no term for its continuance, then the States have a right to secede from it at pleasure.[122] This doctrine is, no doubt, perfectly true. But precisely such was the compact from which the Southern States wished to withdraw; no period was prescribed for its continuance. Yet the North, who had trampled it underfoot, punished the South with indeed the most terrible of all wars, because she was pleased to regard secession as a violation of that "most sacred compact."

No man, as we have seen, could well be more inconsistent on any subject, than "the great expounder" was in relation to the most important of all questions respecting the Constitution. It was, with him, either a compact between the States, or not a compact between the States, according to the exigencies of the occasion. He could be equally eloquent on both sides of the question. He complained, in 1850, that the South had changed her opinions on the subject of slavery. Might not the South complain, that he. had no opinions, or at least no convictions, to change? The man who really seeks the truth, and, when found, clings to it as the choicest treasure of his soul, may well leave his consistency to take care of itself. But the man who seeks place, or power, or popularity more, than the truth, should indeed have a good memory. The one may, and indeed will, sometimes change his opinions, but then, in the midst of all his changes, he will be ever true, like the needle, which only turns until it finds the pole. Whereas the other, in his variations, is like the weathercock, which shifts with the breeze of the passing hour, and never finds a point of permanent rest. Even the intellect of a Webster, where the moral man is deficient, can furnish no exemption from this law of retributive justice.

Mr. Webster's real opinion, however, seems to have been that the Constitution was a compact between the States. His great speech of 1833 may have convinced others; it certainly did not convince himself; for during the remainder of his life, he habitually and constantly spoke of the Constitution as the compact formed by the States. Especially after his race was nearly run, and, instead of the dazzling prize of the Presidency, he saw before him the darkness of the grave, and the still greater darkness that threatened his native land with ruin; he raised the last solemn utterances of his mighty voice in behalf of "the compact of the Constitution," declaring that as it had been "deliberately entered into by the States," so the States should religiously observe "all its stipulations."

Chapter XIV

The Will of the People in the Making of the Constitution

When I come to consider "the sovereignty of the people," about which so much has been said, we shall see the fallacy of the position, which is everywhere assumed by Mr. Webster and his school, that "the aggregate community, the collected will of the people, is sovereign."[123] We shall then see, that this doctrine is utterly without foundation in history, and without support from reason. Or the contrary, it will then be rendered manifest, that the people of America have never existed as one nation *clothed with sovereign authority;* an idea which has no founzdation in fact, and which has grown out of the popular use of language and the passions of politicians.

But, at present, I merely wish to point out a few of the absurdities flowing from this doctrine, that the Constitution was ordained by "the aggregate community, the collected will of the people" of America, acting as one sovereign political society. This argument alone, this *reductio ad absurdum,* is amply sufficient, unless I am greatly mistaken, to shatter that already shattered hypothesis.

Mr. Justice Story, quoting the Declaration of Independence, says: "It is the right of the people, (plainly intending the majority of the people,) to alter, or to abolish it, and to institute a new government, laying its foundation on such principles, and organizing its powers in such forms as to them shall seem most likely to effect their safety and happiness."[124] Now this is what is meant by the sovereignty of the people in America. But will anyone contend, that the people of the United States, that is, a majority of them, may alter, or amend, the government of the Union? If they are, indeed, one people in the political sense of the word, then are they sovereign; and if as such they made the Constitution of the United States, then, according to all our American ideas and doctrines, they have the right to alter or amend that Constitution at their pleasure. No, more; they have the right to *pull down the existing government,* and to set up a new one in its place.

But who will accept such a consequence? This right of sovereignty, if it exist, or if the one people exist to whom it naturally belongs, it is, according to the universally received doctrine of this continent, inherent and *inalienable*. No laws or constitutions can take it away, or abridge and limit its exercise. Who will say, then, that the people of the United States, "plainly meaning the majority of them," have such a right or authority? No one. Plainly and inevitably as this consequence flows from the fundamental position of Story and Webster, that the sovereign people of America ordained the Constitution, it will be avowed by no one, who has any reputation to lose, and who has the least respect for the reputation he possesses. Mr. Lincoln has avowed this consequence. But in this instance, as in many others, his logic has taken advantage of his want of information.

This consequence flows so naturally and so necessarily from the premises, that Mr. Justice Story has, in one place, inadvertently drawn it; or rather it has incidentally drawn itself. "The people of the United States," says he, "have a right to abolish, or alter the Constitution of the United States."[125] True, if they made it; but they did not make it, and therefore they have the right neither to alter nor to abolish it. The power that made, is the power to unmake. Mr. Justice Story did not mean, that is, he did not *deliberately* mean, that the people of the United States, or the majority of them, could alter or abolish the Constitution; for he was too well informed to be capable of such a blunder. But in this instance, as in many others, his logic, speaking the language of nature and of truth, got the better of his artificial and false hypothesis.

If the people of the United States are, in reality, one sovereign political community, and as such, ordained the Constitution, then they have the most absolute control over all the parts; and the States bear the same relation to this one grand and overshadowing sovereignty, that counties sustain to a State. They may be divided, or moulded, or abolished, at the pleasure of the whole people. But everybody knows better than this. Mr. Lincoln did, it is true, endorse this conclusion, in the first speech he ever made to the American public. When the long silence was broken, and, as President elect, he addressed his first word to an anxious country, he likened the relation between the States and the Union to that of counties to a State. Until then, there were many intelligent and well-informed persons, who did not believe, that there was one individual in the United States capable of taking such a view of the Constitution, except among political preachers or parsons.[126] But however absurd, it is only the necessary consequence of the premises laid down by Mr. Justice Story and Mr. Webster. It will, however, be regarded by every student of the Constitution in the light of a *reductio ad absurdum,* which, instead of establishing the conclusion to which it leads, only shatters and demolishes the position from which it flows.

Chapter XV

Do the People of America Form One Nation?

We have seen, in the preceding chapter, some of the absurdities flowing from the assumption, that the people of America form one nation, or constitute one political community. But as this is the first and all-comprehending falsehood, of the Northern theory of the Constitution, by which its history has been so sadly blurred, if not obliterated, and by which its most solemn provisions have been repealed, so we shall go beyond the foregoing *reductio ad absurdum*, and show that it has no foundation whatever in the facts of history. I was about to say, that it has not the shadow of such a foundation; but, in reality, it has precisely such a shadow in the vague popular use of language, to which the passions of interested partisans have given the appearance of substance. And it is out of this substance, thus created from a shadow, that have been manufactured those tremendous rights of national power, by which the clearly-reserved rights of the States have been crushed, and the most unjust war of the modern world justified. I purpose, therefore, to pursue this monstrous abortion of night and darkness, into the secret recesses of its history, and leave neither its substance nor its shadow in existence. Fortunately, in the prosecution of this design, it is only necessary to cross-examine those willing witnesses by whom this fiction has been created, and compare their testimony with itself, in order to show that they are utterly unworthy of credit as historians of the American Union. I shall begin with Mr. Justice Story, who attempts to show that the people of America formed one nation or State.

This celebrated commentator strains all the powers of language, and avails himself of every possible appearance, to make the colonies of America "one people," even before they severed their dependence on the British crown. Thus, he says: "The colonies were fellow-subjects, and for many purposes *one people.* Every colonist had a right to inhabit, if he pleased, in any other colony; and as a British subject, he was capable of inheriting lands by descent in every other colony. The commercial intercourse of the colonies, too, was regulated by the laws of the British empire; and could not be restrained, or obstructed, by colonial legislation. The remarks of Mr. Chief Justice Jay on this subject are equally just and striking: 'All the people of this country were then subjects of the king of Great Britain, and owed allegiance to him; and all the civil authority then existing, or exercised here, flowed from the head of the British empire. They were, in a strict sense, fellow-subjects, and in a variety of respects, *one people.*' "[127]

Now all this signifies just exactly nothing as to the purpose which the author bits in view. For, no matter in what respects the colonies were "one people," if they were not one in the political sense of the words; or if they had no political power as one people, then the germ of the national *oneness* did not exist among them. But this is conceded by Mr. Justice Story himself. "The colonies," says he, "were independent of each other in respect to their domestic concerns."[128] Each was independent of the legislation of another, and of all the others combined, it they had pleased to combine. In many respects, indeed, the whole human race may be said to be one. They have a common origin, a common psychology, a common physiology, and they are all subjects of the same great Ruler of the world. But this does not make all men "one people" in the political sense of the words. In like manner, those things which the colonists had in common, and which are so carefully enumerated by Mr. Justice Story, do not make them one political community; the only sense in which their oneness could have any logical connection with his design. No, so palpably is this the case, that he fails to make the impression on his own mind, which he seems so desirous to make on that of his readers; and the hypothesis that the colonies were "one people," is utterly dispelled by his own explicit admission. For, says he, "Though the colonies had a common origin, and owed a common allegiance, and the inhabitants of each were British subjects, *they had no direct political connection with each other.* Each was independent of all the others; each, in a limited sense, was sovereign within its own territory. There was neither allegiance nor confederacy between them. The Assembly of one province could not make laws for another, nor confer privileges which were to be enjoyed or exercised in another, farther than they could be in any independent foreign state. As colonies, they were also excluded from all connection with foreign states. They were known only as dependencies, and they followed the fate of the parent country, both in peace and war, without having assigned to them, in the intercourse or diplomacy of nations, any distinct or independent existence. They did not possess the power of forming any league or treaty among themselves, which would acquire an obligatory force, without the assent of the parent State. And though their mutual wants and necessities often induced them to associate for common purposes of defence, these confederacies were of a casual and temporary nature, and were allowed as an indulgence, rather than as a right. They made several efforts to procure the establishment of some general superintending government over them all, but their own differences of opinion, as well as the jealousy of the crown, made these efforts abortive."[129]

It is impossible for language to be more precise and explicit. Hence, in whatever other respects the colonies may have formed "one people," we are here authorized, by the undisputed and the indisputable facts of history, to consider them as separate and independent of each other, in the political sense of the terms. And this is all our argument needs.

Mr. Justice Story, not satisfied with the oneness of the people of the colonies before their separation from Great Britain, which he has been at so much pains to establish, next endeavors to show, that they were certainly moulded into one nation by the Declaration of Independence. If they were "one people" before, it is difficult to conceive how they were made so by that Declaration. To that act, says he, "union was as vital, as freedom or independence."[130] But what sort of union? Did the people unite and become one nation, in the sense that it was a sovereign political community; so that the whole could make a Constitution and laws for the parts? If not, then the assertion misses the mark aimed at, and must go for nothing. But no one pretends, for a single moment, that they became one people in any such sense of the words. Mr. Justice Story himself admits, that such union was temporary, and designed to perish with the common danger which had called it into existence. "The union thus formed," says he, "grew out of the exigencies of the times; and from its nature and objects might be deemed temporary, extending only to the maintenance of the common liberties and independence of the States, and to terminate with the return of peace with Great Britain, and the accomplishment of the ends of the revolutionary contest."[131] Thus, it is conceded that they became "one people," not to ordain a Constitution or to enact laws, but only to resist a common enemy, and to continue united only during the presence of the common danger. This union was, according to Judge Story's own admission, more imperfect and fragile than that which, from the operation of a similar cause, had sprung up among the States of Greece, the Swiss Cantons, the United Netherlands, or the members of the German Diet. Yet no one has ever considered any one of these unions as forming one nation, or people, as contradistinguished from, a federation of sovereign and independent States. Such attempts, indeed, to prove that the colonies, or the States of America were one nation, or political community, are simply desperate. They are scarcely, made, before they are overthrown by the hand that reared them.

But let us admit, for the sake of argument, that the colonies formed one people before their separation from Great Britain, and that they were again made one people by the Declaration of Independence. Then no one colony could lawfully act without the concurrence of the others; as the parts would not be independent of the whole. Accordingly, Mr. Justice Story declares, that "the 14 the colonies did not severally act for themselves, and proclaim their own independence."[132] But it is well known, that Virginia did so. "Virginia," says Judge Story, "on the 29th June, 1776, (five days before the Declaration of Independence,) declared the government of the country as formally exercised under the crown of Great Britain, *totally dissolved,* and proceeded to form a new Constitution."[133] No, she had already formed a new Constitution, in pursuance of her resolution of the 15th of the preceding month, and she adopted it on the 29th of June, 1776. Yet Virginia has never been regarded as tainted with treason, or rebellion against the people of America, because she thus proclaimed her own separate independence, and established her own Constitution. On the contrary, she has ever been honored, by her sister colonies and States, for this bold and independent act.

This is not the only insuperable difficulty in the way of the hypothesis, that the colonies were made one people by the Declaration of Independence. For, if this hypothesis be adopted, we must believe that this one people were afterwards broken up into separate and independent States by an act of Confederation! In the case of Gibbons and Ogden,[134] the Supreme Court of the United States, say, (and the words are quoted with approbation by Mr. Justice Story,)[135] "As preliminary to the very able discussion of the Constitution which we have heard from the bar, and as having some influence on its construction, reference has been made to the situation of these States, *anterior to its formation*. It has been said, *that they were sovereign, were completely independent, and were connected with each other only by a league. This is true.*"[136] Now, if this be true, as the Supreme Court of the United States affirm, and as Mr. Justice Story admits, how were this one people broken up into so many separate, *"sovereign,"* and *"completely independent"* States? This must have been done by the Articles of Confederation; since it is only in the presence of these Articles, that this fine theory about the oneness of the American people disappears, and the States once more shine out as free and independent sovereignties. No other cause can be assigned for the change.

It is perfectly certain, indeed, that if the people of America were one nation, or political community, prior to the adoption of those Articles, they then became divided into separate, distinct, and independent States. For, according to those Articles, *"each State retains its sovereignty, freedom, and independence."* Each State retains! This language implies, indeed, that each State was free, sovereign and independent before those Articles were adopted. But then this is only one of the difficulties in the way of the theory of Judge Story.

If they were not free and sovereign States before, if, on the contrary, they were one people, or nation, or political community, then it were absurd to speak of their union as an act of confederation. For it would, indeed, have been an act of separation, and not of confederation. It would have been the dividing of one nation into separate and sovereign States, and not the uniting of such States into one Confederacy. This is another of the difficulties, which stand in the way of the theory of Judge Story, and of the Northern school of politicians.

Again, if one people were thus divided into free, sovereign and independent States, by the Articles of Confederation; then it is very inaccurate in Judge Story, to say, as he always does, that the States granted the powers by which the Confederacy was formed. He should, on the contrary, have spoken only of powers resumed by the States, or restored to them by the American people.

But we may now take leave of his theory and all its insuperable difficulties. It is sufficient for my purpose, that after the Articles of Confederation were agreed upon, as the supreme law, the States were then free, sovereign and independent. It is asserted by the Supreme Court of the United States, as well as by Judge Story himself, that anterior to the adoption of the Constitution the States *"were sovereign, were completely independent, and were connected only by a league."* It was in this capacity, it was as free, sovereign and completely independent States, that they laid aside the old, and entered into the now, "Articles of Union," as the Constitution is everywhere called in the proceedings of the Convention of 1787. *This is conceded.* Hence, the situation of the colonies before their separation from the mother country, or of the States before the adoption of the Articles of Confederation, has nothing to do with our present inquiry; which relates to the character in which the people, or the peoples of America, ordained the Constitution of the United States. If anyone has a mind to amuse himself by building up or pulling down speculations or hypothesis on this subject, he may do so to his heart's content. It is sufficient for every practical purpose, that when they came to adopt the new form of government, each State was a completely free, sovereign, and independent. political community, and in that capacity *acceded* to the compact of the Constitution.

The Attempt of Mr. Curtis to Show That the People of America Formed One Nation, or Political Community

Mr. Curtis, in his extended and elaborate History of the Constitution of the United States, seems to vie with the introductory sketch of Judge Story, in the establishment of the foregoing conclusion, that it was created by and rests on, "the political union of the *people* of the United States, as distinguished from the *States* of which they are the citizens."[137] For this purpose, it is necessary to show, in the first place, that such a political union of the whole people of the country had an existence. Accordingly, the facts of history are recast and moulded in order to suit this hypothesis. If possible, the conflict between fact and theory is, in his work, even more glaring than it is in that of Mr. Justice Story."The people of the different colonies" were, says he, "in several important senses, *one people.*"[138]

This is true. But it is not even pretended, by Mr. Curtis, that this was a political union; he only says, that it enabled them to effect such a union. He admits, on the contrary, in the most explicit terms, "that the colonies had no direct political connection with each other before the Revolution commenced, but that each was a distinct community, with its own separate political organization, and without any power of legislation for any but its own inhabitants; that, as political communities, and upon the principles of their organizations, they possessed no power of forming any union among themselves, for any purposes whatever, without the sanction of the Crown or the Parliament of England."[139]

"It is apparent," says he, "that previously to the Declaration of Independence, the people of the several colonies had established *a national government* of a revolutionary character, which undertook to act, and did act, in the name and with the general consent of the inhabitants of the country."[140] Thus, even previous to the Declaration of Independence, the people of the colonies formed one nation, and established "a national government." A nation, with a national government, and yet dependent colonies!

"This government," says he, "was established by the Union in one body of delegates representing the people of each colony." That is, each colony, acknowledged to be perfectly and wholly independent of every other, sends delegates to one body; and this body, whose duty it is to advise and recommend measures to the several colonies, is "a national government!" Surely, if such an advisory council may be called a government at all, it is anything rather than *national* in its character. It is, in fact, merely the shadow of a federal government.

Mr. Curtis himself is evidently not satisfied with the "one nation," in this stage of its development, or purely verbal existence. Hence, he insists, with Mr. Justice Story, that the colonies were really made one nation by the Declaration of Independence. "The body by which this step was taken," says he, "constituted the actual government of *the nation, at the time,*"[141] that is, while they were yet dependent colonies! "It severed the political connection between the people of this country and the people of England, and at once erected the different colonies into free and independent States."[142] Thus, the colonies formed "one nation" before their separation from Great Britain, and afterwards became "free and independent States." Or, in other words, the nation preceded the States; an opinion for which Mr. Lincoln has been most unconscionably laughed at. This opinion is still more explicitly advanced by Mr. Curtis, in another portion of his history. "The fact," says be, "that these local or State governments were not formed until a Union of the people of the different colonies for national purposes had *already taken place,* and until the national power had authorized and recommended their establishment, is of great importance in the Constitutional history of our country; for it shows that no colony, acting separately for itself, dissolved its own allegiance to the British crown, but that this allegiance was dissolved by the supreme authority of the people of all the colonies," &c., &c.[143] This fact, which is deemed of so much importance in the constitutional history of this country, happens, as we have seen, to be a fiction; and a fiction, too, in direct conflict with the well-known fact, that Virginia declared her own separate independence.

But if, by the Declaration of Independence, the colonies became "free and independent States," how could that act have moulded them into one sovereign political community, or nation? This is one of the mysteries, which I am glad it is not incumbent on me to solve. Was the Declaration of Independence itself necessarily, or *ex vi termini, a* declaration of independence, and, at the same time, one of subjection to a higher authority?

If we may adopt Mr. Curtis as a guide, we must answer this question in the affirmative. For, says he, although the colonies were thereby "erected into free and independent States," "the people of the country became henceforth the rightful sovereign of the country; they became united in a national corporate capacity, *as one people;* they could thereafter enter into treaties and contract alliances with foreign nations, could levy war and conclude peace, *and do all other acts pertaining to the exercise of a national sovereignty.*"[144] If so, then of course they could ordain Constitutions and enact laws; they could set up, or pull down, or modify the parts, called States, as if they were counties, or mere districts of people. For such is the power of one sovereign State, or nation, over its various members.

But, unfortunately for this bold assertion, Mr. Curtis himself tells us, on the very next page of his work, that "on the same, day on which the committee for preparing the Declaration of Independence was appointed, another, committee, consisting of a member from each colony, was directed *to prepare and digest the form of a confederation to be entered into between* these colonies," that is, after they should become free and independent States. "This committee," he continues, "reported a draft of Articles of Confederation on the 12th of July, &c." These Articles were discussed, postponed, resumed, amended, and, finally, adopted.

Now whence resulted the powers conferred by these Articles of Confederation? Were they not granted by the "free and independent States"? Most assuredly they were; no one has ever had the hardihood to deny so plain a fact, except by implication. But if all the powers of the new "national government," as it is called by Mr. Curtis, were granted by "free and independent States," each acting for itself, as everyone acknowledges it to have done; then for what conceivable purpose has he conjured up the phantom of a pre-existing national sovereignty of the whole people of the country?

It is certain, that this phantom has been completely laid by Mr. Curtis himself. The whole elaborate illusion, which it has cost him so much pains to get up, is thus dispelled by a plain, simple and unpremeditated statement of unquestionable facts, by the author himself. "The parties to this instrument," says he, referring to the Articles of Confederation, "were *free, sovereign and independent political communities,—each* possessing within itself *all* the powers of legislation and government over its own citizens, *which any political society can possess. But, by this* instrument, *these several States* became united for certain purposes."[145] Surely, all this must have been absent from the mind of Mr. Curtis, when he spoke of the people of the several States as having been previously merged into one absolutely sovereign political community. But it seems to be requiring too much to expect a Massachusetts politician to remember anything he may have said on any preceding page of his work.

Nor is this all. For it is also conceded that the States, which were "free, sovereign and independent political communities" before they adopted the Articles of Confederation, retained the same prerogatives, or attributes, after that event. "The Articles," says he, "declared, as *would indeed he implied, in such circumstances, without any express declaration,* that each State retained its sovereignty, freedom, and independence."[146] It was, then, in this condition of "free, sovereign, and independent political communities," that the States passed from the old to the new Articles of union, or severally agreed to the compact of the Constitution. Why, then, conjure up shadows and phantoms of a national unity only to dispel them? The cause of secession only demands the fact, that the States, as "free, sovereign, and independent political communities," formed and entered into the new "Articles of Union," and this fact is conceded both by Story and Curtis.

THE USE OF THE TERM PEOPLE

Much of the inconsistency and contradiction in the views above examined, is due to the ambiguities of the word *people,* and the utter confusion of its loose, floating significations, with its technical or scientific sense. We sometimes pronounce a people one, because they have a common origin, or a common language, or a common religion, or even because they inhabit the same portion of the globe. Thus, we speak of "the people of Europe," or "the people of America," without intending to convey the idea that they are a people in the political sense of the term. When we say, however, that "the people are sovereign," we use the word in a more restricted sense. We then speak of the *people* in the political or technical sense of the term.

This includes only the qualified voters of the community, or those by whom Constitutions may be ordained, and re-modelled. For no other persons participate in the exercise of the sovereign power. Women and minors are excluded, as well as some other classes, even in our American States. It is in this limited sense of the word, that the *people* are said to make compacts, or Constitutions and laws, either by themselves or by their agents.

If Mr. Justice Story had borne this in mind, he might have saved himself from all his criticisms on the doctrine of a social contract based on the ground that "infants, minors, married women, persons insane, and many others,"[147] take no part in the formation of civil societies, or in the creation of constitutions and governments. No one includes such persons in the idea of a people, when these are said to be sovereign. Hence, his "limitations and qualifications" of the doctrine in question, have exclusively arisen from his own misapprehension. Something more than a mere natural person is necessary to constitute one of "the people," one of the multitudinous sovereignty of an American State. "The idea of a people," says Burke, evidently using the term in its restricted or political sense, "is the idea of a corporation; it is wholly artificial, and made, like all other legal fictions, by common agreement."[148] That is, says he, "in a rude state of nature, there is no such thing as one people. *A number of men, in themselves, can have no collective capacity.*"

Or, in other words, something more than a number of men is necessary to make a people, or State. It must be agreed and settled, as to who shall take part in the exercise of political power, before constitutions and laws may be ordained or re-modelled by them.

But in vain did Burke, and Hobbes, and other writers on the philosophy of politics, endeavor to "fix, with some degree of distinctness, an idea of what we mean when we say, the PEOPLE."[149] Their labors seem to have been lost upon the politicians of the Massachusetts school; and, in some instances, at least, they appear to have only cast their pearls before swine. For one of the great lights of that school kindles into a blaze of fiery indignation against Mr. Burke, for simply advancing the incontestable truth, that what we call a PEOPLE is, in the political sense of the word, the result of an agreement or mutual understanding of a community of persons. "Oh, that mine enemy had said it!" the admirers of Mr. Burke may well exclaim, "cries this great light of Massachusetts. That some scoffing Voltaire, some impious Rousseau had uttered it! Had uttered it? Rousseau did utter the same thing, &c."[150] This is true. For widely as Edmund Burke and Rousseau differed on most points, they agreed in this, that it is not nature, but art, which determines the question, as to who shall participate in the exercise of political power, or constitute a people, in the political sense of the word. Even "the impious Rousseau" is sometimes right, and nearly, if not quite, always so when he agrees with Edmund Burke.

In his attempt to show that the Constitution was adopted by the people, and not by the States, Mr. Justice Story deceives himself by means of the ambiguities of the term *people,* and repeatedly contradicts his own positions. "The States never, in fact," says he, "did, in their political capacity, as contradistinguished from the people thereof, ratify the Constitution."[151] This is very true, if by States in their political capacity, he means, as he seems to do, the State governments. But this is not to the purpose. Everyone admits, that the Constitution was ratified, not by the Governments, but by the people of the States. Nor does anyone deny, that the term *State* is sometimes used to signify the government of a State. Thus, we often say, that the State does so and so, when the thing is done by its Government. But the question is, may we not say, that the Constitution was ratified by the States, as well as by the people of the States? Or, in other words, are not the terms *State* and *People* properly used as equivalent expressions? These words were, as we have already most abundantly seen, habitually used as convertible terms by the Convention of 1787.

We may truly say, indeed, with Judge Story, that the Constitution was not ratified by the States, as contradistinguished from the people; because it is not very easy to distinguish a thing from itself. In assuming this position, Mr. Justice Story forgets what he had said in the preceding Book of his Commentaries, namely, "the State and the people of the State, are equivalent expressions."[152] "No, the State," he again says, "by which we mean the people composing the State, may divide its sovereign powers among various functionaries, &c"[153] Here the term *people* is clearly used to include only the qualified voters, or those who share the sovereign power; and, in this sense, they are called "the State." It is precisely in this sense, that the Constitution was ratified by the peoples, or the States. We may, and indeed should, distinguish between the meanings of the term *State,* when it is figuratively used to signify the government of a State, and when it is used to signify the State itself. But we shall never distinguish the people of a State from the State itself, until we can find a State which is not composed of people.

But the attempt is made to show, that, in adopting the Constitution, the States acted as mere districts of people, and not in their sovereign political capacity.[154] But if this were so, then the different districts would have been considered together in making up the final result, and the majority of the one grand, national whole would have ordained the Constitution. The fact, however, the undenied and the undeniable fact, is quite otherwise. Each State, with all its own laws, and institutions and government, either went in, or remained out, at its own sovereign will and pleasure. In the words of the *Federalist,* it was "only to be bound by its own voluntary act." No other State, nor all other States combined, nor the whole people of America, had the least authority to control its decision This was an absolutely free, sovereign and independent act of each State. It may be doubted, indeed, if there was ever a more superficial gloss, or a more pitiful subterfuge, than the assertion of Judge Story, that the States adopted the Constitution, not as States, but only "as districts of people" composing one great State or nation. It is at war with facts; it is at war with his own repeated admissions; and it is at war with the plainest dictates of truth, as well as with the unanswerable arguments of the *Federalist.* Sad, indeed, must have been the condition to which the great sophist was reduced, when he could stoop to so palpable a gloss on one of the plainest facts in the history of the Constitution!

CONCLUSION

Mr. Justice Story has, I am aware, as well as Mr. Webster, laid great stress on the fact, that the Constitution addresses the language of authority to the States. "The language of a compact is," says he, "I will, or will not do this; that of a law is, then shalt, or shalt not do it."[155] This is what the act of entering into a compact signifies, but it is not usually the language of the instrument itself. On the contrary, the Articles of Confederation, which are universally admitted to form a compact, use precisely the same style as the Constitution. Both say what *shall,* and what *shall not,* be done by the States. Precisely the same style is also employed in the formation of compacts or treaties between wholly separate and independent powers. No, in the most ordinary articles of co-partnership, it is usual to say, in the same manner, what *shall,* and what *shall not,* be done by the parties thereto. Yet all such instruments rest upon the agreement of the parties, and derive their binding force from their voluntary act.

There is a very simple law of language, which seems to have escaped the attention of these great expounders of the Constitution. The language of written contracts usually speaks of the parties in the third person, and not for them in the first person. Hence, they necessarily assume the imperative style; laying down what *shall,* and not saying what *will,* be done by them. It would have been ridiculous, indeed, if the Constitution had said, No State *will* emit bills of credit, or coin money, and so forth, instead of saying, as it does, that no State *shall* do such acts. Like other written contracts, it says *shall,* of course, because it speaks of the parties in the third person, and lays down the obligations imposed upon them by their own consent. This is a very simple, law of language. But that is no reason why it should be overlooked by the great lights of jurisprudence.

"In compacts," says Judge Story, "we ourselves determine and promise, what *shall* be done, before we are obliged to do it." No words could more admirably suit our purpose, or the facts of the case. For each State agreed to the compact of the Constitution, which prescribes "what *shall* be done," before it was bound by it. That "no State *shall* emit bills of credit," and so forth, is precisely the style which, according to Judge Story himself, as well as according to all usage, would be employed in articles of agreement between the States; and hence, to argue for the use of *shall,* instead of *will,* that the Constitution addresses the language of authority from the people of America to the States, is simply ridiculous. "In compacts" says Story, "we ourselves determine and promise what *shall* be done, before we are obliged to do it." And yet, in the face of this obvious fact he argues from the use of *shall* in the Constitution, that it is not what the State "determined and promised," but what they were commanded to do! that it is not, and cannot be a compact between the States at all!

A and B enter into articles of agreement. These articles, according to good usage, say what A *shall* do, and what B *shall* do. What shall we say, then, of these articles? Shall we say, that they do not form an agreement, or contract at all? Shall we say, that A commands B, or "addresses to him the language of authority," as a law-giver speaks to a subject? If so, then B also commands A, and each is evidently the master of the other! Precisely such is the profound logic of Mr. Justice Story!

Chapter XVI

Arguments in Favor of the
Right of Secession

In the preceding chapters, it has, I think, been clearly demonstrated, that the Constitution of the United States was a compact to which the several States were the parties. This, as we have seen, was most explicitly the doctrine maintained by the fathers of the Constitution, and was unequivocally set forth by the *Federalist* in submitting that instrument to the people, and that it is confirmed by all the historical records of the country. If any proposition, indeed, respecting the Constitution can be considered as unanswerably established, it is the doctrine of the *Federalist,* that the act by which it was ordained was "not a *national,* but *a federal* act," having been ratified "by the people of America, *not as individuals composing one nation, but as composing the distinct and independent States to which they belong,*"[156] that the Constitution, "the compact," was established by "the States regarded as distinct and independent sovereigns."[157] It is, then, on this clear, broad, immutable foundation, that the argument in favor of secession rests.

ARGUMENT IN FAVOR OF SECESSION FROM THE DOCTRINE OF
RESERVED RIGHTS

It is frequently asked, by the opponents of secession, where is the right of a State to withdraw from the Union set forth or contained in the Constitution? But this question betrays a gross ignorance with respect to the origin of State rights. These rights are not derived from the Constitution at all; on the contrary, all the rights, powers, or authorities of the Constitution are derived from the States. And all the rights not delegated to the Federal Government by the States, are reserved to the States themselves, — the original fountains of all the powers of "the Constitution of the United States." This is the doctrine set forth by the *"Federalist"* in submitting that instrument or Constitution to the people.

"The principles established in a former paper," says the *Federalist,* "teach us, that the States will retain all preexisting authorities which may not be exclusively delegated to the federal head."[158] In the former paper here referred to, it is said: "All authorities, of which the States are not explicitly divested in favor of the Union, *remain with them in full vigor.*"[159] In the ratifying Convention of Virginia, the same doctrine is set forth as well known to everyone at that day, by John Marshall, who was afterward the illustrious Chief Justice of the Supreme Court of the United States. "The state governments," says he, "did not derive their powers from the general government, but each government derived its powers from the people, and each was to act according to the powers given it. Would any gentleman deny this? He demanded if powers not given, were retained by implication? Could any man say, no? Could any man say, that this power was not retained by the States, since it was not given away? For, says he, does not a power remain till it is given away?"[160]

Neither Marshall nor Hamilton, the author of the numbers of the *Federalist* just quoted, was ever suspected of a desire to lessen the authority of the Federal Union, or to magnify that of the States. Yet, as we have seen, both of them assume as an undeniable principle, that every power which is not delegated by the States to the Federal Union, is retained by them in full vigor. This principle results, indeed, from the fact that all the powers of the Federal Government emanate from the peoples of the several States. The question of Marshall "does not a power remain till it was given away?" admits of but one answer. For if a principal delegates power to an agent of any kind, or for any purpose; the agent only possesses the delegated powers, and all others remain with the principal. Thus, according to the very nature of things, as well as according to the high authority of Hamilton and Marshall; the States retained all the powers which they had not delegated to the Federal Union.

But however plain this principle, or however fully admitted by the advocates of federal authority; the States still insisted that it should be expressly incorporated in the written language of the Constitution. Hence Massachusetts, having ratified the Constitution, used the following language: "As it is the opinion of this Convention, that certain amendments and alterations in said Constitution would remove the fears and quiet the apprehensions of many of the good people of the

commonwealth, and more effectually guard against an undue administration of the Federal Government, the Convention do therefore recommend that the following alterations and provisions be introduced into
said Constitution:

"First, That it be explicitly declared that all powers not expressly
delegated by the aforesaid Constitution, *are reserved to the several
States,* to be by them exercised."[161]

In like manner, and for a like reason, Virginia recommended the
following "Amendment to the Constitution. 1st. That each State in the
Union shall respectively retain every power, jurisdiction, and right,
which is not by this Constitution delegated to the Congress of the
United States, or to the departments of the Federal Government."[162]
North Carolina urged the same amendment to the Constitution, and
in precisely the same words as those employed by Virginia.[163] In the
first amendment proposed by Pennsylvania, we find the following
words: "All the rights of sovereignty, which are not by the said Constitution expressly and plainly vested in the Congress, *shall be deemed to
remain with, and shall be* exercised by the several States in the
Union."[164]

These recommendations, and others to the same effect, secured the
tenth amendment to the Constitution of the United States; which is in
these words: "The powers not delegated to the United States by the
Constitution, nor prohibited by it to the States, *are reserved to the
States, or to the people.*" If reason, if authority, if history, if the words
of the Constitution itself, can establish anything; then may we regard
it as definitively and forever settled, that every power, right, or authority which is not delegated to the Federal Union, is reserved to the
States, or to the people of the States.

I ask, then, where is this great, inherent right of a State to resume
the powers it has delegated, surrendered to the Federal Union? Where
has this peerless right of sovereignty been ceded, surrendered, or given
away? The people may rage, and the politicians imagine a vain thing;
but I appeal to the great charter of American rights and liberties.
Where, then, in the Constitution of the United States, is the sacred and
inviolable right of a sovereign State to resume the powers it has delegated to its agents, given away or surrendered? When the States entered into "the compact of the Constitution," they did so, as it is conceded both by Story and Curtis, at the moment they were "free, sover-

eign, and independent States." Where, then, in that compact, did they delegate, surrender, or give away, the sacred right to resume the powers which they delegated to their agent, the Federal Government; or, in other words, the right to secede from the Union? Let the place in which this right, this greatest of all the rights of sovereignty, has been given away to the Federal Union, be pointed out in the Constitution; or it must be conceded, that it remained with the States. Let it be shown, where "the States are explicitly divested" of this right "in favor of the Union," or it must be admitted, that it "remained with them in full vigor."[165] Ignorance, or passion, or patriotism may "veil this right," but, nevertheless, the question is, where is this right given away in the compact of the Constitution? If it be not given away there; it still exists with the States in all the plenitude of its power. The stars do not cease to shine, or to exist, because they are concealed from view by exhalations from the earth, or by the blaze of noon.

ARGUMENT FROM THE SOVEREIGNTY OF THE STATES

Perhaps no subject has ever been considered with less steadiness of mind, or clearness of analysis, than "the sovereignty of the States." except "the sovereignty of the United States." The powers of the Federal Government are enumerated by one party, in order to show that it is sovereign or supreme; while the opposite party attempts to prove the sovereignty of the States, by dwelling on the powers which belong to their governments. But all this is nothing whatever to the purpose. It merely deals with the branches, not with the roots, of the great subject under discussion; and how long soever these branches may be beaten, it will only make confusion the worse confounded.

In the contest about the significance of the particular powers of the Federal and of the State Governments, the real principle on which the whole controversy hinges is overlooked, and the subject in dispute is darkened by words without knowledge, and buried far under floods of logomacy.

Mr. Webster, for example, thus demolishes the doctrine of State sovereignty: "However men may think this ought to be, the fact is, that the people of the United States have chosen to impose control on State sovereignties. There are those, doubtless, who wish they had been left without restraint; but the Constitution has ordered the matter rather differently. To make war, for instance, is an exercise of sovereignty, but the Constitution declares that no State shall declare war. To coin money is another act of sovereign power; but no State is at liberty to coin money. Again, the Constitution says that no sovereign State shall be so sovereign as to make a treaty. These prohibitions, it must be confessed, are a control on the State sovereignty of South Carolina, as well as of the other States, which does not arise 'from her feelings of honorable justice.' The opinion referred to, therefore, is in defiance of the plainest provisions of the Constitution."[166] Why, then, did he not wind up his unanswerable logic with a *quod erat demonstrandum?*

The truth is, that the whole thing, from beginning to end, is a miserable sophism. His premises are false, and his conclusion, therefore, falls to the ground. The fact is, that the people of the United States imposed no control whatsoever on the States, and had no power to do so. On the contrary, each State, for the sake of union, agreed that it would abstain from the exercise of the right to wage war, to coin money, and to make treaties. She delegated these high powers to the government of the Federal Union. She entered into the compact of the Constitution, as we have seen, in her character of "a distinct and independent sovereign," and was, therefore, "bound only by her own voluntary act."[167] All the powers of the Constitution were delegated, and all its obligations assumed, by the free act of each sovereign State. All the control to which she was liable in the Union was *self-imposed;* and not one particle of it was laid upon her by any authority but her own. The act, indeed, by which she entered into the compact of the Constitution, was an exercise, not an abridgement, of her sovereign power. If she could not enter into such a compact, she would be less than sovereign.

It is supposed by some, certainly by none who have reflected on the subject, that if a State delegates a portion of her powers, or agrees to abstain from the exercise of them; her sovereignty is thereby limited, or abridged. To all such I would commend the words of Vattel: "Several sovereign and independent States," says he, "may unite themselves together by a perpetual confederacy, without ceasing to be, each individually, a perfect State. They will together constitute a federal republic: *their joint deliberations will not impair the sovereignty of each member, though they may, in certain respects, put some restraint on the exercise of it, in virtue of voluntary engagements.*"[168] Everyone should be perfectly familiar with this principle of law. It has been clearly recognized and embodied in the legislation of this country. In the thirteenth Article of the old Confederation, for example, it is expressly declared that "the Union shall be perpetual," and yet, in the second Article, it is said that "each State retains its sovereignty, freedom, and independence." Thus although the States, in and by those Articles, delegated many sovereign powers to the Federal Government; this, in conformity with the principle laid down by Vattel, did "not impair the sovereignty of each member." But since the new Constitution, or Articles of Union, contained no clause declaring it perpetual, or assigning any period for its duration; how much more clearly did each State in the "more perfect Union" retain its sovereignty unimpaired! For, in such case, it is conceded, as we have repeatedly seen by the great lights of American jurisprudence, that a State may secede at pleasure, or resume the powers she may indeed have delegated to the Federal Government.

Indeed, if a State could not thus delegate her sovereign powers, she would cease to be sovereign. She would resemble a minor, who is incapable of entering into contracts. The State, or the people themselves, cannot exercise sovereign powers in person; and hence, if she could not delegate them to her agents, representatives, substitutes, or servants; her sovereignty would be a useless burden to her. Thus, the very circumstance which is supposed, by superficial thinkers, to limit and control the sovereignty of a State, is indispensably necessary to the perfection of that sovereignty. The people are not the less sovereign, because they institute governments, and appoint them as agents to transact their business; although they necessarily delegate a portion of their sovereign powers to these agents, or governments. On the contrary, this is the very highest exercise of sovereignty, and implies the right to alter, amend, or re-model their governments. No, it implies the right of a people to set their government entirely aside, and to substitute another, in its room.

What, then, has all this talk about the powers delegated to the State Governments, or to the Federal Government, to do with the great question of sovereignty? Those governments are not sovereign. They are subordinate to the will of the people, by whom they were created; and a subordinate sovereignty is a contradiction in terms. The only real sovereignty is that which makes, and unmakes, Constitutions and Governments. Or, if anyone is pleased to call any Government whether

State or Federal, sovereign; he should not forget that it is merely a *delegated* sovereignty. It is not original; it is derived. It is not inherent; it comes from without; and, instead of being supreme, it depends on a power greater than itself. It is divisible, and may be divided among different governments, or agents of the supreme power. On the contrary, the sovereign power of a State, or, in other words, the power of the people of a State, is inherent, original, supreme, indivisible, and inalienable. This, at least, is the American doctrine; and it is to be deeply lamented that Americans should, in the ardor and struggle of debate, so frequently forget, or overlook, the very first lessons they have ever learned, and which they certainly do not mean to repudiate or discard.

I have nothing to say, then, about the delegated powers of *this* or *that* government. They have nothing to do with the question. Others may wrangle about those powers, if they please, and beat their brains over them; all I want to know is, *where resides the one power from which all such delegated powers proceed.* The difference between this *one power* and the powers of the government it creates, is the difference between the sun and its rays, or the creator and its manifold creations. Where, then, does this one sovereign power reside? It resides, as we have seen, in each State, and not in the people of the United States. The people of the United States, indeed, were not one people, or nation, in the political sense of the word, and were never clothed with any sovereign power whatever. The late war was, it is true, carried on "to preserve the life of the nation." But there was no such nation. Its substance was a sham, and its life was a lie.[169]

As the one sovereign power, which makes, and therefore unmakes, Constitutions and Governments, resides in each State; so each State had the right to secede from the Federal Government. As each State, however, only made or adopted that Government for itself; so she could unmake it as to herself only. That is, she had no power to destroy the Federal Union, but only to withdraw from it, and let it move on in its own sphere. In the exercise of her original, inherent, indivisible, and inalienable sovereignty, she merely seceded from the Union to which he had acceded, and asked to be let alone. But she could not escape the despotic, all-devouring Lie, by which her sovereignty had been denied, and her rights denounced as "a pestilential heresy." No, by which she had been stripped of her character as a State, and degraded to the rank of a county. Was that the purpose for which, as a sovereign State, she entered into "the more perfect Union?"

"No man," says Mr. Webster, "makes a question that the people are the source of all political power. . .There is no other doctrine of government here."[170] This is conceded. The people make, and the people unmake, Constitutions. This is the universally received doctrine in America. It is asserted by Calhoun as strenuously as by Webster.

But the Constitution was made by the people of the several States, each acting for itself, and bound by no action but its own. Hence, as each State *acceded* to the compact of the Constitution, so each State may, if it choose, *secede* from that compact. If the premise is true, the conclusion is conceded; *and the premise has been demonstrated.* In acceding to the compact of the Constitution, each State made the Union as to itself; and, in seceding therefrom, it unmakes the Union only as to itself. And it does so by virtue of its own inherent, and inalienable sovereignty.

If it should be said, that the people of the several States made, but cannot unmake, the compact of the Constitution as to themselves; it would follow that the people of 1788 alone were sovereign. But the people of this generation are sovereign as well as the people of that generation. The attribute of sovereignty is, according to the American doctrine, inherent and inalienable. The people of Virginia, then, in the year 1788, did not, and could not, absorb and monopolize the sovereignty of all subsequent generations, so as to deprive them of its exercise. If this could be so, then the sovereign people of one age, or generation, might deprive the sovereign people of all ages and generations of their power and freedom. But this cannot be. The living, as well as the dead, are sovereign. As the people of Virginia in 1788 acceded to the Union, because they believed it would be for their good; so the people of Virginia in 1861 had a right to secede from the Union, because they believed it had been made to work their insufferable harm. Deny this, and you assert the sovereignty of the people of Virginia of 1788, at the expense of the sovereignty of the people of Virginia for all future ages. Or, in other words, you take all power, and sovereignty, and freedom from all other ages and generations, in order to concentrate and bury them with a past, departed, inexperienced, and perhaps fatally deluded generation. The whole American doctrine of the sovereignty of the people is false, or else it must be asserted for the living as well as for the dead; and even if it is false, it is nevertheless the doctrine by which the right of secession should be tried.

At the time the Constitution was adopted, or "the more perfect Union" formed; the people of New England took the lead of all others in their devotion to State-sovereignty and State-rights. Thus, in her Constitution of 1780, Massachusetts declared: "The people of this commonwealth have the sole and exclusive right of governing themselves, as a free, sovereign, and independent State; and do, and forever hereafter shall, exercise and enjoy every power, jurisdiction, and right, which is not, or may not hereafter, be by them expressly delegated to the United States of America, in Congress assembled." Precisely the same language, word for word, is contained in the Constitution of New Hampshire, which was made twelve years after that of Massachusetts. Thus, after the new Union was formed, New Hampshire, in the words of Massachusetts, declared herself a "free, sovereign, and independent State." "Paris," it has been said, "is France." It is more certain that "Massachusetts is New England."

How did it happen, then, that Massachusetts in 1780, and consequently New England, took the lead of all the members of the Union in her devotion to the doctrine of State-sovereignty; and yet, in 1861, more fiercely denounced that very doctrine as "a pestilential heresy" than any other State in existence? The answer is plain. The mystery is easily solved. Or rather, it is no mystery at all to anyone acquainted with the character, or the history, of Massachusetts. Never has she been in the ascendency, as in 1861, or with the majority working the Union for her benefit, that it did not appear to her eyes, like the full moon, a great world of light full of inexpressible beneficence and beauty. Nor has she ever been in the minority, feeling the pressure of the Union, or its demands upon her purse, that it did not rapidly wane, and appear to her emptied of all its glory. Hence, in 1861, so great was the glory of the Union to her enravished eyes, that it blotted out the States; just as the meridian sun blots out the stars. She forgets her primitive creed; or, if she remembers it at all, it is only to denounce it as the creed of "rebels and traitors." On the other hand, when, in 1815, Massachusetts felt the Union in her pockets; all its glory vanished, and the Rights of the States, and the Sovereignty of the States, came out to her keen vision like stars after the setting of the sun. This has been the great misfortune of the South, that the world did not turn around quite as fast at her end of the Union as it did in New England; and that it did not turn exactly in the same direction. The creed of the fathers, the creed of all sections in 1787, the creed of all the States for more than thirty years after the formation of the "more perfect Union," was substantially the creed of the South in 1861.

There she stood. But, in the meantime, Massachusetts, and consequently all New England, having made one entire revolution, denounced her primitive creed, — still the creed of the South, that the States are "free, sovereign, and independent," as the invention of rebels and traitors, designing to put the glorious Union out of joint. True, the South did dislocate the Union, and breed fiery discord; but then, this was simply by standing still, and refusing to follow the rapid revolution of New England.

ARGUMENT FROM THE SILENCE OF THE CONSTITUTION

It is a remarkable fact, that, in the Constitution of the United States, there is not a word relating to the *perpetuity* or continuance of the Government established by it. This momentous question is passed over in profound silence. Nor was this omission an act of forgetfulness. It was, on the contrary, the result of deliberate design. The existing Articles of Confederation expressly provided that the government established by them should be "perpetual," and should never be changed without the unanimous consent of all the States of the Union. This provision was deliberately struck out, or not permitted to appear in the new Constitution.

In the act of receding from the compact of the Union, which had expressly pronounced itself "perpetual," the fathers had not the face to declare that the new compact should last forever. Time had demonstrated the futility of such a provision. The Convention of 1787 had been most sadly hampered by it in their design to erect a new form of government, as appears from the Madison Papers, and other accounts of its proceedings. Hence, they wisely determined to leave no such obstacle in the way of the free action of future generations, in case they should wish to new-model their government. It is certain that *no such obstacle* is found in the Constitution framed by them.

Now what is the inference from this fact, from this omission? If the framers of the Constitution designed to make it perpetually binding, why did they not say so? Why did they depart from the plan before them, and refuse to say so? Only one answer can be given to this question. They did not intend to repeat the folly of seeking to render perpetual, by mere dint of words, those Articles of Union between Sovereign States, whose binding force and perpetuity must necessarily depend on the justice with which they should be observed by the parties to them, or on their adaptation to the great ends for which they were enacted. The perpetuity, or continuance, of the new Union was frequently alluded to and considered in the Convention of 1787, and yet there is not one syllable on the subject in the Constitution made by them. This speaks volumes.

It is argued, in the *Federalist*,[171] that as the old Articles of Confederation had utterly failed in consequence of defects which no one had foreseen; so the real objections to the new Constitution, whatever they might be, would in all probability remain to be disclosed by time and experience. Reasoning from the past, it was concluded, that no one could foresee its real defects, or how great they might prove in practice. Would it not, then, have been infinitely absurd to pronounce it perpetual, or seek to stamp it with the attribute of immortality?

The truth is, that the new Constitution was designed by its authors to last just as long as it should be faithfully observed by the parties to it, or as it should answer the great ends of its creation, and no longer. On the failure of either of these conditions, then, in their view, the power by which it was ordained possessed the inherent and indefeasible right to withdraw from it. Otherwise there would be no remedy, not even in the sovereign power itself, for the greatest of all political evils or abuses. Otherwise we should have to repudiate and reject the great principle of American freedom, which has never been called into question by any statesman of the New World, or over which the cloud of suspicion has ever been cast by any American citizen.

What, then, is the position assumed by those who deny the right of secession? In asserting that a State has no right to withdraw from the Union, they declare that the Constitution, or Articles of Union, is perpetually binding. That is to say, by a forced construction, they introduce into the Constitution, the very provision which its framers most deliberately refused to insert therein! They refused to say, that the new compact should be perpetual; and yet these interpreters declare, that they designed to make it perpetual!

Both Story and Webster admit, as we have repeatedly seen, that if sovereign States enter into a compact or Confederation, without expressly prescribing any period for the continuance of the Union; then any State has the right to secede at pleasure. This is the true inference to be drawn from the silence of the Constitution as to the continuance of the Union; an inference too clear and unquestionable to be denied by either a Story or a Webster. If they have sought to evade its force, or obscure the right of secession; this is by assuming the ground, so fully exploded in the preceding pages, that the Constitution was not a compact between the States of the Union.

"It is sometimes asked," says Mr. Motley, "why the Constitution did not make a special provision against the right of secession. How could it do so?"[172] Why, simply, by transferring the words of the old Constitution to the now, and saying "the union shall be perpetual." There is no impossibility in the case. The thing had been done once, and it might easily have been done again, if the framers of the Constitution had desired to do it. Many words, phrases, and provisions of the old Constitution were transferred by them to the new; and if they had wished to do so, they might just as easily have transferred those words, "the union shall be perpetual," or last till all the parties consent to a separation. "How could they do so?" asks Mr. Motley; and I reply, how could he ask so silly a question?

"It would have been puerile," says he, "for the Constitution to say formally to each State, thou shalt not secede." There was no necessity, perhaps, that the Convention should have been very formal in the language it addresses to the States. But would it have been puerile, or ridiculous, if the Convention had said, "the Union shall be perpetual." Who can doubt that if these words had been inserted in the new Constitution, that Mr. Motley would have wielded them as an unanswerable argument against the right of secession? Indeed, these words answer that purpose so well, that Dr. Hodge borrows them from the old Articles of Confederation, and passes them off as "the very words" of the Constitution, in order to demonstrate the palpable absurdity of secession; in order to show that secession is in direct and open defiance of "the avowed design of the compact" of 1787. These words were, indeed, the very ones he needed to demolish the right of secession; and his need was so great, that he came at them in no very legitimate way. Could anything be more feeble, or puerile, than Mr. Motley's attempt to account for the silence of the Convention on the momentous subject of secession? or more clearly illustrate the difficulty of getting rid of the argument from that silence in favor of secession? The truth is, that the Convention, in its desire to secede from the old compact, was so greatly embarrassed by the clause declaring that "the Union shall be perpetual," that it deliberately removed that obstacle from the path of future legislation; and, whether it was intended by the Convention or not, the legal effect of this was to establish the right of secession under the new compact between the same parties.

ARGUMENT FROM THE FUNDAMENTAL PRINCIPLE OF THE UNION

"To render a Federation desirable," says Mr. John Stuart Mill, "several conditions are necessary. *The first of these is, that there should be a sufficient amount of mutual sympathy among the populations.*"[173] This sentiment recommends itself to the good sense of every man in the world; no, to every man who is not insane from the influence of passion. Even Mr. Greeley, before the war, could say: "We hope never to live in a Republic, whereof one section is pinned to another by bayonets." Such is indeed the desire of every good man, no, of every rational being; for, as Mr. Mill says, no union of States is desirable, unless it be held together by the cement of good feeling, as well as of interest.

In like manner, John Quincy Adams says: "The indissoluble link of union between the people of the several States of this confederated nation is, after all, not in the *right,* but in the *heart.* If the day should ever come, (may Heaven avert it) when the affections of the people of these States shall be alienated from each other; when the fraternal spirit shall give way to cold indifference, or collision of interest shall fester into hatred, the bands of political associations will not long hold together parties no longer attracted by the magnetism of conciliated interests and kindly sympathies; and far better will it be for the people of the disunited states to part in friendship from each other, than to be held together by constraint. Then will be the time for reverting to the precedents which occurred at the formation and adoption of the Constitution, to form again a more perfect union, by dissolving that which could no longer bind, and to leave the separated parts to be re-united by the law of political gravitation to the centre."

"Better," says Mr. Adams, "to part in friendship, than to be held together by restraint." History, it is said repeats itself. Some of the Greek States, wishing to part in peace from their confederates, were held together by force of arms. This, says Freeman, in his learned work on Federal Government, ultimately proved injurious to those who drew the sword of coercion.

ARGUMENT FROM THE RIGHT OF SELF-GOVERNMENT

The thirteen Colonies, in the Declaration of Independence, justified their separation on the distinct ground, that all "governments" derive "their just powers from the consent of the governed." It was in obedience to this great principle, that the American Union became a free and voluntary association of States. This, by its very nature, excludes the idea of coercion. For, if States are compelled to remain in the Union against their will, this is subjugation, and not a co-partnership in honor, interest, freedom, and glory. It destroys the autonomy, annihilates the freedom, and extinguishes the glory of the subjugated States. The system is transformed. It is no longer a sisterhood of free States, but the vassalage of some, and the dominion of others.

This is so obvious, that it was declared at first, even by the most zealous advocates of President Lincoln, that one no intended to coerce a State. What then? Did they mean to let it go in peace? No, they neither intended to coerce a seceding State, nor let it depart! But how was such a thing possible? Why, these admirable casuists, by a most refined and subtle distinction, determined that they would not coerce a State, but only the people of whom it is composed! The State secedes. The citizens acknowledge their allegiance to the State, and determine to obey the ordinance of secession. And thereupon the Federal Government resolves to wage war, not upon the State itself, but only upon the people of the State! Happy State! Miserable people! The one may depart; but the other must come back! But if the Federal Government had only waged war upon the State, how would it have proceeded otherwise than it did?

The authors of this very nice distinction, were evidently driven to assume such a position, by the horror which Madison, Ellsworth, Mason, Hamilton, and other fathers of the Constitution, were known to have expressed at the idea of the coercion of a State. No, they would not coerce a State; they would not be guilty of the horrid thing so eloquently denounced by the fathers; they would only wage war on the men, women, and children of whom the State is composed! How admirable the acuteness! How wonderful the logic.

In 1848, Mr. Lincoln had not forgotten his very first, and nearly his very last, lesson in the science of government. He had read it in the Declaration of Independence; he had heard it recited in school; he had heard it most eloquently spouted every fourth of July. How, then, could he forget it, without some very powerful motive? No humble rail-splitter, no honest citizen, could forget such a lesson. It requires a great politician, or a President, to forget, despise, and trample such things under foot. Hence, in 1848, the humble citizen, Abraham Lincoln, like every other American citizen, publicly declared, that "any people whatever have the right to abolish the existing government, and form a new one that suits them better. This is a most valuable, a most sacred right."

Yes, any people whatever: the thirteen British Colonies; the Greeks; the States of South America; Poland; Hungary; any and every people under the wide expanse of heaven; *except* the people of the South. But why except the South? The reason is plain. It was, indeed, most perfectly and fully explained by Mr. Lincoln himself. When asked, as President of the United States, "why not let the South go?" his simple, direct, and honest answer revealed one secret of the wise policy of the Washington Cabinet. "Let the South go!" said he, *"where, then, shall we get our revenue?"* There lies the secret. The Declaration of Independence is great; the voice of all the fathers is mighty; but then they yield us no revenue.

The right of self-government is "a most valuable, a most sacred right," but in this particular case, it gives us no revenue. Hence, this "most valuable, this most sacred right," may and should shine upon every other land under heaven; but here it must "pale its ineffectual fires," and sink into utter insignificance and contempt in the august presence of the "ALMIGHTY DOLLAR."

As the object of the Black Republicans, in wishing to retain the South, was not to lose revenue, so now that they have the South, the only use they have for her is to lay taxes and other burdens of government upon her. In an open and shameless violation of the great principle of 1776, the South is united to the North by the tie of "taxation without representation." Is this then "the sacred right" of self-government? The Union waged a seven years war to establish that right, and a four years war to demolish it.

Every American citizen has taken in the idea of self-government with his mother's milk; has heard it from all his most venerated guides, teachers, and oracles; has proclaimed it himself, perhaps, all his life as "a most valuable, and a most sacred right." Hence, he should not be required, all on a sudden, to proclaim the diametrically opposite doctrine. He should be allowed some little time, at least, to clear his throat for the opposite utterance. Is it not quite natural, then, that his early and life-long prejudice in favor of the right of self-government, should have clung to the Editor of the *Tribune,* the great organ of the Republican party, even while that party was preparing the way for its subversion? True, it was but an organ; yet had it so long, and so earnestly, proclaimed the great right of self-government, that some little time, at least, should have been allowed for it to come right around to the diametrically opposite position. Accordingly, on the 9th of November, three days after Mr. Lincoln's election, that organ uttered the sentiments: "If the cotton States shall become satisfied that they can do better out of the Union than in it, we insist on letting them go in peace . . . We must ever resist the right of any State to remain in the Union and nullify or defy the laws thereof. To withdraw from the union is quite another matter; and whenever any considerable section of our Union shall deliberately resolve to go out, *we shall resist all coercive measures designed to keep it in.* We hope never to live in a Republic whereof one section is pinned to another by bayonets."

Again, on the 17th December, just before the secession of South Carolina, the same organ said: "If it [the Declaration of Independence] justifies the secession from the British Empire of three millions of colonists in 1776, we do not see why it would not justify the secession of five millions of southerners from the federal union in 1861. If we are mistaken on this point, why does not someone show us *wherein and why?* For our own part, *while we deny the right of slave-holders to hold slaves against the will of the latter, we cannot see how twenty millions of people can hold ten, or even five, in a detested Union with them by military force* . . . If seven or eight contiguous States should present themselves authoritatively at Washington, saying, 'We hate the Federal Union; we have withdrawn from it; we give you the choice between acquiescing in our secession and arranging amicably all incidental questions on the one hand and attempting to subdue us on the other, we could not stand up for coercion, for subjugation, for we do not think it would be just; we hold the right of self-government even when invoked on behalf of those who deny it to others. So much for the question of principle.'"..."Any attempt to compel them by force to remain would be contrary to the principles enunciated in the immortal Declaration of Independence, contrary to the fundamental ideas on which human liberty is based."

On the 23d February, 1861, after the cotton States had formed their confederacy, the *Tribune* used this language: "*We have repeatedly said, and we once more insist,* that the great principle embodied by Jefferson in the Declaration of American Independence, that Governments derive their just powers from the consent of the governed, is sound and just; *and that if the slave States, the cotton States, or the gulf States only, choose to form an independent nation,* they have a clear moral right to do so. *Whenever it shall be clear that the great body of Southern people have become conclusively alienated from the Union, and anxious to escape from it,* we will do our best to forward their views."

President Buchanan, from whose interesting book the above extracts have been taken, adds: "In a similar spirit, leading Republicans everywhere scornfully exclaimed, 'Let them go;' 'We can do better without them;' 'Let the Union slide,' and other language of the same import."

Before the war, it was indignantly denied, that the abolitionists constituted more than a small minority of the Republicans. How is it since the war? Does not almost every man of them now claim that he has always been an abolitionist, and, as such, come in for his share of glory in the forced emancipation of the slaves? It is certain, that of all the men in the Union, the abolitionists of the Republican party were the most active asserters, and the most powerful promoters, of secession and disunion. They everywhere proclaimed, not only the right, but the sacred duty of secession. William Lloyd Garrison led the way. "In the expressive and pertinent language of Scripture," said he, the Constitution "was a covenant with death, and an agreement with hell, null and void before God, from the first moment of its inception the framers of which were recreant to duty, and the supporters of which are equally guilty."[174] Yet, how strange! the men of this school enlisted in the ranks, and fought under the banner of Mr. Lincoln; who was bound by his oath to support that "covenant with death and agreement with hell!" Did they fight for the Constitution? Did they heartily join in the cry for the Union?

Again, he said, "the motto inscribed on the banner of Freedom is, no Union with slave-holders"[175]. . ."Our motto is, no Union with slave-holders, either religious or political."[176] [I am holier than thou!] "In withdrawing from the American Union, we have the God of justice with us."[177] Did this man, then, or his followers, fight for the Union? "Circulate," he cried, "a declaration of disunion from slave-holders throughout the country. Hold mass meetings—assemble in Conventions—nail your banners to the mast."[178] Did these men, then, take down their banners, trample its motto in the dust, and join the loud war-cry for the Union of the fathers? If so, then it was not because they hated that Union the less, but because they hated Southerners the more.

Now this man William Lloyd Garrison was an honest fanatic. He just came right down with a direct sledge-hammer force on all slave-holders, and on all the poor, pitiful, pulling hypocrites, who pretended to desire to preserve the Constitution and the Union; and who, to that end, labored to explain away the provisions of that "sacred compact," as they delighted to call the Constitution.

"Those provisions," said they, "were meant to cover slavery," yet "as they may be fairly interpreted to mean something exactly the reverse, it is allowable to give them such an interpretation, *especially as the cause of Freedom will he thereby promoted.*"[179] In thus stating this hypocritical position, Mr. Garrison must have had Mr. Sumner in his mind's eye. But with honest scorn and contempt he tears the mean fabric to tatters, and scatters it to the winds! "This," says he, "is to advocate fraud and violence to one of the contracting parties, *whose co-operation was secured only by an express agreement and undertaking between them both, in regard to the clauses alluded to;* and that such a construction, if enforced by laws and penalties, would unquestionably lead to civil war, *and the aggrieved party would justly claim to have been betrayed,* and robbed of their Constitutional rights."[180]

"No honest use can be made of it," says he, "in opposition to the plain intention of its framers, *except to declare the contract at an end, and to refuse to serve under it.*"[181] It is of no use to lie, said he, that the Constitution is "a contract" between the States; an "express agreement and undertaking" between the North and the South. He will not have this "express agreement" explained away.

"It is objected," say's he, "that slaves are held as property, and therefore, as the clauses refers to persons, it cannot mean slaves. Slaves are
recognized not merely as property, but also as persons,—as having a
mixed character—as combining the human with the brute. This is par-
adoxical, we admit; but slavery is a paradox—the American Constitution is a paradox—the American Union is a paradox—the American
Government is a paradox—and if any one of these is to be repudiated
on that ground, they all are. That it is the duty of the friends of freedom to deny the binding authority of them all, *and to secede from all,
we distinctly affirm.*"[182]

Such were the sentiments of Mr. Lloyd Garrison, in 1844, delivered
in their annual address to the Anti-Slavery society of America, as its
president. Precisely the same sentiments were entertained by the two
learned secretaries of that society, namely, Wendell Phillips and Maria
Weston Chapman, as well as by all its leading members. They proclaimed the duty of secession from the Constitution, from the Union,
and from the Government of America. They wished to have nothing
to do with slave-holders. In the mild and conciliatory language of their
president, they longed to get away and to live apart from those *"incorrigible men-stealers, merciless tyrants, and blood-thirsty assassins."*[183]

Such was the gentle and persuasive language, and such were the
loyal sentiments, of the abolitionists from 1844 to 1861. The following
resolutions were passed at a meeting of the American Anti-Slavery
Society:

Resolved, That secession from the United States Government is the
duty of every Abolitionist, since no one can take office or deposit his
vote under the Constitution without violating his anti-slavery principles, and rendering himself an abettor to the slave-holder in his sin.

Resolved, That years of warfare against the slave power has convinced us that every act done in support of the American Union rivets
the chain of the slave—that the only exodus of the slave to freedom,
unless it be one of blood, must be over the remains of the present
American Church and the grave of the present Union.

Resolved, That the Abolitionists of this country should make it one
of the primary objects of this agitation to dissolve the American Union.

Yet of all the war-spirits in the country, these very men were the
loudest and fiercest in their cries for a war of coercion to put down
secession, as rebellion and treason. In its burning hate of the Union,

the *Tribune* had become poetical, and addressed THE AMERICAN FLAG as follows:

Tear down that flaunting lie!
Half-mast the starry flag!
Insult no sunny sky
With hate's polluted rag!

But, all on a sudden, that "polluted rag" became the most sacred ensign of freedom that ever floated between heaven and earth! The cry has gone forth: "This Union is a lie! The American Union is an imposition . . . I am for its overthrow. . .Up with the flag of disunion, that we may have a glorious Republic of our own." But from the same person, the opposite cry is heard: "Down with the flag of disunion, and up with the flag of the Union, that we may 'preserve the life of the nation, 'the glorious Republic of the fathers.' " Even the despised Constitution, "the antiquated parchment" of Henry Ward Beecher, becomes all at once young, and fresh, and beautiful again; and that Reverend gentleman stands before the world at Exeter Hall as the representative of the "constitutional union" party of this country.

Is there, in the history of the world, another instance of a change so sudden, so complete, and so wonderful in the avowed sentiments of any great body of men, as that which took place among the abolitionists of this country in 1861? Now whence all this intense love of the Union, where recently there had been such deadly hate? Whence this new-born desire to be forever associated with "the merciless tyrants, the blood-thirsty assassins" of the South? The truth is, they did not love the Union then, and they do not want the Union now. They raised the cry of "the Union," because, as one of their leaders said, they believed they could "win on the Union." And having ridden into power on "the Union," and consolidated their power in the name of "the Union," they now resist the persistent efforts of President Johnson to restore the Union.

But Mr. Greeley has, in his "American Conflict," made a most awkward and unsatisfactory attempt to explain the course of the Union-hating and the Union-loving *Tribune*. It was, perhaps, a little difficult for him to speak out all that was in him on this delicate subject. The truth seems to be: 1. That the word which went forth from President

Lincoln, "If we let the South go, where shall we get our revenue?" is one of the causes of the great change in question. Several books had, in 1860, been published to illustrate the subject of "Southern Wealth and Northern Profits," and, upon reflection, the North concluded that, after all, she had some use for the South. She was naturally indignant at the thought of losing the bird, which had so long laid for her the golden egg. 2. Secession offered a splendid opportunity, or occasion, on which to wreak a little wrath on the slave-holders of the South, on those "incorrigible men-stealers, merciless tyrants, and bloodthirsty assassins," who so richly deserved to die. But it would, of course, be much more respectable to kill them as "rebels and traitors," than merely as slave-holders. Hence, the very men who had been foremost and fiercest in preaching the duty of secession and disunion, became, all on a sudden, the most clamorous for the blood of secessionists as traitors to "the glorious Union." As the cynic, Diogenes, trampled on the robe of Plato's pride with a still greater pride; so the abolitionists panted for the blood of "blood-thirsty assassins" with a still greater thirst. Hence, more than any other class of men, they insisted that Mr. Lincoln, however reluctant, should "cry havoc, and let slip the dogs of war." 3. Secession furnished a fine pretext, a glorious occasion, for the forced emancipation of the slaves at the South. Hence, just before Mr. Lincoln publicly declared that he had neither the wish, nor the power, to interfere with slavery in the States, the word privately went forth from a member of his Cabinet, that secession should be punished with the emancipation of the blacks; and with the utter devastation of the South by fire and sword.[184] This word was, of course, intended for "the faithful." For if, at that early day, such a design had been publicly avowed, it would have filled the North with amazement, horror, and disgust. But has it not been accomplished to the very letter?

Such were the causes, especially the last two, by which, it seems to me, so wonderful a revolution was produced in the political views and aspirations of the Northern abolitionists. The change appeared like magic. "The antiquated parchment" was renovated; the "polluted rag" was purified; and the Union became, not only habitable, but the only fit habitation for free men. But, then, the Union was not to be "the more perfect Union" of the fathers; the Constitution was not to be the compact of 1787; and "hate's polluted rag" was to be consecrated and glorified by hate. On the contrary, the Union was to be cast into the furnace of war, seven times heated, and to come forth free from the sin of slavery, and cemented, not by "the mutual sympathy of its populations," but by their blood. It was to be a new Union; a bright and beautiful emanation, not from the consent of the governed, but from the sovereign, the supreme, the sublime will of the Northern abolitionists. How lustily they joined in the war-cry for the Union, this was in order that they might the more effectually overthrow it, and ordain, one of their own in its place. Is not this the true secret of their new-born love for "the glorious Union?"

Previous to the war, it was frequently alleged, that the abolitionists constituted only a small minority in the Republican party. It is certain, that they controlled the policy of Mr. Lincoln's administration. "The higher law," "the law written on the hearts and consciences of freemen," was the rule of their conduct. For the Constitution, for the compact of 1787, for that "covenant with death and agreement with hell," they cared less than nothing; except when it agreed with their own will, or could be made a pretext for their dark designs. The fact, that there was not the shadow of an authority for coercion in the Constitution, had not the least weight with them. No, if the power to coerce had been expressly denied to the Federal Government in the Constitution; this provision would have been easily explained away, or overruled by "the law written on the hearts and consciences of freemen." It would have been but a "straw to the fire in the blood."

President Buchanan could not find the power to coerce a State in the Constitution he had sworn to support. In like manner, Professor Bernard, of Oxford, England, finding no authority for the coercion of a State in the Constitution of 1787, pronounces it wrong. The same ground is taken by Mr. Freeman, of the same University, in his learned work on Federal Government. But if coercion is a wrong under the Constitution; then, surely, secession is a Constitutional right. Every man has the legal right to do anything, which is not forbidden by the law of the land. He may not have the *moral,* but he has *the legal,* right to do it. A miserly act, for example, especially in a rich man, is morally and socially wrong. But if there is no law against it, then, however rich the man may be, he has the *legal* right to do it. We may despise the act; we may abhor it; and we may denounce it as bitterly as anyone ever denounced secession. But still, in the case supposed, the act is done in the exercise of a *legal* right; which everyone is bound to recognize and respect. This ambiguity in the term *right* has, indeed; been the source of no little darkness and confusion in the discussion of moral and political questions. Mr. Buchanan seems to have been confused by this ambiguity, when he denied both the *right* of coercion and the *right* of secession. Surely, both positions cannot be true, in the legal sense of the term *right*. For, if we say, that coercion is a constitutional wrong, or usurpation, is not this saying that the Constitution permits secession, or, in other words, that it is a Constitutional right?

This appears so clear to my mind, that when Mr. Buchanan denied the right of secession, I suppose he merely intended to condemn secession as a moral or social wrong. This is the way in which he must be understood, if we would not make him contradict himself. He may have dreaded, he may have abhorred, the act of secession; and he may, therefore, have pronounced it wrong in the forum of conscience. But if the Constitution does not authorize coercion, then it permits secession; or, in other words, secession is a Constitutional right, which every power on earth is bound to respect as existing under the supreme law of the land; a Constitutional right, which the Federal Government could deny only by an act of usurpation.

Coercion is unconstitutional. Coercion is wrong. Coercion strikes down and demolishes the great fundamental principle of the Declaration of Independence, the sacred right of self-government itself. Coercion wages war on the autonomy of free States. Secession, on the other hand, asserts the right of self-government for every free, sovereign, and independent State in existence.

Virginia did not favor secession. But when the hour of trial came, she stood in the imminent, deadly breach between the secession of South Carolina and the coercion of Massachusetts; receiving into her own broad bosom the fatal shafts of war, till she fell crushed, bleeding and exhausted to the earth. I appeal to the universe, then, if her course was not noble, heroic, sublime.

Massachusetts has, on the contrary, favored both secession and coercion by terms. The pilgrim fathers of Massachusetts delighted in two things; first, in the freedom from persecution for themselves; and, secondly, in the sweet privilege and power to persecute others. In like manner, their sons have rejoiced in two things; first, in the right of self-government for themselves; and, secondly, in the denial of that right to others.

ARGUMENT FROM THE OPINION OF WELL-INFORMED AND INTELLIGENT FOREIGNERS

The position that secession is a Constitutional right, flowing from the idea that the Constitution is a compact between sovereign States, is adopted by many impartial foreigners, who have been at the pains to examine our institutions for themselves. Thus, says M. De Tocqueville, in his celebrated work on *Democracy in America*: "The Union was formed by *the voluntary agreement of the States;* and in uniting together they have not forfeited their nationality, *nor have they been reduced to the condition of one and the same people. If one of the States choose to withdraw from the compact, it would be difficult to disprove its right of doing so, and the Federal Government would have no means of maintaining its claims directly either by force or right.*"[185] In like manner, Dr. Mackay says: "The Federal Government exists on sufferance only. Any State may, at any time, *Constitutionally withdraw from the Union, and thus virtually dissolve it.* It was not certainly created with the idea that the States, or several of them, would desire a separation; *but whenever they choose to do it, they have no obstacle in the Constitution."* Mr. Spence also, to whom we owe this extract from Dr. Mackay, comes to the conclusion, in his able work on "The American Union," that secession is a Constitutional right. No, he unanswerably establishes this conclusion, by facts which lie on the very surface of American history, and which, however they may be concealed or obscured by the influence of party passions at home, cannot escape the scrutiny of impartial foreigners, who may simply desire to ascertain the truth in regard to such questions. After referring to the opinions of M. De Tocqueville and Dr. Mackay, Mr. Spence very justly remarks: "Here, secession is plainly declared a Constitutional right, not by excited Southerners, *but by impartial men of unquestionable ability.*"[186]

An intelligent foreigner, as De Lolme, in his admirable treatise on the Constitution of England observes, possesses some very decided advantages in the study of the fundamental institutions of a country. This is specially true in regard to all questions, which have been drawn into the vortex of party politics, and mixed up with the struggle for power and the emoluments of office. Never has its justness been more forcibly illustrated, than in regard to the conflicting theories of the Constitution of the United States. Though Lord Brougham, to select only one example, most profoundly sympathized with the abolitionists of the North; yet, in spite of all his natural affinities, the simple facts of history constrained him to adopt the Southern view of the Constitution. Hence, in his work on Political Philosophy, he says: "It is plainly impossible to consider the Constitution which professes to govern this whole Union, *this Federacy of States,* as anything other than a treaty."[187] Accordingly, he speaks of the American Union of States, as "the Great League." It required no great research, or profound logic, to reach this conclusion. On the contrary, it requires, as we have seen, the utmost effort to keep facts in the background, and all the resources of the most perverse ingenuity, to come to any other conclusion. It is, indeed, only necessary to know a few facts, with which every student of our history is perfectly familiar, and which are well-stated by Lord Brougham, in order to recognise the fundamental principle of the "Great League." "The affairs of the colonies," says he, "having during the revolutionary war been conducted by a Congress of delegates for each, on the restoration of peace, and the final establishment of their independence, they formed this *Federal* Constitution, *which was only gradually adopted by the different members of the Great League. Nine States having ratified it,* the new form of government went into operation on the 4th of March, 1789. Before the end of 1790 it had received the assent of the remaining States." These facts alone, it is believed, are absolutely decisive in favor of the position, that the American Union was a voluntary association of States, or a compact to which the States were the parties. Hence it is that foreigners, whether impartial or prejudiced against the South, adopt the Southern view of the Constitution, when they examine the subject with the least care.

It is natural, indeed, that foreigners, before they examine the subject, should look upon the American people as one consolidated nation; for that is the external appearance which they present to those who view the affairs of this continent from a distance. But like a multiple star, which in the distance seems to be a single luminary to the naked eye, the American Union is no sooner approached, or more closely examined, than it is resolved into a constellation of sister States. Nothing but party passion, it is believed, can resist so plain a conclusion; just as the clearest revelations of the telescope were vehemently denied by many of the most learned contemporaries of Galileo. Hence, it is that De Tocqueville, and Mackay, and Spence, and Brougham, and Cantu,[188] and Heeren,[189] as well as other philosophers, jurists and historians among the most enlightened portions of Europe, so readily adopt the Southern view of the Constitution, and pronounce the American Union a confederation of States.

ARGUMENT FROM THE VIRGINIA ORDINANCE OF RATIFICATION

A great many unfounded objections were urged against the Constitution by its enemies. Mr. Madison has, in the thirty-eighth number of the *Federalist,* drawn a powerful picture of "the incoherence of the objections to the plan proposed," that is, to the Constitution of 1787. Now this chaos of conflicting objections, which were raised by the enemies of the Constitution in order to defeat its adoption, could not truly reflect the nature and design of that plan for the government of the Union. Yet, however strange it may seem, Mr. Justice Story and Mr. Webster have, as we have seen,[190] selected one of these objections to show what the Constitution is; though this very objection had been most triumphantly refuted by Mr. Madison, both in the *Federalist* and in the ratifying Convention of Virginia. By the same sort of logic, if logic it may be called, they might have fastened almost any other absurd interpretation on the Constitution, as well as the construction that it was ordained by the people of America as one nation, and not by the several States. By appealing to the objections of Patrick Henry alone, as an authority, they might have proved that there was "not one federal feature" in the Constitution of 1787, as well as a dozen other glaring absurdities; and that the fathers of the Constitution did not know what they were about when they called the work of their own hands, *"The Federal Government of these States."*

In the ratifying Convention of Virginia, Patrick Henry frequently dwelt, with great earnestness, on the danger of entering into a new and untried Union, from which there might be no escape. Virginia is now free, said he, and the mistress of her own destiny. But once in the new Union, the power of the General Government may be wielded for her injury and oppression. This result was, in fact, eloquently predicted by Patrick Henry, George Mason, William Grayson, and other members of the same Convention. This argument proceeded on the supposition, either that Virginia would not have the right to secede from the Union, or else that this right would be denied by her oppressors. The debates in the Virginia Convention of 1788 are, indeed, replete with passages of burning eloquence, which predict the calamities that would fall on that noble State, as well as on other Southern States, from the oppressions of "the Northern majority." Hence, the people of Virginia, in their ordinance of ratification, took the precaution to guard against this danger, by expressly reserving the right to resume the powers delegated to the Federal Government "whensoever the same shall be perverted to their injury or oppression."

The view which Virginia has taken of her own ordinance is disputed. The words of this ordinance are as follows: "We, the delegates of the people of Virginia, duly elected, &c. . . Do in the name, and in behalf of the people of Virginia, declare and make known, that *the powers granted under the Constitution, being derived from the people of the United States, be returned by them whensoever the same shall be perverted to their injury or oppression."*

Mr. Webster understood these words, "the people of the United States," precisely as he understood them in the preamble to the Constitution. Hence, he quotes the Virginia ordinance of ratification, in order to show that the Constitution was established, not by the States, nor by the people of the States, but by "the people of the United States in the aggregate," or as one nation. But, as we have repeatedly seen, this is a false view of the words in question. They were not so understood by the Virginia Convention of 1788. In that Convention, Mr. Madison most clearly and fully explained these words, precisely as he had previously done in *The Federalist.* The powers of the new government are derived, said he, from the people of the United States, "but not the people as composing one great society, *but the people as composing thirteen sovereignties."*

Such was the meaning of the words in question, as explained by James Madison, to whom the Convention looked for information on the subject, and by whom they were led to adopt and ratify the Constitution. Yet these words are quoted by Webster, Everett, and other politicians of Massachusetts, in order to show that, in the opinion of the Virginia Convention of 1788, the Constitution of the United States was ordained by the people of America as one nation; and that the people of America as one nation may, therefore, resume the delegated powers "whensoever they shall be perverted to their injury or oppression." To this interpretation and inference, there are several insuperable objections.

In the first place, the Constitution was not to be established by the people of America as one nation, or by "the people of the United States as one great society," and this fact was perfectly well known to the Virginia Convention of 1788. It has already been sufficiently demonstrated, that the Constitution was ordained, not by the people of America as one great society, but by each People acting for itself alone, and to be bound exclusively by its own voluntary act. It would be a gross solecism in language, as well as in logic, to say that the people of the United States as one great society, might *resume* powers which were not delegated by them. The sovereignty which delegates, is the sovereignty which resumes; and it is absurd to speak of a resumption of powers by any other authority, whether real or imaginary.

In the second place, the evil intended to be remedied shows the true meaning of the words in question. The Virginia people did not fear, that the people of the United States might pervert the powers of the Federal Government for their own oppression. Their fears were for the weak, not for the strong; not for the people of the United States in the aggregate, but for the Southern States in the minority; and especially for the State of Virginia. They feared, as the burning eloquence of Henry, and Mason, and Monroe, and Grayson evinced, that the new Government would "operate as a faction of seven States to oppress six," that the Northern majority would, sooner or later, trample on the Southern minority. They feared, in the language of Grayson, that the new Union would be made "to exchange the poverty of the North for the riches of the South." In the words of Henry, "This Government subjects everything to the Northern majority. Is there not, then, a settled purpose to check the Southern interest? We thus put unbounded power over our property in hands not having a common interest with us. How can the Southern members prevent the adoption of the most oppressive mode of taxation in the Southern States, as there is a majority in favor of the Northern States? Sir, this is a picture so horrid, so wretched, so dreadful, that I need no longer dwell upon it."[191] Did the Convention of Virginia, then, seek to quiet these dreadful apprehensions, by declaring, that the people of the United States "as one great society," might resume the powers of the Federal Government whensoever they should be perverted to their oppression? By declaring, that this one great society, or rather the majority of this society, might resume the powers of the Federal Government whensoever they should be pleased to use them for the oppression of the minority? Could any possible interpretation render any legislation more absolutely ridiculous? It puts the remedy in the hands of those from whom the evil is expected to proceed! It gives the shield of defence to the very power which holds the terrible sword of destruction!

The Convention of Virginia spoke "in behalf of the people of Virginia," and not in behalf of the overbearing majority, by whom it was feared these people might be crushed. They sought to protect, not the people of America, who needed no protection, but the people of Virginia. Hence, as the people of Virginia had delegated powers to the Federal Government, they reserved "in behalf of the people of Virginia," the right to resume those powers whensoever they should be perverted to their injury or oppression.

Now this reservation enures to the benefit of all the parties to the Constitutional compact; for as all such compacts are mutual, so no one party can be under any greater obligation than another. Hence, a condition in favor of one is a condition in favor of all. This well-known principle was assorted by Mr. Calhoun in the great debate of 1833, with the remark that he presumed it would not be denied by Mr. Webster; and it was not denied by him. Hence any State, as well as Virginia, had the express right to resume the powers delegated by her to the Federal Government, in case they should be perverted to her injury or oppression.

But, it may be asked, were the powers of the Federal Government perverted to the injury or oppression of any Southern State? It might be easily shown, that they were indeed perverted to the injury and oppression of more States than one; but this is unnecessary, since the parties to the compact, the sovereign States by whom it was ratified, are the judges of this question.[192]

Chapter XVII

Arguments Against the Right of Secession

Having considered the arguments in favor of the right of secession, it is, in the next place, proper to analyze and discuss those which have been most confidently urged against that right. Among these, none have been relied on with greater confidence, than those which are supposed to flow from the express language of the Constitution. This class of arguments shall, therefore, occupy the first place in the following examination and discussion.

ARGUMENT FROM "THE VERY WORDS" OF THE CONSTITUTION

Now this argument comes directly to the point. Let us see, then, these "very words and avowed design of the compact"[193] of 1787, by which the right of secession is repudiated and rejected. "The contracting parties," we are told, stipulate that "the Union shall be perpetual."[194] Again, the same writer says, "these States are pledged to a perpetual Union," quoting, as he supposes, the very words of the Constitution. But, unfortunately for his confident argument, these words are not to be found in the Constitution at all. They are evidently taken from the old Articles of Confederation!

Would it not be well, if learned doctors of divinity would only condescend to read the Constitution, before they undertake to interpret it for the benefit of their confiding flocks? Especially, should they not take some little pains to ascertain "the very words of the compact" of 1787, before they erect on its very words the grave charge of treason against their "Southern brethren?"

The Constitution, says an English writer, does "expressly prohibit the States from entering into any treaty, alliance, or confederation, such as the so-called Southern Confederacy."[195] This argument is relied on with great confidence. It may be found in all the books, pamphlets, and publications, with which the opponents of secession have flooded the

English public on the "American Question." Yet, as it appears to me, it clearly admits of two perfectly satisfactory replies.

In the first place, the Constitution, or the new "Articles of Union," is obligatory only upon the members of the Union. No one supposes that the States could, while remaining in the Union, form any other "treaty, alliance, or confederation." But their duty while in the Union is one thing, and their right to withdraw from the Union is quite another. In the articles of any partnership, whether great or small, a clause may be inserted forbidding the parties to enter into any other partnership of the same kind, or for the same, purpose. Indeed this is often done. But who, for a moment, ever imagined that such a clause would render the partnership perpetual, or forever prevent any of its members from withdrawing from the firm?

In the second place, the words in question were transferred from the old to the new "Articles of Union." Thus, say the old Articles, "No two or more States shall enter into any treaty, confederation, or alliance whatever between them."[196] Now this clause was binding as long as the Confederation continued. But did it prohibit "any two or more States" from withdrawing from the Union, in order to establish "a more perfect" one? By no means. It is, on the contrary, perfectly notorious, that some of the States did withdraw from that Union in order to form the Union of 1787. Hence, nothing but the blind force of passion can render this clause more obligatory in the new "Articles of Union," or in the Constitution, than it was in the old one.

No, if words could have made any union of States perpetual, the old Articles of Confederation would still form the supreme law of the American Union. For the thirteenth Article expressly declares, that "the articles of this confederation shall be observed by every State, and *the Union shall be perpetual;* nor shall any alteration at any time hereafter be made in any of them, unless such alterations be agreed to by a Congress of the United States, *and be afterward confirmed by the Legislatures of every State."* Yet, in spite of these words, some of the States did withdraw from that "perpetual union," and formed a new one. The people of 1787 refused to be bound by the people of 1778. They deemed themselves no less sovereign than their predecessors. Hence, in the words of the English writer above-quoted, "the plan of course failed, *like all similar attempts to fetter future legislation."*[197]

No words, and no principle of law or justice, could render such

Articles of Union forever binding on free, sovereign, and independent States. Nothing but passion, or brute force, could have compelled the millions of 1865 to bond their necks to the legislation of 1787 against their will. The Union of 1787 owed its existence to secession from a voluntary association of States; and, being itself a voluntary association of States, it could not escape from the law of its creation. The right of secession was, indeed, the law both of its origin and its existence.

The English writer, who argues so confidently against the right of secession from the words of the Constitution, does not seem to have been at all aware that those words were borrowed from the old Articles of Confederation, or that the Convention of 1787 had understood them very differently from himself. The people of this country were bound by the legislation of 1787, not by Mr. Ludlow's mistakes and blunders respecting that legislation.

The right of coercion is sometimes deduced from that clause of the Constitution, which contains the President's oath of office, and which requires him to "preserve, protect, and defend the Constitution of the United States." This is, indeed, the great argument against secession from the words of the Constitution. But it is a gross solecism; *a petitio principii* as plain as possible. For, if by and under the Constitution, a State has a right to secede from the Union; then the President is sworn to preserve, not to destroy, this Constitutional right. Hence, when it is argued that the President is bound to coerce in order to preserve, protect, and defend the Constitution; it is assumed that, in the view of the Constitution, secession is wrong and coercion is right; which is very clearly to beg the question. It takes the very point in dispute for granted. Such an argument, such a fallacy, may lave satisfied those who were passionately bent on coercion; but, in the eye of reason, it is wholly destitute of force. If a State had the Constitutional right to secede, and did secede, then she was out of the Union; and the President had no more power to execute the laws of the United States within her limits, than he had to enforce them in the dominions of Great Britain, or France, or Russia. The President's oath of office requires him, not to usurp any power, but only to exercise those which are conferred on him by the Constitution.

Argument from the Wisdom of the Fathers

An argument against the right of secession is deduced from the wisdom of the framers of the Constitution. It is supposed, that men who were so remarkable for their sagacity and wisdom, would not have undertaken to erect a grand Confederacy of States, and yet have been so absurd as to allow a State to secede from it. It is argued, that they could not have intended to astonish the world with the "extraordinary spectacle of a nation existing only at the will of each of its constituent parts."[198]

This argument, which is urged by Judge Story, and others, amounts simply to this, that the fathers of the Constitution could not have been such fools as to make a compact between the States. For it is conceded, that this extraordinary spectacle, this wonderful exhibition of weakness, results from the doctrine that the Constitution is a compact between the States. The conclusions, says Mr. Justice Story, "which naturally flow from the doctrine that the Constitution is a compact between the States," "go to the extent of reducing the government to a mere confederacy during pleasure; and of thus presenting the extraordinary spectacle of a nation existing only at the will of each of its constituent parts." Hence, in the opinion of Judge Story, all that is wonderful in this spectacle resolves itself into the most unaccountable fact, that the fathers should have framed "a compact between the States"! A thing which has been frequently done in the history of the world, and which, as we have seen, was actually done by the Convention of 1787. It is *impossible*, exclaims Judge Story; we simply reply, *it is a fact*. A learned doctor, in one of Moliere's plays, argues that, after taking his remedy, it was impossible that his patient should have died. But the poor servant, who was not blessed with half the doctor's learning or ingenuity, was weak enough to believe that the fact of his death was some little evidence of its possibility. The question is, not what the fathers in the opinion of one of the sons, ought to have done, but what they have actually done.

The son in question, for example, is shocked and astonished at the "extraordinary spectacle of a nation existing at the will of its constituent parts." If this very learned son had only possessed a little more wisdom, he would never have discovered, perhaps, this wonderful spectacle of "a nation," with "its constituent parts," or subordinate fractions.

He would, on the contrary, have seen that the sovereign States which he calls "the constituent parts," or the fractions, of his imaginary nation, are really the units of a confederation. I am rather inclined to doubt, therefore, whether such a son is the fittest of all possible tribunals before which to try the wisdom of the fathers.

After all, perhaps, it was no want of wisdom in the fathers, but only the conceit of wisdom in ourselves, which causes their work to present so "extraordinary a spectacle." Indeed, if we infer the nature of their work, not from an examination of what they have actually done, but from their wisdom, do we not reason from our own notions of wisdom? And are we not in danger of interpolating their conceptions with our own devices? The better method is to listen to the great teacher, Time, which estimates their wisdom from the nature of their work, and not the nature of their work from their wisdom.

The question is, not what the fathers, as reasonable men, ought to have done; but what they have actually done. Perhaps their wisdom, even if perfect in itself, was sometimes held in abeyance by the prejudices, the passions, and the interests by which it was surrounded. But, for the sake of argument, let us suppose that the new Constitution was made perpetually binding on the States, that the right of secession was excluded; and then ask ourselves, what sort of spectacle would such a work present to the minds of reasonable men? Would it not appear far more extraordinary, than if the right of secession had been recognized? Let us examine and see.

The scheme of a perpetual Union, excluding the right of secession, proceeded on the supposition, that a perpetual peace, good faith and good will, would subsist among the States. This was the idea of Madison. The predictions of George Mason and others, in which they foretold the wrongs and aggressions of the Northern States, if armed with the formidable powers of the new government,[199] Mr. Madison just set aside as unfounded and uncharitable suspicions.[200] Now, in regard to this point, we need not ask who was the wiser of the two, George Mason or James Madison, nor need we try the question by any imperfect notions of our own. For Time has pronounced its irreversible verdict in favor of the wisdom of George Mason.

Again, as each State bound its citizens to render allegiance to the Federal Government by its own voluntary act, namely, the act of accession to the Constitution; so, if by her own sovereign will in the same way expressed, she may absolve them from that allegiance; we can well understand the reasonableness of the arrangement. But if she may not secede, or withdraw the allegiance of her citizens from the Federal Government; then it would be impossible for them to escape the crime of treason. For, although the State should be driven by oppression to withdraw from the Union, her citizens would, according to such a scheme, be indissolubly bound by a double allegiance. Hence, if they should follow or obey their own State, they might be pursued and hunted down as traitors to the Federal Government. Or, if forsaking the State to which their allegiance was originally and exclusively due, they should adhere to the Federal Government, they would be traitors to their own State, and so regarded. There would be no possible escape for them. Now, were such a scheme wise, or reasonable, or just? Would it not, on the contrary, present a monstrous spectacle of cruelty and oppression? Can we believe that the fathers, in order to secure the liberty of their descendants, erected such an engine of tyranny? Can we believe that they intended, in any event, to crush and grind their posterity thus between the upper and the nether millstones of the two governments? But whatever they may have intended, or designed, such is the horrible character of the two governments in one, as explained by the very learned son in question. If his explanation be true, then it must be admitted, that the fathers, with all their wisdom, first con-structed one of the most horrible engines of oppression the world has ever seen, and then pronounced it a scheme to "secure the blessings of liberty to themselves and their posterity." But I have too much re-spect for the wisdom of the fathers to construe their work into any such tremendous and terrific engine of oppression. On the contrary, I believe that as the allegiance of the citizen was originally and exclu-sively due to his State, and was extended to the Federal Constitution only by a sovereign act of his State; so, by a like sovereign act, the State may reclaim his supreme allegiance. Otherwise, the machine invented by the Convention of 1787, would divide the citizen from himself; putting the noblest and warmest affections of his heart on the one side, and his highest allegiance on the other; so that, in case of a conflict between his State and the Federal Union, he must be inevitably lacerated and torn by the frightful collision. The fathers always admit-ted, that the noblest and warmest affections of the citizen would clus-ter around and cling to the State in which he was born, and to which his allegiance was, at first, exclusively due.[201] Did they mean, then, that in case of a conflict between a State and the Union, and the secession of the former, the strongest affections of the citizen should be with the one, and his supreme allegiance with the other. I have too much respect for the wisdom and the goodness of the fathers, to impute so horrible an intention to them; or that they designed, in any event, to set the citizen against himself, and rend him asunder by such a conflict between the elements of his nature. I believe, on the contrary, that it is the intention of the fundamental law instituted by them, that the allegiance of the citizen should go with his affections; and cling to the sovereign will of the State in which he lives, whether that leads him into or out of the Union.

"It is not easy," said one of the most sagacious of the fathers, "to be wise for the present; much less for the future." How true! and especially with reference to the institution of a new government! Perhaps, if the fathers had only had a little more of this wisdom for the future, they would have more profoundly considered the great question of secession, and settled it beyond the possibility of dispute in the Constitution framed by them. If, for instance, in the solemn compact between the States, they had expressly declared that any one of the sovereign parties to it might secede at pleasure; this would, it is believed, have produced the most happy result. The known and established fact, that the Union depended on the will of its members, would certainly tend to beget that mutual forbearance, moderation, good-will, and sympathy, without which no federation of States is desirable. The wisdom of the fathers might, in such case, have appeared far less conspicuous to some of the sons; and yet it might have saved the sons from the terrible war of words, and deeds, and blood, by which the civilization of the 19th century has been so horribly disgraced. It might have appeared a most "extraordinary spectacle" in theory; and yet, in practice, it might have spared the world the infinitely more extraordinary spectacle of the war of 1861.

I shall conclude my reflections on this argument, with the following judicious observations of Mr. Spence: "It would appear," says he, "the true policy of such a confederation to remove all doubt, and carry out clearly the principles of its origin, *by openly declaring the right of secession.* Had this been done from the first, there would probably have been no secession this day. The surest way to end the desire for any object, is to give unlimited command of it. Secession has mainly occurred because it was denied. How beneficial the consequence, had it been an admitted right for the last forty years! In place of the despotic use of political power, in contempt of the feelings or interests of other portions of the country, whether of the slave-owners or monopolists, there would have been all along *a tempering, moderating* influence. Abolitionism, in all its extremes of virulence, has been permitted by the North because the South was considered to be fast. It might writhe under it, but it must abide. But for this unfortunate belief, the intelligence of the North would have said, 'If to gratify your passionate opinions, you indulge in such language as this, addressed to your fellow-citizens, they will separate from us; we will not have the Union destroyed, at your bidding and pleasure.' In like manner, when the manufacturers desired to increase protection to outrageous monopoly, that intelligence of the North would have said to them, 'Our sister States shall not be driven from the Union in order to increase your profits.' The same rule will apply to external affairs. Texas would not have been annexed and beslaved, no Mexican spoliations—no war of 1813—no Ostend manifestoes need have defaced the history of the country. Throughout the range of political affairs there would have been present that influence so constantly absent consideration for others. The sovereignty of the people is a despotism untempered by division or check. The denial of secession has invited it to act despotically—to do simply as it listed, regardless of those supposed to have no escape from endurance. The more the subject is examined, the more plainly it will appear that under an admitted right of secession, there would never have grown up to dangerous magnitude those causes which now produce,—and that in so terrible a form—the disruption of the Union. Without those causes, had the feelings and interests of others been fairly and temperately considered, the Union might have existed as firmly this day as at any former period of its history."[202]

ARGUMENT FROM THE OPINION OF MR. MADISON

In the Biographical Memoir of Daniel Webster, prefixed to his works, Mr. Everett says: "The opinion entertained of this speech, (the speech of 1833), by the individual who, of all the people in America, was the best qualified to estimate its value, may be seen from the following letter of Mr. Madison, which has never before been published."

MONTPELIER, *March 15th, 1833.*
My Dear Sir:
I return my thanks for the copy of your late very powerful speech
in the Senate of the United States. It crushes nullification, and
must hasten an abandonment of secession.

Now on what ground Mr. Madison could have based this opinion,
at least in so far as it relates to secession, it is difficult to conceive. The
fundamental premise of Mr. Webster, that "the Constitution is not a
compact between sovereign States," and which is adopted as the title
of his speech, was certainly not approved by Mr. Madison; for this premise, beside being in direct opposition to the doctrine of his whole life,
is denied again in the very letter in which the above compliment is
found. Mr. Webster has very little to say against secession. His argument is almost exclusively directed against "nullification," the point
then in debate between himself and Mr. Calhoun. But the little he has
to say against secession, is based on the idea that the Constitution is
not a compact between sovereign States. Every argument, and every
assertion, levelled by him against secession (and they are but few in
number), have no other than this false foundation. Hence, Mr. Madison
could not have approved or applauded the argument of Mr. Webster
against secession, because he regarded his premise as sound; for he
was most profoundly convinced that it was false. On what ground,
then, could Mr. Madison have admired this argument?

If the Constitution is a compact between sovereign States, as Mr.
Madison always contended it was, then Mr. Webster admits, as we
have seen, that the right of secession follows. Thus, this right is conceded by Mr. Webster to flow from the premise which Mr. Madison
always regarded as perfectly and unquestionably true. How, in the face
of such a concession, Mr. Madison could have pronounced the opinion,
that Mr. Webster's argument "must hasten the abandonment of secession," it is exceedingly difficult to conceive. The acknowledgment that
the right of secession flows from a position too plain to be denied,
would tend, as one would suppose, to hasten its adoption, rather than
its abandonment. How then could Mr. Madison have said otherwise?

The truth seems to be, that Mr. Madison was more solicitous to preserve the integrity of the Union, than the coherency of his own thoughts. He commends Lycurgus for having sacrificed his life to secure the perpetuity of the institutions he had taken so much pains to establish.[203] For the same purpose, Mr. Madison sacrificed, not his life, but his logic.

Is it not truly wonderful, that Mr. Madison who, on most subjects, sees so clearly and reasons so well, should fall into such inanities about secession? From his conduct, as well as from his confession in *The Federalist*,[204] it is evident, that he considered it a duty to veil the idea of this right, unless a proper occasion should arise for its assertion. But how imperfectly his arguments and opinions perform this high office of concealment! He would, no doubt, have done better, if better arguments against the right of secession could have been found or invented. As it is, the ineffable weakness of his views in opposition to the right of secession, shows how high and impregnable is the position which that right occupies.

Mr. Madison greatly feared that Virginia and New York would, in their ordinances of ratification, expressly reserve the right to secede from the Union. This apprehension is most vividly set forth in his correspondence with Mr. Hamilton, in regard to the proposed conditional ratification of New York; from which it has been most confidently inferred, that neither Virginia nor New York did reserve such right. But what Mr. Madison desired, and what those States did, are two very distinct things. If we really wish to know what those States did, we should; it seems to me, *look at their recorded acts,* rather than at what Mr. Madison desired them to do. The conditional ratification of Virginia was in direct opposition to the wishes of Mr. Madison. His wish, then, however great his influence, could not always control the action of his own State, much less that of New York.

Hamilton and Madison both desired a strong "national government." It was owing to their influence, that the first resolution of the Convention of 1787 in favor of such a government, was passed. But, as we have seen,[205] although that resolution was afterward set aside by the Convention, Mr. Webster and Judge Story argue from its momentary existence, that the Convention of 1787 actually established "a national government." In like manner, it is most confidently inferred from the wish of Mr. Madison, expressed in his private correspondence, that neither Virginia nor New York expressly reserved the right of secession in its ordinance of ratification! Was Mr. Madison's wish the law of Virginia and of New York? And if we want to know what those States actually did, must Mr. Madison's wish pass for everything, and their solemnly recorded acts for nothing?

Mr. Madison, as his correspondence shows, was extremely anxious to prevent a conditional ratification of the Constitution in New York, as well as in Virginia. He even went so far as to advance the extraordinary proposition, that a conditional ratification would be "no ratification at all," and would "not make New York a member of the new Union." But after Virginia had ratified the Constitution on the express condition, that its powers should not be perverted to her injury or oppression, and had reserved the right to resume the delegated powers in case that condition should be violated; Mr. Madison retraced his, steps, and freely admitted that Virginia was really in the Union! He writes to Hamilton at once, and to Washington, in order to do away with the impression, that a conditional ratification is "no ratification at all," and would not make any State a "member of the new Union." In regard to the conditional ratification of Virginia, he says: it contains *"some plain and general truths, that do not impair the validity of the act."*

Now from these words of Mr. Madison, it has been strenuously argued, that Virginia did not reserve the right to resume the powers she had delegated to the Federal Government! It is true, as Mr. Madison said, that the plain truths referred to, did not impair the validity of the Virginia act of ratification. No one has ever doubted the validity of that act; or that it made Virginia a member of the new Union. Nor could anyone ever dream of doubting such a thing; unless he had previously embraced Mr. Madison's most extraordinary proposition, that a conditional ratification is no ratification at all. But, while there is no question whatever as to the validity of the act, it is denied, that it was unconditionally and eternally binding on the State of Virginia, or that it could never be repealed by the sovereign power by which it was enacted. Is it not wonderful, then, that Mr. Madison's words merely asserting the validity of the act in question, which no one has ever denied, should be so confidently quoted to prove, that the act must, in any event, stand forever, unrepealed and unrepealable, by the power by which it was ordained?

Now what is "the plain and general truth" to which Mr. Madison refers as contained in the Virginia ordinance of ratification? It is the truth, that the powers delegated to the Federal Government may be resumed in case of their perversion; and that they may be resumed by the authority which delegated them. This was a plain truth then, and this is a plain truth now. It is indeed universally conceded. Neither Story, nor Webster, nor Everett, nor Motley, has one syllable to say against this plain and incontestable truth. Hence, if Virginia delegated powers to the Federal Government; then Virginia, and Virginia alone, had the right to resume those powers. This would have been the case, even if no express reservation of that right had been contained in her ordinance of ratification. But did Mr. Madison deny, that the powers in question were delegated by the State of Virginia? If so, then he denied a plain fact; and a fact, too, which he invariably and earnestly proclaimed from the beginning to the end of his career. Even if he denied that fact by implication, this would have proved only his inconsistency, and furnished another instance of the blinding influence of his extreme desire to veil the right of secession.

ARGUMENT FROM THE OPINION OF HAMILTON

"However gross a heresy," says Hamilton, "it may be to maintain, that *a party to a compact* has a right to revoke that *compact,* the doctrine itself has had respectable advocates."[206] This, it should be observed, is said in relation to the old Articles of Confederation, which are universally admitted to have formed a compact between sovereign States. It was, then, the opinion of Hamilton, that a *State* had no *right* to secede from a confederacy of States, or from the compact by which they are united. If he means to assert, that it has no *natural* or *moral* right to secede *at pleasure* from a compact, I have at present no controversy with him. But if he means that it has no legal, or constitutional right to do so, then his own opinion is "a gross heresy," which has but few respectable advocates at the present day.

For, as we have already seen, both Story and Webster concede, that the constitutional right of secession belongs to States, which are united by a compact. Now, after such a concession, is it not too late to quote the opinion of Hamilton to prove, that the very inference conceded is "a gross heresy"? Yet this is done by Mr. Justice Story. In one paragraph, he admits that if the Constitution is a compact between the

States, then each State may secede from that compact at pleasure; and yet, in the very next paragraph, he proves out of the *Federalist,*[207] that "even under the confederation," which is admitted to have been founded on a compact between the States,[208] "it was deemed a gross heresy to maintain, *that a party to a compact* has a right to revoke that *compact,*"[209] or to set it aside at pleasure. Thus the very inference which he admits in one breath, he pronounces a gross heresy in the next, and proves it to be such by the authority of Hamilton!

The doctrine which both Story and Webster have been constrained to admit, is no doubt entitled to more consideration than the naked and unsupported opinion of Hamilton. This opinion seems, indeed, to have grown out of his deep and intense desire to consolidate the Union, rather than form his legal studies and knowledge. He was only thirty years of age when the *Federalist* was written; and his life, with the exception of four years, had been passed in the active duties of the camp, or in his college studies. Hence, however great his powers, his knowledge of jurisprudence, and of the opinions of the learned, must have been exceedingly limited, when compared with those who have devoted their lives to this study. If, then, Story and Webster are constrained to admit the right of a State to secede from a confederacy bound by a mutual compact; this may surely be taken as an indication of the real teachings of the law on the point in question, and regarded as a higher authority, than the bare opinion of Hamilton. This would be so, even if no progress had been made in the science of international law since the time of Hamilton; but, in fact, there has been great progress in this science during the present century; especially in regard to the doctrine of compacts between States.

Enlightened by the principles of that doctrine, Mr. Justice Story could not deny the right of one of the parties to secede from such "a compact." Hence, he attempted the more than herculean labor of recasting the whole political history of his country, and moulding it into conformity with his wonderful hypothesis, that the Constitution of the United States is not a compact between States at all. He first asserts truly, that a State may secede from such a compact, and then proves out of Hamilton that his own assertion is "a gross heresy"! "That gross heresy," says Hamilton, "has had respectable advocates." Mr. Justice Story himself is one of those advocates. Nor is this all. The Convention of 1787 advocated the same heresy; and, moreover, even embodied it in their legislation. Hamilton insisted in that Convention, that the States had no right to revoke the existing compact between them, or to secede from it in order to form another, without the consent of each and every State in the Union. But his opinion was overruled by the Convention; and the States did, in pursuance of the decision of the Convention, withdraw from the existing compact to form a new one. Mr. Hamilton may have been right, and the States may have been wrong; but, however this may be, their decision established the supreme law of the land. The advocates of the right of some of the parties to a compact between States to revoke that compact, or to withdraw from it, may not have been as respectable as the opponents of this doctrine; it is certain that they prevailed in the Convention of 1787, and embodied their own views in the legislation of the United States. That legislation should be our guide, not the defeated opinion of Mr. Hamilton. Or, at least if we happen to believe that legislation to have been right, and if in conformity with the opinion of Mr. Justice Story, we happen also to believe that a State may secede from a compact between States; may we not humbly hope, that this will not be deemed so "gross a heresy" as to be treated as treason and rebellion?

ARGUMENT FROM THE VERY IDEA OF A NATION

The "very idea of a nation," it is said, is utterly inconsistent with the right of secession. But what is a nation? "It is a body politic," we are told, "independent of all others, and *indissolubly* one. *That is, indissoluble at the mere option of its constituent parts.*"[210] Thus, the whole question is begged, and the whole controversy completely settled, by the definition of the "very idea of a nation."

How great the triumphs of such logic, and how wonderful the displays of such genius! Setting out from "the very idea of a nation" in the abstract, and, absolutely unembarrassed by any other idea or knowledge in the wide world, this argument just reaches, at one simple bound, the conclusion, that "as the Abberville district cannot secede from South Carolina; so South Carolina cannot secede from the United States," a profound view and striking illustration which the President from Illinois borrowed from the Preacher of Princeton.[211]

ARGUMENT FROM THE PURCHASE OF LOUISIANA, FLORIDA, &C.

It is, we are told, absurd to suppose that the people would have expended so much money for the purchase of Louisiana, Texas, and Florida, if those States could secede from the Union.[212] It is not at all probable, that those territories were purchased under the belief that they would desire to secede, whether they possessed the right to do so or not. And besides, it might be easily shown, that long being before those States did secede, the government of the United States had realized far more from them than she gave for them; which was only a few millions of dollars. Hence, even on the theory and the practice of secession, the purchase was far from being absurd. On the contrary, it was a highly profitable bargain; and in order to justify it, or to show that it was reasonable, it is not at all necessary to suppose that the sovereign peoples of those States, with their Constitutional rights and privileges, were also purchased with the pitiful sum paid for their annexation to the United States. They were admitted as sovereign States, with all the rights of the original parties to the compact; and as such were entitled to the full benefit of all its provisions.

Indeed, this *ad captandum* argument appears exceedingly weak, if not absolutely ridiculous. Can any purchases made by any parties to a compact, alter the terms of that compact, or make it more binding that it was before? If a State retained its sovereignty in the Union, and, consequently, had a right to resume the powers which it had delegated to the Federal Government; this right was not affected by the purchase of Louisiana, or Florida. To purchase those Territories is one thing, and to sell the sovereignty of each and every State in the original Union is quite another. If any State should withdraw from the original compact, and thereby dissolve the Union as to itself; then the purchase of such Territories should be considered in the final settlement between the parties. But to argue, that they were indissolubly and eternally bound together because they made such purchases, seems, to say the least, a little ridiculous.

ARGUMENT FROM ANALOGY

How wonderful whatsoever it may seem, Mr. Justice Story argues from analogy as follows: As an individual has no right to secede from a State government; so a State has no right to secede from the government of the Union. Now this argument proceeds on the supposition, that a sovereign State bears the same relation to the Federal Government, which it concurred with other States in creating, that a county, not only but that an individual, bears to a State. Mr. Justice Story was far too learned to endorse so monstrous a heresy explicitly; but it is, nevertheless, tacitly assumed as the basis of his argument from analogy against the right of secession. His whole theory of the Constitution points, it is true, to the conclusion so openly avowed by the Rev. Dr. Hodge and Mr. Lincoln, which views a State as merely a county of one great consolidated nation; but he never reached this conclusion himself, except surreptitiously, as in the above argument from analogy.

But even admitting this false conclusion as a postulate, the argument of Judge Story is by no means as conclusive as it appears to his own mind. For the right of an individual to secede from a State government, is daily exercised by someone or other in every part of the world. An individual cannot, it is true, remain under the government of a State, continuing to enjoy its protection, and, at the same time, refuse to obey its mandates. But this were *nullification,* not *secession.* The only way in which an individual can secede from a State, is to withdraw from the limits of its dominion; and this right is daily exercised in every part of the civilized world, without being called in question by anyone. The Puritans themselves, by whom Massachusetts was originally settled, withdrew from the government of Great Britain; and quietly marched off, undisturbed by his Majesty, first into Holland, and then into the New World. Now suppose this right had been denied to them? Suppose fire and sword had been used to compel the Pilgrim Fathers, those meek and holy apostles of freedom, to remain under the government they detested; would they not have made the world ring with their outcries at the perpetration of such injustice and tyranny? But they were allowed to withdraw to the New World; and there set up the government of their choice. The colony of Massachusetts Bay, then, owed its existence to the acknowledged right of individuals to secede from the government of a State, and enjoy one whose "powers are derived from the consent of the governed."

But a State, united in a confederacy with other States, can secede from the government of the union, without the necessity of changing its location. This makes a difference in the exercise of the right, though not in the right itself. It is indeed quite impossible for a whole State, or people, to change its location, or abandon their homes. If the Southern States could have done so, the exodus would, no doubt, have been most gratifying to some of the descendants of the Pilgrim Fathers of New England. This is evident from the eloquent address of Mr. Henry Ward Beecher to the excited thousands of Exeter Hall in 1863. In reply to the question, "Why not let the South go?" he exclaimed, "Oh that the South would go! but then they must leave us their lands." If they had only left their lands and homes, and plunged into the gulf of Mexico; this great enemy of secession would have hailed the event as one most auspicious for the spread, the aggrandizement, and the glory of the race to which he belongs. It would have appeared to him, no doubt, like the herd of swine which, being possessed of devils, madly rushed into the sea, and disappeared from the world. But when they seceded, without proposing to leave their lands behind; this made all the difference imaginable; being an outrageous violation of one of the great fundamental article's of the Puritan creed, which, in early times, was expressly set forth by the Colony of Connecticut in solemn conclave assembled. It was then and there decided, that "the earth is the inheritance of the saints of the Lord," the saints having, in their declaration, as is believed, an eye to the beautiful locations and lands of the Indians. It is certain, if we may judge from the speech of Mr. Beecher in Exeter Hall, that some of the most influential of the saints had a longing and passionate eye for the beautiful lands of the sunny South.

The truth is, that every constitutional compact, whether between the people of a single State, or between sovereign States themselves, forms a voluntary association; the one between individuals, and the other between sovereign States. Hence, if the right of secession be denied in either case, and the denial enforced by the sword of coercion; the nature of the polity is changed, and freedom is at an end. *It is no longer a government by consent, but a government of force. Conquest is substituted for compact, and the dream of liberty is over.*

No man has contributed more to this dire result, than Mr. Justice Story, who not only exhausted all the stores of his own erudition, and exerted all the powers of his own mind, to prove that the Constitution was not a compact between the States, but also enlisted the great powers and eloquence of Mr. Webster in the advocacy of the same monstrous heresy. This concealed the great fundamental principle of the

Constitution, and kept out of view the all-important truth laid down by Mr. Mill, that the very first condition necessary to a desirable federation of States, "is a sufficient amount of sympathy among its populations." Nor is this all. His theory of the Constitution fell in with the corrupt and the corrupting tendency of the age; the tendency, namely, to deny the sacred obligation of "The Compact of the Constitution." For how can any compact be held sacred, which is held not to be a compact at all, but only the emanation, or creature, of the sovereign will by which its restraints are abhorred? May not the creator do what he pleases with its own? May not the one great nation, the one sovereign people of America, take some little liberties with the work of its hands, instead of being scrupulously bound by it as a compact between the States? No, may it not take some little liberties with the rights of she States themselves; since the States, as well as the Constitution, were created by its own sovereign will and pleasure? May it not, in short, treat the States as counties?

It is possible, indeed, that no learning, or logic, or eloquence could have resisted this terrible tendency, or stemmed the mighty torrent of corruption it continually fed and augmented. But this is no reason why learning, and logic, and eloquence should have favored its progress. That progress was slow, but sure. All power slowly gravitated toward the federal centre, and was there consolidated by false theories of the Constitution. In the towering audacity of that central power, assuming to itself all the glories of the *one grand nation,* it was gradually forgotten that honor, and justice in the observance of the original compact, (no longer regarded as a compact,) and mutual sympathy among the peoples, it was intended to unite, are the indispensable conditions of a free and happy Federation of States; and for these sacred ties of "the glorious Union," were substituted the sacrilegious bonds of fraud, force, and ferocity. It is no wonder, then, that secession should, in the end, have been regarded as the greatest of all crimes; since the Union was then held together, not by the mutual sympathy or the conciliated interests of its peoples, but by "the cohesive power of public plunder." Mr. Justice Story, be it said to his eternal shame, took the lead in constructing the theory of that scheme of despotic power, and the politicians of Massachusetts in reducing it to practice. John C. Calhoun, on the contrary, lived and died in opposing all the powers of his gigantic intellect to its overwhelming torrents, both in theory and in practice.

Chapter XVIII

Is Secession Treason?

The doctrine of secession consists of two propositions: the first asserts that the Constitution was a compact between the States; and the second that a State, or one of the parties, had a right to secede from such a compact. The second proposition is simply an inference from the first. Now, if secession is at all tainted with treason, the crime must lurk in the one or the other of these propositions.

Is it treasonable, then, to assert that the Constitution was a compact between the States, or the members of the Union? No one, it is presumed, will venture on so bold an assertion; for, as we have seen, this was the doctrine of the fathers of the Constitution themselves. It has been shown, by an articulate reference to their writings, that it was clearly and unequivocally the doctrine of Madison, and Morris, and Hamilton, as well as of other celebrated architects of the Constitution. Who, then, will pronounce it treason, or treasonable? *The Federalist,* in submitting the Constitution to the people and in pleading the cause of its adoption, did not hesitate to say, as a fact then perfectly well and universally known, that the Constitution was "the compact"[213] to which "the States as distinct and independent sovereigns"[214] were the parties. Did *The Federalist* espouse treasonable sentiments? Both Hamilton and Madison, the two great architects of the Constitution, most earnestly and eloquently recommended it to the people in *The Federalist* and elsewhere as the compact between thirteen sovereign and independent states. Is that doctrine treason, then? Is there the least sign, or symptom, or shadow of treason connected with that sentiment of the fathers? Are those "untrue to their country," who say, with all the most illustrious fathers of the Union, that the Constitution was a compact between the States? On the contrary, are not those untrue to themselves, to their country, and to their God, who, in the midst of so many unquestionably proofs on all sides around them, can assert that the Constitution is not a compact? Is it "the dialect of treason" to say that "the States *acceded* to the Constitution?" In other words, is the language of Wilson, and Morris, and Randolph, and Franklin, and Jefferson, and Washington, to be denounced as "the dialect of treason?" Is it treason to understand the Constitution as it was understood by the great patriots and statesmen from whose wisdom it proceeded? Is it treason to adhere to their views, sentiments, and language? Or is it loyalty to depart from their views, sentiments, and language; denouncing them as the inventions of modern rebels, and blood-thirsty traitors? No one can, or will, venture to answer this question in the affirmative. Ignorance and passion may have done so in times past. But who can read the history of his country, who can behold the great fact, that the constitution is a compact between the states blazing all over its ample pages, written there by the fathers of the Republic themselves, and then deliberately pronounce it a treasonable sentiment? Can any man do so? Has any man sufficient strength of continence for such an achievement? If so, then indeed must his front of brass, and his heart of iron, forever remain an incomprehensible mystery to all reasonable men. No, if any party or majority, aided by the united strength of all their countenances, should pronounce such a fact treasonable; this would only prove that they must have been ignorant of the history of their country. But, whether from ignorance, or from malice, or from both, shall it ever be the lot of American citizens to live in a land in which truth shall be treason, and history rebellion? Shall it ever come to this—Oh ye blessed spirits of departed heroes and patriots!—shall it ever come to this, that a dungeon and a halter awaits the man who may have the most devoutly cherished thy sentiments, and the most implicitly trod in thy footsteps?

No! it will be admitted, that the doctrine of the fathers is not treason. Whether that doctrine be true or false, it will be admitted, that it is entitled to the respect of all who respect the founders of the Republic. Even if the fathers did not understand their own work,—a thought which is itself almost akin to treason—it is certainly not an unpardonable heresy to agree with them, or to adopt their view of the Constitution of the United States.

Will it be said, then, that it is treasonable to assert, that a State may secede from a compact between States? If so, then Story and Webster were both traitors; for, as we have over and over again seen, these most admired expounders of the Constitution expressly concede, that a State may secede at pleasure from such a compact. But, here again, even if Story and Webster were mistaken in this principle of law; it is surely absurd to denounce such an error as treason or rebellion.

Nor is this all. Precisely the same inference is drawn by another great expounder of the Constitution, namely, by William Rawle, of Philadelphia. The legal opinion of Mr. Rawle is entitled to great respect. Mr. Buchanan, late President of the United States, speaks of him as follows: "The right of secession found advocates afterwards in men of distinguished abilities and unquestioned patriotism. In 1825 it was maintained by Mr. William Rawle, of Philadelphia, an eminent and universally respected lawyer, in the 23d [32d] chapter of his 'View of the Constitution of the United States.' In speaking of him his biographer says that 'in 1791 he was appointed District Attorney of the United States;' and 'the situation of Attorney General was more than once tendered to him by Washington, but as often declined,' for domestic reasons."[215] Now Mr. Rawle wrote his "View," not as a partisan, but simply as a jurist in the calm and impartial investigation of truth; having no conceivable motive to reject the plain teachings of history and law. Indeed, as we have seen, he agreed with Story and Webster in regard to the principle of law, and differed from them only in regard to facts. Hence, if they had not denied that the Constitution was made by the States, they would have been compelled, like Mr. Rawle. to admit the right of secession.

"The Union is an association of republics," says Mr. Rawle . . . Again, "we have associated as republics . . . But the mere *compact,* without the means to enforce it, would be of little value."[216] Having announced the truth, that the Constitution is a compact between republics, he drew the inference from this which is admitted to follow by Story and Webster. That is, he inferred the right of secession; just as if there could be no question on so plain a point of law. "It depends on the State itself," said he, "to retain or abolish the principle of representation, because it depends on the state itself whether it continues a member of the union." Again, he says, "*the states may withdraw from the union,* but while they continue, they must retain the character of republics," as well as comply with every stipulation of the constitutional compact . . . "The secession of a State from the Union," he continues, "depends on the will of the people. The Constitution of the United States is to a certain extent, incorporated with the Constitutions of the several

States by the act of the people". . ."Nothing is more certain than that the act [secession] should be deliberate, clear, and unequivocal. The perspicuity and solemnity of the original obligation require correspondent qualities in its dissolution."

Now this is the language of a man, of an eminent jurist, who was the contemporary and friend of Washington. He lived before the rise of those new ideas, and dazzling images of power, which afterward obscured "the perspicuity and solemnity" of the act by which each State had acceded to the compact of the Constitution. Was not this man of "distinguished abilities and unquestioned patriotism," then, right both in regard to his premise and to his conclusion? He took, as we have seen, precisely the same view of the Constitution as that taken by all his great contemporaries, the fathers of the Constitution themselves; and he only inferred from this view the right of secession, which, according to Story and Webster, is a legitimate inference?

But even if he was not right, if Rawle, and Story, and Webster were all in error as to the justness of this inference; still were it not the very height of absurdity, the very climax of intolerance, the very quintessence of malice and persecuting bigotry to pronounce such an opinion treason?

If, then, any poor benighted son of the South was really guilty of treason on account of secession; this must have been either because he understood the Constitution no better than those who made it, or because he knew the law of compacts no better than the most celebrated jurists of America? On which horn of this dilemma shall he be hanged? Shall he be tried and found guilty of treason, for not understanding the Constitution better than Morris, and Madison, and Hamilton, and Washington; or for not knowing the law of compacts better than Rawle, and Story, and Webster? If found guilty on either ground, it is to be hoped that his counsel will move an arrest of judgment, that such distressing ignorance was his misfortune, not his fault.

MASSACHUSETTS AND THE HARTFORD CONVENTION

The facts, proofs, and authorities going to establish the right of secession are, indeed, so redundant, so overflowing, indeed, so absolutely overwhelming, that many of them have been necessarily omitted in the foregoing argument. One of them is, however, quite too important and striking to be entirely neglected. Hence it shall be introduced in the present place.

The Virginia Resolutions of 1798 were submitted, as the reader is doubtless aware, to the Legislatures of every State in the Union. These Resolutions contained, as we have repeatedly seen, the very doctrine so eloquently denounced by Mr. Webster in 1833; the doctrine, namely, that the Constitution is a compact between the States of the Union. This doctrine was, in fact, made the groundwork of that celebrated manifesto. Now it is a remarkable fact, that not one of the Legislatures, who replied to the Resolutions of 1798 called this great fundamental position in question. No one at that early day, so near the origin of the Constitution, seems to have dreamed that such a doctrine was tainted with heresy, much less with treason. Not a single Legislature seems to have imagined, for one moment, that the United States, or the States United, did not form a Confederacy, or that its Constitution was not a compact. In the answer of the Legislature of Massachusetts. Mr. Story's and Mr. Webster's own State, by far the most able and elaborate of all the replies to the Resolutions in question, there is not one syllable or sign of opposition to the doctrine, that the States formed a Confederacy, or that their Constitution was a compact between them. On the contrary, Massachusetts, then and there, in her great manifesto in opposition to that of Virginia, expressly recognized the truth of that doctrine. That is, in conformity with the uniform and universal usage of the day, she spoke of the desire of Massachusetts to "co-operate with its confederate states,"[217] and also of "that solemn compact, which is declared to be the supreme law of the land."[218] Massachusetts was not, then, one of that mighty cloud of witnesses, composed alike of "friends and foes," which Mr. Webster, with his great dark eye "in a fine frenzy rolling," fancied that he saw in the air, all uniting in the solemn declaration, as with the voice of doom, that *compact* is no more, that *confederacy* has fallen, and that henceforth the sovereign will of the one grand nation, the people of America, shall reign forever and ever! On the contrary, poor simple-hearted Massachusetts of 1799 imagined, that a compact, that even a "solemn compact," not only might be, but actually was, "the supreme law of the land," and that it was under or by virtue of that solemn compact that she had, only eleven years before, "confederated" with her sister States!

Nor is this all. Massachusetts continued, for some years longer, true to the first great article in the creed of the fathers. Indeed circumstances greatly favored her fidelity, and deepened the fervor of her faith. The acquisition of Louisiana, which added a vast empire to the Southern end of the Union, produced a profound dissatisfaction throughout Massachusetts and the other New England States; causing "the glorious Union" to wane, and the sovereignty of the States to wax, mightily in their eyes. "At an early period after the formation of the Constitution," as Mr. Buchanan truly says, "many influential individuals of New England became dissatisfied with the union between the Northern and Southern States, *and wished to dissolve it.*" "This design," according to Mr. John Quincy Adams, "had been formed in the winter of 1803–4, immediately after and in consequence of the acquisition of Louisiana."[219] The embargo and non-intercourse laws, which were designed to bring England to terms without the dire necessity of war, augmented the already great dissatisfaction of New England; because they affected her commercial interests, and thereby touched her in by the most sensitive portion of her frame. She cried aloud for war! She cried, down with all your embargo and non-intercourse laws, and up with the flag of armed resistance! Impatient at the slow movements of the South, she taunted her with cowardice, and courteously as well as elegantly declared, that the South could not be "kicked into a war with England." But she was mistaken; she did not fully comprehend the South; the South is, perhaps, too easily "kicked into a war." It is certain, that the South in the persons of her two young, ardent, enthusiastic, and chivalrous representatives, Henry Clay, of Kentucky, and John C. Calhoun, of South Carolina, responded to the loud, vehement war-cry of New England. Their eloquence shook the nation. The spirit of armed resistance was roused; and the war with Great Britain proclaimed. But, alas! this did not help the commerce of New England. The remedy proved worse than the evil. Her ravenous pockets, instead of being filled with gold and satisfied, became still more and more alive to the dreadful state of things, and, thereupon, she endeavored to "kick the South" out of the war with Great Britain. In this, the dark hour of her agony and distress, she suddenly discovered that war is, at best, a most unholy and unchristian thing; not to be entered on lightly, or *without counting the cost.* She also discovered, that, after all, the number of her seaman, impressed by the tyranny of Great Britain, had been greatly exaggerated (by whom?); and that consequently the cause of quarrel was far too small to justify so unholy and so unchristian, that is to say, so unprofitable a war.

In the dark hour of her distress, the glorious rights of the States came out, and showered down their radiance on all New England, like the stars at night. The sovereignty of her own beloved Massachusetts, indeed, then totally eclipsed the full moon of the once "glorious Union," just as completely as if Massachusetts had been "the whole earth." I speak from the record; from that secret, silent record of the Hartford Convention, in which all the profound dissatisfaction of New England with the Union culminated; and into which her sons, in spite of all their prying curiosity, have no desire whatever to look. Mr. Webster, for example, in his great debate with Mr. Hayne, of South Carolina, in 1830, solemnly declared that he had never read the proceedings of that famous Convention. No wonder!

"Events may prove," says the Journal of the Hartford Convention, January 4th, 1815, "that the causes of our calamities are deep and permanent. They may be found to proceed, not merely from blindness of prejudice, pride of opinion, violence of party spirit, or the confusion of the times; *but they may be traced to implacable combinations of individuals, or of states, to monopolize power and office, and to trample without remorse upon the rights and interests of the commercial sections of the Union.*" Now, if we only substitute the term *agricultural* for *commercial* in the above passage; how admirably will it express the complaint of the South, which, for long years of endurance, was treated with such imperial scorn and implacable contempt by the States of New England!

"Whenever it shall appear," continues the Journal, "that these causes are radical and permanent, *a separation by equitable arrangement, will be preferable to an alliance by constraint,* among nominal friends, but real enemies, inflamed by mutual hatred and jealousies, and inviting, by intestine divisions, contempt and aggressions from abroad."[220] Precisely thus, and not otherwise, reasoned the South in 1861; and asked for "a separation by equitable arrangement," instead of "an alliance by contrast" with "nominal friends, but real enemies, inflamed by mutual hatred and jealousies." But the great boon was contemptuously refused; because the sentiments of New England had undergone a radical and total revolution. The reason is, that those were the sentiments of New England in the minority, and these the sentiments of

New England in the majority. Holy indeed was her horror of "an alliance by Constraint," when she was the party in danger of being constrained; but no sooner had she acquired the power to constrain, than such an alliance appeared altogether pure and just in her unselfish eyes!

The Journal of this Convention has much to say about "the constitutional compact," and hence, if it had only been read by Mr. Webster, he must have been familiar with this mode of expression, which so seriously offended him in the resolutions of Mr. Calhoun in 1833, and called forth his fine burst of eloquence in defence of the rights of that "noun substantive," the Constitution. He must have discovered also, that in the opinion of Massachusetts in 1815, the rights of sovereign States are at least as important as those of any noun substantive in the language. For, in the words of that Convention, the power of conscription is "not delegated to Congress by the Constitution, and *the exercise of it would not be less dangerous to their liberties,* than hostile to the sovereignty of the states."[221] . . ."It must be the duty of the State to watch over the *rights reserved,* as of the United States to exercise the *powers which were delegated.*"[222]

The Hartford Convention, towering in the strength of its State rights sentiments, continues: "That acts of Congress in violation of the Constitution are absolutely void, is an undeniable position. It does not, however, consist with the respect from a Confederate state towards the General Government, to fly to open resistance upon every infraction of the Constitution. The mode and the energy of the opposition should always conform to the nature of the violation, the intention of the authors, the extent of the evil inflicted, the determination manifested to persist in it, and the danger of delay. But in cases of deliberate, dangerous, and palpable infractions of the Constitution, affecting the sovereignty of the state, and liberties of the people; *it is not only the right, but the duty, of such State to interpose its authority for their protection, in the manner best calculated to secure that end.* When emergencies occur which are either beyond the reach of judicial tribunals, or too pressing to admit of delay incident to their forms, states, which have no common umpire, must be their own judges, and execute their own decisions."[223] Now, if possible, this comes directly and plainly to the point, than the Resolutions of 1798. It not only sets forth the doctrine, it sometimes employs the very language of those Resolutions.

Having finished its work, and appointed commissioners to lay the complaints of New England before the Government of the United States, the Convention resolved, that "if these should fail," it would be the duty of the New England States to hold another Convention at Boston, on the 3d Thursday of June, with such powers and instructions as so momentous a crisis may require.[224] No such Convention ever assembled at Boston, or elsewhere; for in the meantime, the great trouble had come to an end. How, or by what means? Mr. Webster, though he confesses ignorance as to the proceedings of the Hartford Convention, is nevertheless perfectly ready with an answer to this question. In his senatorial debate with Mr. Hayne, in 1830, he tells the world, that Massachusetts gave up all opposition as soon as the Supreme Court of the United States decided the laws of which she complained to be constitutional; thus showing her loyalty under the most severe and trying circumstances! This was, perhaps, a thrust at South Carolina; who, as Mr. Webster supposed, stood far apart from Massachusetts in the heresy, that, in great and trying emergencies, "the States, who have no common umpire, are to be their own judges, and to execute their own decisions." How little he knew the history of his own State! Hence, he could fondly imagine, that Massachusetts had always been willing and ready to bow to the Supreme Court as the common umpire between the States, and proudly pointed to her conduct in 1815, bending and groaning under the burden of the laws, and yet loyally submitting to the high tribunal by whom it was fastened upon her shoulders! The truth is, as we have just seen, that Massachusetts had resolved to take that very emergency into her own hands; *to be her own judge, and to execute her own decision.* She cared indeed as little for the Supreme Court, in such an emergency, as she did for the other Courts of the Union; whose decisions had been repeatedly treated with contempt, and resisted with impunity, by her very loyal citizens during the great trouble of the war.

Why, then, did Massachusetts submit at last? Why did so great a change come over the spirit of her dream? The answer is a very simple one. It is told in the printed proceedings of the Hartford Convention. The story is certainly not so well adapted to the purposes of poetry, or of oratory, as the fine fiction invented by Mr. Webster; but it has, at least, the homely merit of truth. Harrison Gray Otis, T. H. Perkins, and W. Sullivan, the commissioners appointed by the Convention to lay the grievances of New England before the Government of the United States, reported that they had declined to do so, *"because they found, on their arrival at Washington, that peace had been concluded."*[225] That was the secret of the submission of Massachusetts. The war with Great Britain was at an end; the embargo and non intercourse would, of course, no longer vex her righteous soul; she could unfurl the wings of her commerce to every breeze, and bring in harvests of gold from every quarter of the globe. That was the secret of her great-hearted loyalty and submission. She no longer had anything to submit to!

Sidney Smith complains of "exegesis," that it spoils so many fine sermons; not allowing the preacher to ramble in his rhetoric, or to flourish at random, without regard to the real sense of his text. The same complaint maybe urged against the simple truth of history. How many splendid orations, and grand soaring flights of rhetoric, will it not spoil for the people of New England! How many self-flattering and, glorious illusions will it not dispel!

"That their object was," said John Quincy Adams, "and had been for several years, a dissolution of the Union, and the establishment of a separate Confederation, he knew from unequivocal evidence, although not provable in a court of law; and that in case of a civil war, the aid of Great Britain to effect that purpose would be assuredly resorted to, as it would be indispensably necessary to their design."[226]

This design, says Mr. Adams, he had communicated to Mr. Jefferson, in 1809. Again, while President of the United States, Mr. Adams said: "That project, I repeat, had gone to the length of fixing upon a military leader for its execution; and although the circumstances of the times never admitted of its execution, nor even of its full development, I had no doubt in 1808 and 1809, and have no doubt at this time, that it is the key of all the great movements of the Federal Party in New England, [and that party was then in the ascendency in New England,] from that time forward until its final catastrophe in the Hartford Convention."[227]

"It is but fair to observe," says Mr. Buchanan, "that these statements were denied by the parties implicated, but were still adhered to and again reaffirmed by Mr. Adams."[228] True, it is but fair that their denial should be known, and estimated at its true value. But who could expect any men to acknowledge their complicity in such a design? If, in the dark hour of their country's trial, engaged in a war with the greatest

nation upon earth, they could conceive the idea of deserting her standard, and even of invoking the aid and the arms of her powerful enemy
to make their desertion good, is it to be supposed that, after the
scheme had failed or blown over, they would have pleaded guilty to
such a design? Nor is this all. What did they mean by appointing another Convention to be held at Boston? Did they mean nothing? Or if
they had any honorable design, — any design which need not shrink
from the light of day, — why has it never been avowed by them? The
truth is, if anyone shall carefully examine the proceedings of the Hartford Convention, and the previous history of New England which
culminated in that Convention, he can hardly fail to perceive, that the
positive testimony of John Quincy Adams, is most powerfully corrobo-
rated by circumstances. The conclusion of Mr. Buchanan appears perfectly true; "that this body [the Hartford Convention] manifested their
purpose to dissolve the Union, should Congress refuse to redress the
grievances of which they complained."

Four years before the date of the Hartford Convention, Mr. Josiah
Quincy, an influential member of Congress from Massachusetts, publicly declared the right of secession. The extract from his speech on the
14th January, 1811, is hackneyed; but it is, nevertheless, significant of
what was then passing in the mind of Massachusetts. It is also exceedingly significant; because it was uttered in opposition to the admission
of Louisiana into the Union as a State. "If this bill passes," said he, "it
is my deliberate opinion that it is virtually a dissolution of the Union;
that it will free the States from their moral obligation and, as it will be
the right of all, so it will be the duty of some, definitely to prepare for
separation, amicably if they can, violently if they must." Upon the
purchase of Louisiana in 1803, the Legislature of Massachusetts passed
the following resolution: "*Resolved,* That the annexation of Louisiana
to the Union, transcends the Constitutional power of the Government
of the United States. It formed a new Confederacy to which *the States
united by the former compact,* are not bound to adhere." Thus, as we
have seen, Massachusetts from the foundation of the Federal Government down to 1815, held the Constitution to be a compact between the
States, and the Union to be a Confederacy. In her ordinance of ratification in 1788; in her reply to the Resolutions of 1798; in her own
resolution of 1803–4; she most distinctly announced this doctrine.
Hence, it seems impossible to doubt the statement of John Quincy

Adams,[229] that the Hartford Convention deduced the right of secession from the fact, that the Constitution was a compact between the States of the Confederacy. This was a clearly legal inference. Rawle, Story, and Webster all admit it to be such. Thus the fathers, one and all, laid down the great premise or postulate of the doctrine of secession at the very foundation of the Union; and the New England States, in 1815, deliberately drew the inference, and asserted the right of secession. Yet these States, in 1861, took the lead of all others in the fierceness and the bitterness of their denunciation of secession as treason and rebellion! The first to assert for themselves, and yet the first to persecute in others, this great right!

It is thus that Josiah Quincy, the Webster of 1815, asserted the fundamental principle or postulate of secession "Touching the general nature of that instrument called the Constitution of the United States, there is no obscurity; it has no fabled descent, like the palladium of ancient Troy, from the heavens. Its origin is not confused by the mists of time, or hidden by the darkness of past, unexplained ages; *it is the fabric of our day.* Some now living had a share in its construction; all of us stood by, and saw the rising edifice. *There can be no doubt about its nature. It is a political compact.*" Is this the same Josiah Quincy, or was it his son, who, in 1861, made himself so conspicuous by denouncing secession as treason? It is certainly the same Josiah Quincy, who, in 1811, was called to order in Congress for asserting the right of secession, and voted to be in order. How rapidly the New England world turns upon its political axis! In 1815, as secession was the right of all, so it was the duty of some, of the States; and, in 1861, it was treason and rebellion!

DID THE SOUTH CONDEMN SECESSION IN 1815?

The South, it has been repeatedly asserted, condemned the secession of 1815 as treason, and is, therefore, estopped from complaining of the same sentiment in 1861. "This," it is urged,"may be said to be *res adjudicata.* All parties are committed against the right of secession."

Now, even if the facts were as alleged, still this would be a one-sided logic. For if the South, in 1815, condemned secession, it was the secession which New England had approved; and if the North, in 1861, denounced secession, it was precisely the right which the South had asserted. Hence, it is just as true, that all parties were committed *for,* as that all parties were committed *against,* the right of secession.

If, as is supposed, the minority was, in both instances, in favor of the right of secession, and the majority opposed to it; this would have been nothing very strange or wonderful. It would only have illustrated the saying of Aristotle, which all history confirms, that "the weak always desire what is equal and just; but the powerful pay no regard to it."

But the facts have not been accurately stated. It is true, that the South, as well as other portions of the Union, vehemently condemned the Hartford Convention. No Convention, or assembly, was ever more odious to the great body of the people of the United States. But its proceedings were secret; and, till the appearance of Mr. Adams' letter of Dec. 30th, 1828, its precise object or design was not generally known. It maybe doubted, indeed, if it was ever condemned by any portion of the South, on the simple ground, that it claimed for the New England States merely the right to secede from the Union, and to be let alone. It was, however, known to the South, that the New England States had insisted on a war with Great Britain in order to defend and secure the rights of their seamen. It was also known, that while the South was engaged in this war, the New England States not only failed to do their duty, but denounced the war they had instigated, and the government by which it was carried on. It is true that, by these pro-ceedings, the wrath of the South was awakened, and that she denoun-ced them as treason; because they gave "aid and comfort" to the en-emy. From all that had preceded, how could the South know, indeed, but that the Hartford Convention had formed the dark design of ap-pealing to arms against the Government of the United States, and of joining Great Britain in the war against the people of this country?

Even if the South had known, that New England merely designed, in 1815, to secede from the Union; still her indignation would not have been without just cause. For, having got the South into a war with Great Britain, was that the time for her to desert the standard of her country, and leave the other States exposed to the full brunt of its fury? The clearest right may, indeed, be exercised in such a manner, and under such circumstances, as to render it odious. The right of secession has, no doubt, been made to appear treasonable, by its association with the Hartford Convention of 1815.

Far otherwise was the conduct of the South. She held no secret Conventions. All her proceedings were as open as the day. The United

States were at peace with all the world. It was under these circumstances, that the States of the South, each in its own Convention assembled, withdrew from the Union, and asked to be let alone. But the South was not permitted to enjoy the government of her choice. On the contrary, she was subjugated, impoverished, and ruined, with the avowed design to bring her back into the Union; and now that she is knocking at the door of the Union, she is not allowed to enter. What, then, is left to her sons and daughters but to weep over the inconsistency and wickedness of mankind; and, if possible, to pray for their enemies?

THOMAS JEFFERSON ON THE RIGHT OF SECESSION

Mr. Jefferson was not one of the architects of the Constitution; yet has more stress been laid on his *supposed* opposition to the right of secession, than upon that of any other statesman of America, especially by foreign writers. We are gravely told, with the usual information of such writers, that "Mr. Jefferson was, *in after life,* the foremost champion of State's rights."[230] We are also informed, that "he would certainly have turned away with abhorrence from the consequences to which these [rights] have since been driven."[231] This last sentiment is, perhaps, conformed to the general opinion at the North on the same subject. But is it true?

It is certain, in the first place, that Mr. Jefferson himself deduced the right of nullification from the doctrine of State-rights; not "in after life," but in 1799, before he was President of the United States. Mr. Everett, I am aware, insinuates that Mr. Jefferson never favored the doctrine of nullification. "Such, in brief," says he, "was the main purport of the Virginia and Kentucky resolutions." The sort of interposition indeed was left in studied obscurity. Not a word was dropped of secession from the Union. Mr. Nicholas' resolution in 1799 hinted at "nullification" as the appropriate remedy for an unconstitutional law, but what was meant by the ill-sounding word was not explained.[232] Now this statement is of a piece with the main substance of that grand swelling oration of the great Massachusetts declaimer. It is utterly devoid of truth.

In the first place, Mr. Jefferson himself in his correspondence, replied to the enquiry, of the son of Mr. Nicholas, that his father was not the author of the resolutions in question. Mr. Jefferson says: "I drew and delivered them to him."[233]

Nor is this all. "Two copies of these resolutions," says the editor of Mr. Jefferson's works, "are preserved among the manuscripts of the author, both in his own handwriting. One is a rough draft, and the other very neatly and carefully prepared. The probability is, that they are the original of the Kentucky Resolutions on the same subject."[234] Let us see, then, the very language of these Resolutions, and the manner in which they "hinted at nullification."

The first resolution is in these words: *"Resolved,* That the several States composing the United States of America, are not united on the principle of unlimited submission of their general government; but that, by a compact under the style and title of the Constitution of the United States, and of amendments thereto, they constitute a general government for special purposes; and that whensoever the general government assumes undelegated powers its acts are unauthoritative, void, and of no force, *that to this compact each State acceded as a State, and is an integral party, its co-States forming, as to itself, the other party; that the government created by this compact was not made the exclusive or final judge of the extent of the powers delegated to itself; since that would have made its discretion, not the Constitution, the measure of its powers; but that, as in all cases of compact among powers having no common judge, each party has an equal right to judge for itself, as well of infractions as of the mode and measure of redress."*[235] So much for the postulate.

The conclusion is in these words: *"Resolved,* That . . . where powers are assumed which have not been delegated, a nullification of the act is the rightful remedy; that every State has a natural right in cases not within the compact, *[casus non fœderis]* to nullify of their own authority all assumptions of power by others within their limits; that without this right, they would be under the dominion, absolute and unlimited, of whosoever might exercise this right of judgment for them; that nevertheless, this commonwealth, from motives of regard and respect for its co-States, has wished to communicate with them on the subject; *that with them alone it is proper to communicate, they alone being the parties to judge in the last resort of the powers exercised under it, Congress being not a party, but merely the creature of the compact, and subject as to its assumptions of power to the final judgment of those by whom, and for whose use itself and its powers were all created and mod-ified,"* & c. Such is the language of Thomas Jefferson! Is it merely a modest "hint at nullification?" Some alterations were made in the re-solutions, as penned by Mr. Jefferson, before they were passed by the Legislature of Kentucky. But the first resolution above given was not altered at all; it was passed precisely as it came from the pen of Mr. Jefferson, *with only one dissenting vote!* In the resolutions as passed by the State of Kentucky, we find these words: "That the principle and construction contended for by sundry of the State Legislatures, that the General Government is the exclusive judge of the extent of the powers delegated to it, stop nothing short of *despotism*—since the discretion of those who administer the government, and not the Constitution, would be the measure of their powers: *That the several States who formed that instrument being sovereign and independent, have the unquestionable right to judge of the infraction;* and, that a nullification by those sovereignties, of all unauthorized acts done under color of that instrument is the rightful remedy."[236]

Such is the language, which Mr. Everett so very modestly calls a "hint at nullification"!

He must be a dull logician, indeed, or a partial one, who does. not see, that both nullification and secession flow from the great funda-mental doctrine of the Virginia and the Kentucky Resolutions. If, ac-cording to that doctrine, stated in the very words of Massachusetts, "the States, who have no common umpire, are to be their own judges, and to execute their own decisions," then most assuredly they may pronounce in favor of either nullification or secession. Any State may, it is true, bring reproach on this right of sovereignty, by the manner in which it is exercised. I have, indeed, always doubted whether nullification was a wise, or judicious, exercise of the right of State sovereignty. It is certain, that Mr. Webster, as well as many others, has pointed out so many inconveniences, not to say absurdities, connected with the *act* of nullification; that the *right* has usually been rejected with contempt. But the exercise of a right is one thing; and the exis-tence of that right is another. A man may, in his own affairs, judge unwisely; but does that prove that he had no right to judge for himself? In like manner, it does not follow, that a sovereign State has no right to be her own judge; because she may judge unwisely. It is, then, false reasoning to conclude that a State has no right to nullify, because the act of nullification is full of inconveniences, or even absurdities. Yet this kind of sophistry is precisely the amount of all the logic, which has been urged against nullification. If a man, who has the right to judge for himself in his own business, makes an unwise decision; shall the right, therefore, be taken from him, and given to another? Shall his decision be declared null and void; and the decision of some other person substituted in its place? Nothing could be more unjust and despotic. Nor will any sovereign State submit to be treated in a similar manner by any unauthorized power on earth. The act of nullification has, no doubt, brought reproach on the doctrine of State-rights, and especially on the right of secession; but then this has been just because men have failed to think accurately and profoundly on the subject. They have confounded the propriety, or judiciousness of an act, with the right of the party to do the act, than which a worse solecism could hardly be perpetrated.

Nullification is, however, but indirectly connected with secession. This right flows, as we have seen, directly from the doctrine of Mr. Jefferson, "that as in all other cases of compact, among parties having no common judge, each party has an equal right to judge for itself, as well of infractions as of the mode and measure of redress." To say that a State has the right to judge of infractions of the compact of the Constitution by the Federal Government, and also of the mode and measure of redress; and, at the same time, that it has no right to decide upon secession as the proper remedy; is, it seems to me, simply a contradiction in terms. Now the question is, was Mr. Jefferson guilty of this act of glaring inconsistency, or self-contradiction?

He "would have turned away with abhorrence," it is said, "from the consequences" which have been deduced from the doctrine of State rights. In this bold assertion, the writer had special reference to the right of secession; which his history of the United States, as it is called, was written to demolish. Hundreds have, indeed, attempted to throw the great weight of Mr. Jefferson's authority in the scale against the right of secession, by means of the following extract from his works: "If to rid ourselves of the present rule of Massachusetts and Connecticut, we break the Union, will the evil stop there? Suppose the New England States alone cut off, will our nature be changed? Are we not men still to the South of that, and with all the passions of men! Immediately, we shall see a Pennsylvania and a Virginia party arise in the residuary confederacy. What a game too will the one party have in their hands, by eternally threatening the other that unless they do so and so, they will join their Northern neighbors. If we reduce our Union to Virginia and North Carolina, immediately the conflict will be established between the representatives of these two States, and they will end by breaking into their separate units."

Now this partial extract, which has gone the rounds of the civilized world, gives an utterly false view of Mr. Jefferson's opinion. The context to the above passage, which is sometimes permitted to accompany it, shows that Mr. Jefferson really believed in the right of secession, and only argued against the intemperate and too hasty exercise of that right. "If" says he, in the sentence immediately preceding the above extract, "on the temporary superiority of one party, the other is to resort to a scission of the Union, no federal government can exist."

How perfectly true! If, for so trifling a cause, any union of States should be dissolved, it would soon be resolved into its original units. The union would not long exist, and it would not deserve to exist, if its members were such fools as to resort to the right of secession "on the temporary success" of every party therein. But to argue, as Mr. Jefferson does, against the too hasty and intemperate exercise of the right, is to acknowledge the existence of the right itself.

In the Declaration of Independence, Mr. Jefferson said, "that long established governments should not be changed *for light and transient causes.*" Nor, however clear the constitutional right, would he have dissolved the Union for such causes. But does he say, that he would not advocate a scission of the Union for any cause whatever? That in no event whatever, he would resort to the right of secession? There is no such doctrine in his writings; no such glaring self-contradiction in any portion of his works.

On the contrary, in consultation as to what the Kentucky Resolutions of 1798 and 1799 should contain, he wished the following sentiments to be incorporated therein: "Expressing in affectionate and conciliatory language our warm attachment to the Union with our sister States, and to the instrument and principles by which we are united; that we are willing to sacrifice to this everything but the rights of self-government in those important points which we have never yielded, and in which alone we see liberty, safety and happiness."[237] Is it not perfectly obvious, from this passage, that Mr. Jefferson had not been so dazzled by the glories of the new Union, as to forget the immortal principles of the Declaration of Independence?

Devoted to the Union, but still adhering to the great principles of 1776, he immediately adds, that we are "not at all disposed to make every measure of error or of wrong, a cause of scission." Could language more clearly, or more necessarily imply, that there are measures of error, or of wrong, which he would make a ground of scission, or secession from the Union? Or could any doctrine be more clearly asserted, than is the opinion of Mr. Jefferson, that the States, and the States alone, are to be the judges whether the measure of error, or of wrong, which justifies her secession, has been filled or otherwise?

THE POLITICAL CREED OF THE STATE-RIGHTS PARTY

The Virginia Resolutions of 1798 and the Kentucky Resolutions of 1798 and 1799, the former from the pen of "the father of the Constitution," and the latter from the pen of the author of the Declaration of Independence; constituted, for at least forty years, the political creed of the great State-Rights party. They were, as everyone knows, the manifestoes on which Thomas Jefferson went before the people, in 1800, as candidate for the Presidency of the United States? They were also inscribed on the banners of the party by which Madison, and Monroe, and Jackson, and other candidates, were supported for the same high office. Were they, then, at that time, deemed treasonable by the people, or by their leaders? Let us glance at the record and see.

In 1800, Mr. Jefferson beat his opponent, John Adams, then President of the United States, by a majority of eight votes in the electoral college, or by a vote of 73 to 65.

In 1804, Mr. Jefferson, the champion of State-Rights, beat his opponent by the overwhelming majority of 162 votes to 14. In the Northern States alone, Mr. Jefferson received 85 votes, and his opponent receiving only 9.

In 1808, Mr. Madison beat his opponent by a vote of 122 to 47; and, in spite of the dissatisfaction of the New England States, he received from the whole North a majority of 50 to 39 votes.

In 1812, he defeated DeWitt Clinton, a distinguished citizen, and formerly Governor of New York, by a majority of 128 to 89; receiving in the Northern States only 40 votes to his rival's 80.

In 1816, James Monroe of Virginia, received 183 votes, and his opponent only 34; and more than one-half of these 183 votes were given by Northern States.

In 1820, Mr. Monroe was elected over John Quincy Adams, of Massachusetts, by the majority of 231 votes to 13. Two other candidates were in the field at the same time, Crawford and Jackson; both of whom together received only 11 votes.

This vote, however, can hardly be regarded as a test of the popularity of the doctrine of State-Rights; since this was, in 1820, professed by all the candidates for the Presidency. Yet this fact shows, that the opposite party had been so often and so completely defeated, that it refused to nominate a candidate. But James Monroe, the successor of Jefferson and Madison, and well known as an ardent advocate of the doctrine of State sovereignty, swept the whole country, and carried everything before him like a tornado. Henceforth, all aspirants for the Presidency bowed down to that great symbol of political truth and power, the Virginia Resolutions of 1798. Even Mr. Webster approached them with evident signs of awe, and never ventured to speak of them otherwise than in terms of marked respect, if not of veneration. No living soul dared to breath the suspicion that any one of their doctrines was treasonable.

How, then, did it happen, that those doctrines were afterward arraigned by Story and Webster as at war with the Constitution of the United States? How did it happen, that, without the most distant allusion to the Virginia Resolutions, under which so many battles had been fought and so many victories won, the great orator of New England had the audacity to declare, that all the fathers of the Constitution, that all the publications of friends and foes, denied the Constitution to be a compact between sovereign States? The foregoing brief sketch of the progress of opinion in regard to the nature of the Constitution would be incomplete without an answer to this question; without some notice of the causes by which so marvellous a revolution was produced.

THE DECLINE OF THE DOCTRINE OF THE SOVEREIGNTY OF THE STATES, AND ITS CAUSES

Mr. Dane says: "That for forty years one great party has received the Constitution, as a federative compact among the States, and the other party, not as such a compact, but in the main national and popular."[238] Now, as we have seen in this chapter, the above statement is not true. The federal party itself, with Hamilton at its head, admitted the Constitution to be a compact between the States. The State of Massachusetts, the great leading State of that party, always held the Constitution to be such a compact previous to the year 1830. She held this doctrine, as we just seen, in 1788, in 1799, in 1803; and she. continued to hold it until, in 1815, it culminated in the avowed right of secession. There is, then, no truth in the statement, that for forty years one great party denied the Constitution to be a federative compact among the States. One great party, it is true, showed a strong disposition to deny the sovereignty of the States in the Union, and to assert the sovereignty of the Federal Government. But the doctrine imputed to it was not one of its heresies.

Neither Mr. Dane, nor Judge Story who quotes his words, is pleased to inform the reader that "the great party," which is asserted to have sanctioned their own heresy, was swept from existence by the other great party. It sank so low, in fact, after the war of 1812, and became so odious, that none was so humble as to do it reverence.

Nor do they inform the reader, that the great leaders of this very party in New England, became in 1815, when in distress, the warmest of all existing advocates for the rights and the sovereignty of individual States. They do not even drop a hint, that those leaders, those staunch advocates of the sovereignty of the Federal Government, were the first to insist on the right of secession; a fact which would have detracted very much from the weight of their authority against the doctrine of "a federative compact among States," even if they had ever rejected that doctrine.

History acquits the old federal party of the monstrous heresy imputed to it. Having been chief agents themselves in framing "the federative compact" for the States; and having anxiously watched the States as, one after another, each acceded to that compact; such a heresy, such a perversion of the facts falling under their own observation, would have been utterly beyond their power. How, then, and why, did the heresy in question raise its head in the Northern States?

This question is easily answered.

1. The doctrine of a compact is attended with one great inconvenience; the inconvenience, namely, that if it be violated by one of the

parties, the other parties are absolved from its obligations. This great inconvenience is set forth by Dr. Paley; to whose chapter on the subject, in his Political Philosophy, Mr. Justice Story refers. Now this doctrine makes the stability of the Federal Compact depend on the good faith of all the parties; which seemed quite too frail a foundation for the Union. Hence, the doctrine of a federative compact, which, for forty years I had been held by both the great parties of the United States, was explained away, and the will of the strongest substituted in its place. According to his theory, then, the Union rested, not on the justice of the parties, but on the despotic power of the dominant faction. He thus placed the Union, by his construction, on what he conceived to be a more solid foundation "than a federative compact between the States." But this, as we have seen, was to subvert the foundation laid by the fathers of the Union; and, in order to make good his theory, he had to falsify the whole political history of the United States during the first forty years of the existence of the new Union; especially the views and the authority of its founders.

2. The right of secession had never been seriously considered by any party, so long as the Union was prosperous and happy. But, during the period from 1803 to 1815, the great leaders of New England, regarding their section as grievously oppressed in the Union, revolved the great theme in mind, and, for the first time in the history of parties, deliberately asserted the right of secession. In view of this alarming event, it became still more important, in the opinion of Mr. Justice Story and other constructionists, to deny the doctrine of a federative compact, from which, as he saw and admitted, so frightful a consequence necessarily resulted.

3. This denial became the more indispensable, in Judge Story's opinion; because Mr. William Rawle had, in 1825, asserted the right of secession in his work in the Constitution. Mr. Justice Story alludes to the opinion of Mr. Rawle, and, deploring it, he bent all his energies and erudition to demolish the doctrine of a federative compact, from which that right necessarily results. Thus, according to his theory, the Union was to be hooped with bands of iron, and not trusted to the mutual sympathy and good-faith of its members.

4. But, however great and commanding the influence of Story's opinion, or view of the Constitution, it would have been comparatively feeble; if it had not been aided by public events. South Carolina, feel-

ing herself and some of her sister States grievously oppressed in the Union, by the tariffs of 1824 and 1828, planted herself on the great platform of State-Rights, and nullified the act of Congress. The indignation of the North was aroused. Nullification, it was said, led directly to secession, or a dissolution of the Union. The New England States, which had only fifteen years before advocated the right of secession, now led the fierce crusade against its advocates. John C. Calhoun, the great nullifier, was the mark of their fury. It was in this contest, as everyone knows, that the great orator of New England, Mr. Webster, put forth "the greatest intellectual effort of his life," if not of the human mind. The whole North was electrified by his eloquence; and became intoxicated with his fictions.

Much has been said about the Northern and the Southern theories of the Constitution. The true word is, however, the theories of the majority and of the minority. For the Southern theory, as it is called, originated in New England; and, passing from minority to minority, found a permanent resting place in the South. Yet it may, with truth, be called the Southern theory, since the South has always been in the minority in the new Union.

Mr. Webster lived to pronounce a splendid eulogy on the virtues, the patriotism, and the genius of John C. Calhoun, with whom he had so long served in the Senate of the United States. But the successors of Mr. Webster have, for more than eighteen long months, held the bosom friend and the peer of John C. Calhoun in prison at Fortress Monroe, as if he were already a convicted felon and traitor. Yet is it, as we have seen, his only crime, that he sat at the feet of Thomas Jefferson, "the immortal author of the Declaration of Independence," and there learned the right of secession. Shall the people, then, who sang loud hozannas to the great master, follow the equally great disciple with the cry of *crucify him, crucify him?* Or shall it be said, that they voted the Presidency for the one, and a prison for the other?

Chapter XIX

The Causes of Secession

In the preceding chapters, the Constitutional right of secession has, it seems to me, been demonstrated. If so, then in the eye of reason, the Southern States are acquitted of every offence against the Constitution, or the supreme law of the land. But, however clear a legal or constitutional right, it may not be always proper to exercise it. If the Southern States exercised the right of secession merely because they possessed that right, or merely because they were beaten at an election, or for any such "light and transient cause," then they committed a great wrong. Then, although they violated no law of the land, they committed a great and grievous wrong against the moral law of the world, by a capricious exercise of their sovereign right and power. Hence, the vindication of the Southern States in the forum of conscience, as well as in that of the law, demands an exposition of the causes of secession. It would require a volume to do justice to this subject; and yet, at present, a brief sketch is all that can be attempted.

THE BALANCE OF POWER

From the foundation of the American Union to the present day, the provision of its Constitution for the fractional representation of slaves, has been more talked about, and less understood, than any other clause of that "sacred instrument." One would suppose, that if anyone really desired to ascertain the reason or design of this "singular provision," as it is called, he would look into the debates of the Convention by which it was inserted in the Constitution. In these debates, as reported in "The Madison Papers," the reason or design of the fathers in the enactment of that clause is as clear as the noonday sun. Yet, in all that has been written by the North on the subject, there is not even a glimmering of light as to that reason or design. Men make books, says old Burton, as apothecaries make medicines, by pouring them out of one bottle into another. This has most emphatically been the way in which men have made books on "the American Question," and, in the case before us, the bottles were originally filled, not at the pure fountains of historic truth, but from the turbid streams of ignorance, falsehood, and misrepresentation. Yet, for three quarters of a century, has all this vile stuff been continually poured out of one book into another. Accordingly, we find it in a hundred books on both sides of the Atlantic; uttered with just as much confidence as if the authors had some knowledge on the subject.

Thus are we gravely told, and with great confidence, that "the weakest point in the Constitution lies elsewhere. It lies in that truckling to the slave-power which is obvious in it . . . It lies especially in that singular provision for what is termed 'black' or 'slave' representation, whereby alone, amongst all species of property, that in human flesh is made a source of political power."[239] Now, if anything in history is certain, it is that, after a protracted debate, the Convention of 1787 agreed that population, and population alone, should constitute the basis of representation. The slaves were not represented at all as property. This is evident, not only from the debates of the Convention of 1787, but from the very face of the Constitution itself. "Representatives," says that document, "shall be apportioned among the several States which maybe included within this Union, according to their respective numbers, (not one word is said about property), which shall be determined by adding to the whole number of free persons, including those bound to service for a term of years, and excluding Indians not taxed, three-fifths of all *other persons.*" Thus, in this very clause, the slaves are called "persons," and are to be represented as such, not as property. Hence, when Mr. Greeley, in his "American Conflict," wishes to prove that the Constitution regards slaves as "persons," he quotes the clause in question. Mr. Ludlow himself, when it suits his purpose, can recognize the truth, that the Constitution "never speaks of the slave as a property, but as a person." If, indeed, slaves had not been regarded as persons, they would not have been admitted into the basis of representation at all.

Now, did the North truckle to the South, in conceding that slaves are "persons?" Mr. Paterson, of New Jersey, and some other Northern members, endeavored to exclude slaves from the basis of representation on the ground that they were "property," but Mr. Butler and Mr.

C. C. Pinckney, both of South Carolina, insisted that they were "persons," that they were a portion of the laboring and productive "population" of the South, and *as such,* should be included in the basis of representation on a footing of equality with other "inhabitants." The Convention decided that they were "persons." Was this decision correct? Or was it, on the contrary, a mean "truckling to the slave power?"

In the declamations on this subject, it is usually taken for granted by Northern writers, as well as by Mr. Ludlow, that free citizens or voters alone are included in the basis of representation for the North, while three-fifths of the slaves are embraced in it for the South. Hence, this is vehemently denounced as a "singular provision," as a "strange anomaly," as a most undue advantage to the South. But the fact is not so. The assumption is utterly false. By the decision of the Convention, and by the very terms of the Constitution, "the whole number of free persons," whether men, women, children, or paupers, are included in the basis of representation. All "persons," of every age, color, and sex, are included in that basis. Hence, Mr. Ludlow is mistaken in calling the clause in question, "the provision" for "black" representation. The blacks, as such, were included in the general provision, and ranked as equal to the whites. In like manner, Professor Cairnes errs in saying the clause under consideration "is known as the *three-fifths vote.*"[240] No such thing as a "three-fifths vote" is known to the Constitution of the United States, and the name is the coinage of ignorance. The three-fifths clause has nothing to do with votes or voting. No slave could cast the three-fifths, or any fraction, of a vote. The free blacks were, in most cases, denied the exercise of the elective franchise. It was in counting the number, not of those who should vote, but only of those who should make up the basis of representation that five slaves were to be reckoned equal to three white persons, or to three free negroes.

Now, why was this? Had the Convention any rule of vulgar fractions, by which a slave was shown to be only the three-fifths of a person? And if they had, did not the clause in question result from a mathematical calculation, rather than from a "truckling to the slave power?" or, if that was treated as a question of vulgar fractions, why did the Convention stop there? Why not raise other questions of the same kind? Why not consider the problem, if a full-grown slave is only the three-fifths of a person, what fraction of a person is the infant of a day old, before the power of thought, or of local motion, has even begun to infold itself in him or her? The truth is, that the Convention of 1787 indulged in no such contemptible trifling with the great practical questions demanding a solution.

The States were exceedingly jealous of "the sovereignty, freedom, and independence," which they had expressly retained under the Articles of Confederation. The Federal Government claimed, on the other hand, an augmentation of its powers; a claim eloquently urged by the tongues and pens of many of the ablest men in America. Hence arose the great conflict between the States and the central Power; which, from that day to this, has agitated the minds of the Anglo-Americans. In approaching this conflict, the Convention first determined, in outline, the form of the General Government. It was readily agreed, that it should be a Republic, with a Legislature consisting of two branches, a Senate and House of Representatives, a Judiciary, and an Executive. The next question was, what powers shall the States delegate to this General Government, this grand Republic? After debating this question for some time, the Convention discovered that it had begun at the wrong end. None of the parties were willing to say with what powers the new Government should be invested, until it was ascertained what share they were to have in the exercise of those powers. Therefore, the Convention found it necessary to retrace its steps, and begin with the question of the distribution of power among the various members of the Union. In this contest for power, each and every party, of course, claimed "the lion's share." But each and every party could not have "the lion's share." Hence the two memorable quarrels or controversies of the Convention of 1787; the one between "the large and the small States," and the other between "the North and the South." Much is known about the first of these quarrels; but the history of the last yet remains to be written. Its very first chapter is still enveloped in the most profound obscurity. I speak advisedly, and with the proofs on all sides around me, when I say that the Americans themselves have not studied this first chapter in the history of the great quarrel between "the North and the South." Let us look into it, then, and see what it teaches.

In order to adjust and settle the two quarrels above mentioned, Mr. Madison laid down the general principle, that "wherever there is danger of attack, there should be a constitutional power of defence." No principle could have been more reasonable or just, since the object of all government is to protect the weak, or those most exposed to danger, against the aggressions of the powerful. The Convention, without difficulty, agreed to the above principle, when only stated in general terms; but, as usual in such cases, a great difference of opinion arose in regard to the application of the principle.

The small States, for example, fearing lest the large States should "annex" them, or swallow them up in some other way, refused to increase their power in the Union. They insisted, that each State, whether small or great, should have precisely the same power in both branches of Congress. This would have placed all the powers of the Federal Legislature in the hands of the small States. They were willing, indeed, they were eager to possess them all; just as if they had not the least fear that they could ever be tempted to do the least injury to the large States. But the large States, not having this perfect confidence in the justice of their little neighbors, refused to entrust them with the supreme control and destiny of the Union. Hence they refused "the lion's share" to the small States. They contended, however, for this share for themselves. They contended that each State should, in each branch of the Federal Legislature, have a power exactly proportioned to its size or population; an arrangement which would have given the absolute control of the whole government of the thirteen States to three States alone. Yet those three States, (Massachusetts, Pennsylvania, and Virginia) with a perfect unanimity and a burning zeal, contended for this supreme dominion in the new Union. The small States, till then equal in constitutional power with the large ones, resented this as a design to degrade and enslave them. This contest was the most obstinate and violent one of the Convention of 1787. "The truth is," said Alexander Hamilton, in regard to this very quarrel, "it is a contest for power, not for liberty." Each party, in its eagerness to grasp the supreme power, neglected the rights and interests of the other.

This violent contest, which threatened to break up the Convention and blast all hope of a "more perfect Union," was finally settled by one of "the compromises of the Constitution." It was agreed, that the States should retain their equality in the Senate, each having two representatives in that body; and that they should be represented in the other branch of Congress in proportion to their populations. Thus the small States controlled the Senate; and the large ones, the House of Representatives. Hence neither party could oppress the other. As no law could be passed without the concurrence of both Houses of Congress; so it must obtain the consent of the small States in the one, and of the large States in the other. Each class of States held a check upon the power of the other. Thus, where "there was a danger of attack," there was, on both sides, given "a constitutional power of defence." This was, in deed as well as in word, to "establish and ordain liberty." Hence the most violent contest, of the Convention of 1787 ceased to agitate the bosom of the new Union. This admirable arrangement was proposed by Oliver Ellsworth, of Connecticut, and recommended on the ground that, in a Republic, it is always necessary to protect the minority against the tyranny of the majority.

The same principles and policy governed the Convention in its attempt to adjust and settle the great antagonism between the North and the South. Mr. Madison was so deeply impressed with the importance of arming each of these sections with a defensive power against the other, that he proposed "the numbers of free white inhabitants" as the basis of representation in one House of Congress, and the whole population, including blacks as well as whites, as the basis of representation in the other. This distribution of power would have given the North a majority in one branch of the Legislature, and the South a majority in the other. But the proposition failed. Mr. Madison did not urge it, indeed, because, as he said, it presented a cause of quarrel which was but too apt to arise of itself.

After the States were made equal in the Senate, each having two representatives in that body, the North had the entire control of it. As there were eight Northern States, (Delaware was then considered a Northern State), and only five Southern States; so the North had a majority in the Senate of 16 to 10. Hence, if the South was to have any defensive power at all, it should have had a majority of representatives in the other branch of Congress. Accordingly, Southern members insisted on the full representation of the whole population of the South, as well as of the North, in order that their section might have a majority in one branch of the common Legislature. The North, on the contrary, insisted that the slaves should be entirely excluded from the basis of representation, which would have given that section a decided majority in both branches of Congress. Thus, while the South contended for a power of self-defence or protection, the North aimed at no less than absolute control and dominion. The South would not submit. The North and the South were then, as they afterward appeared to De Tocqueville, "more like hostile nations, than rival parties, under one government." The fierce contest for power between them resulted in the compromise of the three-fifths clause of the Constitution. In proposing this clause, Mr. Wilson, of Pennsylvania, said it could not be justified on principle, whether property or population were regarded as the basis of representation, but that it was deemed "necessary as a compromise" between the North and the South. As such it was seconded by Mr. C. C. Pinckney, of South Carolina, and as such it was adopted by the Convention. This clause was, then, a compromise, not between abstract metaphysical principles of government, but between the opposite and conflicting claims of the two rival sections. Did the North, then, "truckle to the slave power"? It is certain, that she grasped at and gained a majority in both branches of the common Legislature. For, in spite of the clause in question, the North had a majority of 36 to 29 in the House of Representatives, as well as of 16 to 10 in the Senate; a share which certainly ought to have satisfied any ordinary lion.

But it is the fate of a democracy to be governed more by words than by ideas, more by "telling cries" than by truth. The cry has always been that the slaves, who had no wills of their own, were represented in Congress; and that this "singular provision," this "strange anomaly," had resulted from a base "truckling to the slave power." But for this provision, says Professor Cairnes,[241] there seemed to be nothing in the Constitution, "which was not calculated to give to numbers, wealth, and intelligence, their due share in the government of the country." Did the general clause, then, which places idiots, paupers, free negroes, and infants of all ages, in the basis of representation, provide for nothing but a representation of "the intelligence and wealth of the country?" The truth is, that none of these clauses were represented in Congress; they were merely considered in the difficult question of the distribution of power among the States and the Sections. The only persons really represented were the voters, who had the legal right to choose their own representatives. It was in this way, and in this way alone, that the Convention sought to secure a representation of the "wealth and intelligence" of the country. But who cared for the truth? The telling cry, that slaves were represented in Congress, inflamed the passions of the North, and served the purpose of demagogues infinitely better than a thousand truths. Hence the world has been filled with clamors about "the slave representation of the South." The deceivers are, however, careful to conceal the fact, that all classes of "persons," except the slaves, are reckoned at their full value in constituting the basis of representation. The women and children of the North alone, many of whom were born in foreign countries and had never been naturalized in America, have been the source of far greater political power, than that which has resulted from the whole population of the South. Is it not much nearer to the truth, then, to say that the South has been governed by the women and children of the North, than that "the North has been governed by the slaves of the South"?

Immense, indeed, has been the advantage of the clause in question to the South! Only let Mr. Ludlow, or one of his school, estimate this advantage, and it is sufficient to astonish the world! It gives to "every poor white" at the South, "however ignorant and miserable," "ten times the political power of the Northerner, be he never so steady, never so wealthy, never so able."[242] How wonderful the disparity! And, considering that "all men are created equal," how infinitely more wonderful, that the wealthy and the able Northerner should have so long and so patiently submitted to such an amazing inequality! What! The rich Northerner, the merchant prince, or the great lord of the loom, only the one-tenth part of the political power of the "poor white" at the South! Is it possible? Mr. Ludlow proves the whole thing by figures; and "figures," it is said, "cannot lie." Let us see, then, this wonderful proof of the wonderful fact. "Suppose," says Mr. Ludlow, "300,000 be the figures of population required to return a representative, then, whilst 300,000 freemen of the North are required for the purpose, 30,000 Southerners, owning collectively 450,000 slaves, or 15 on an average (many plantations employing hundreds) are their equals politically, and every 'poor white,' however ignorant and miserable, has his vanity gratified by standing at the ballot-box the equal of his richest slave-holding neighbor, whilst each of them is equally invested with ten times the political power of the Northerner, be he never so steady, never so wealthy, and never so able." But he must, indeed, have been a most "ignorant and miserable" white, if he could have had his vanity gratified, or his judgment swayed, by any such logical process or conclusion. This specimen of logic, or rather of legerdemain, only assumes that none but "the 30,000 Southerners," with their "450,000 slaves, or fifteen on an average," are included in the basis of representation. But since, in fact, all persons are included in that basis, Mr. Ludlow should have taken some little pains to explain to his poor ignorant readers how it is possible for eight millions of whites to own only four millions of blacks; and yet for each white to own, "on an average," as many as "fifteen slaves." It would seem, without much calculation, that, in such a case, there could be only one slave to every two whites. If so, then if the slaves had been regarded as whole "persons," the Southerner would have had only one and a half times the power of the Northerner. But as, in fact, the slave was counted as little more than the half of a person; so the Southerner possessed only a little more than one and a quarter times as much political power as his Northern neighbor. There was, then, no reason why the vanity of the poor, ignorant white of the South should have been so highly gratified, nor why the pride of the rich nabob of the North should have been so deeply wounded.

But this whole way of viewing the subject is, in reality, puerile. What has the political power of the individual to do with such a question? There is the broad fact, acknowledged by all parties and all sections, that, at the time the Constitution was formed, the South was superior to the North both in wealth and population. Thus, if either wealth or population had been made the basis of representation, and fairly carried out in practice, the South would have had the majority in one branch of Congress. As it was, however, the North resolutely fought for and secured the majority in both branches thereof. Was not this, then, sufficient to gratify the pride of the North, as well to humble that of the South. Suppose that in a society of ten millions of people, eight millions are united by one interest, and the remaining two millions by another interest. Suppose, again, that in order to get the two millions to enter into such a society, each individual of them had been allowed two votes, or twice as much power as an individual of the eight millions. Would this render the two millions secure? Would this give the minority a "defensive power" against the majority? "Ignorant and miserable," indeed, must be the individual in such a minority, if his vanity could be gratified by the possession of twice as much power as an individual of the majority, while that majority had the power to rob him of both his purse and his good name.

The only strange thing in the transaction is, why the South should have consented to enter into so unequal a union with the North. Why she should have entrusted her rights, her interests, her honor, her glory, and her whole destiny, to the care and keeping of a foreign and hostile majority. This seems the more wonderful; because, at that time, every statesman in America regarded nothing as more certain than the tyranny of the majority. "Complaints are everywhere heard," said Mr. Madison, in *The Federalist,* "from our most considerate and virtuous citizens that measures are too often decided, not according to the rules of justice, and the rights of the minor party, but by the superior force of an interested and overbearing majority."[243]

It was the grand object of the Convention of 1787 to correct this tendency, this radical vice, if not this incurable evil, of all democratic republics. The evils under which the country labors, it was said in that Convention, are, on all hands, "traced to the turbulence and violence of democracy," to the injustice and tyranny of the majority. "To secure the public good, and private rights," said *The Federalist,* "against the danger of such a faction, (i.e. of such 'an interested and overbearing majority,') and at the same time to preserve the spirit and the form of a popular government, is then the great object to which our inquiries are directed. Let me add, that it is the great desideratum, by which alone this form of government can be rescued from the opprobrium under which it has so long labored, and be recommended to the esteem and adoption of mankind."[244] Did the South, then, with her eyes open, willingly put her neck in the yoke of such a majority? If, as every Southern statesman knew perfectly well, "it is of great importance in a republic to guard one part of society against the injustice of another part,"[245] did the South really fail to demand such a safeguard? Did she place herself under the rule of the North, without taking any security for her protection, without claiming any "constitutional power of defence?" Nothing was further from her thoughts. If she had been seduced into the Union by the idea, by the immense advantage, that each of her citizens would have a little more power in one branch of Congress than those of the North, she would have been the weakest and most contemptible of creatures.

The citizen of a small State, such as Delaware or Rhode. Island, might have had ten, or twenty, or thirty times the power in the other House of Congress, which a citizen of Pennsylvania or Virginia possessed; and yet this would not have satisfied him unless the small States could have controlled that branch of the Legislature. This control

of the Senate was demanded for the small States, as one of the indispensable conditions of Union, and this demand was conceded to them,
in order that the minority might, in this instance, enjoy that freedom,
and independence, which it had resolutely refused to hold at the mercy
of the majority.

By all the principles, then, of the Convention of 1787, by the great
object for which that Convention assembled, by the very nature and
design of all constitutional republics, they were bound to protect the
minority against the majority. They were, especially, bound to protect
the South against the North; the weaker and the richer sections against
the stronger and the more rapacious. Accordingly, this was the grand
object of the Convention. The design was good; but the execution was
bad. The South insisted on the three-fifths clause, and some Northern
members resisted its enactment; because it was believed, on both sides,
that this would ultimately give the South a majority in the House of
Representatives. It would, as everyone knew, give the North the majority at the outset; but population was, before the adoption of the new
Union, so much more rapidly increasing at the South than at the North,
that the Convention believed that the South would soon gain the
ascendency in the lower House of Congress. The debates of the Convention bear ample and overwhelming testimony to the prevalence of
this belief. The speeches of Madison, Mason, Pinckney, Butler, and
others from the South, as well as of Morris, King, Wilson, and others
from the North, conclusively show that the Convention intended to
allow the South the prospect of a majority in one branch of Congress.
Such was the object and design of the three-fifths clause. Such was the
reason of the Convention for admitting a fraction of the slave population into the basis of representation. From this point of view, that provision appears as reasonable and just to every thinking man, as from
any other it seems strange, singular, anomalous. It was, as Rufus King,
of Massachusetts, declared in the Convention, due to the South, as a
constitutional power of defence, or protection, in the new Union.

This "singular provision," then, about which so much has been said
and so little known, did, according to the design of its authors, lie at
the very foundation of the Constitution of the United States. Neither
the large States nor the small States, neither the North nor the South,
would agree to enlarge the powers of the common government, until
they could first see how those powers were to be distributed among

themselves as the principal parties to "the compact of the Constitution." Neither the North nor the South would, for one moment, have dreamed of entering into the new Union, if it had believed that the other would continue to have a majority in both branches of the Federal Legislature. Neither would have consented thus to hold its rights and interests at the mercy of the other. Each was, as the debates show, perfectly willing to hold the reins of empire and dominion over the other. But while each was thus perfectly willing to rule, it had some little objection against being ruled. It could easily trust itself, but not its rival, with the control of the supreme power, and it was, no doubt, amply prepared to bear with becoming fortitude any hardship or danger, which might result to its ally from such an arrangement in its own favor. Hence the absolute necessity of the compromise in question. On no other terms, or conditions, could the new Union, with its vastly augmented powers, have arisen between the two great sections, which were so violently agitated and repelled by similar electricities. That "compromise," then, that "singular provision," that partial admission of slaves into the basis of representation, was introduced and enacted to adjust the balance of power between the North and the South. It was one of the fundamental principles of the Constitution, without which "the more perfect Union" could not have been formed between the sections.

The three-fifths clause or compromise, then, intended to give the one section, as well as the other, a defensive power in the new Union, was absolutely indispensable to the formation of that Union. Such a defensive power was, indeed, deemed by a majority of the fathers of the Constitution, absolutely indispensable to the safety, freedom, and independence of each of the sections in the Union. Yet, however strange it may seem, no public man in America has, from that day to this, taken the pains to make himself acquainted with the reason and design of that fundamental provision of the Constitution of the United States!

The author of the "American Conflict" regards slaves as "human beings"; and quotes the clause in question, "three-fifths of all other *persons*" to prove that the Constitution regards them in the same light. Why, then, says he, were they not represented "like other human beings, like women and children, and other persons, ignorant, humble, and powerless, like themselves?" The answer is very easy. Although the

Convention did, as their proceedings show, adopt population on the basis of representation; yet was the majority more bent on the possession of power, than on the preservation of their logical consistency. If instead of compromising the difficulty, the South had persisted in pushing the principle adopted by the Convention to its logical conclusion, then would the great design of that body of legislators have been spoiled, and all prospects of the "more perfect Union" blown into thin air. So much for one horn of his formidable dilemma. "If, on the other hand," says he, "you consider them property, mere chattels personal, why should they be represented any more than ships, or houses, or cattle? Here is a nabob, who values his favorite highbred horse at five thousand dollars, and five of his able-bodied negroes at the same amount. Why should his five negroes count as three men in apportioning the representatives in Congress among the several States, while the blooded horse counts for just nothing at all?" Here, again, the answer is perfectly easy. The slaves were not counted as property at all; and, consequently, there was no inconsistency in excluding horses, or other quadrupeds, from the basis of representation. Thus, neither the horn of the dilemma is quite as unanswerable as the author imagines it to be, and utterly fails to show the absurdity of the clause in question as one of the "unsightly and anomalous" excrescences of the slave power.

In reply to the two questions of his own dilemma the author says: "We can only answer that Slavery and Reason travel different roads, and that he strives in vain who labors to make these roads even *seem* parallel." Such is his profound commentary on one of the most important clauses, one of the most indispensable provisions, of the Constitution of his country. He is, in the same spirit, pleased to speak of this provision of the Constitution, as if it had been hastily adopted by the Convention, "without much debate or demur,"[246] and that, too, just after he had quoted the undeniable words of one of the most celebrated members of the Convention, which show that it had "been settled" only "after much difficulty and deliberation."[247] Roger Sherman was right; and Horace Greeley was wrong. The Convention had something more to do than merely to "split the difference" between two hairs, or abstractions; they had to adjust the balance of power between the two great rival sections of the United States, a problem which lay at the very foundation of the new Union, and upon the satisfactory solution of which the whole superstructure was destined to depend.

It is absurd, as well as untrue, to say that such a question was settled without much difficulty. It exercised, to the utmost, all the sagacity and wisdom of the Convention of 1787. That wisdom is, no doubt, utter foolishness to the rabid rage of radical reformers; which never fails to condemn constitutions and laws without even knowing, or caring to know, the reasons on which they are founded.

"Slavery and Reason" have, it is true, often travelled "different roads." But, in the case before us, the South would have been glad to travel the same road with Reason, and follow the principle of the Convention to its logical conclusion. But the sturdy North would not listen to that conclusion. Hence, if the South departed from the road of Reason at all, it was in order to meet the hard demands of the North, and join in the Union, which has proved her ruin.

It proved her ruin, just because the balance of power, which the fathers intended to establish between the two sections, was overthrown and destroyed. That equilibrium, or balance of power, was, in the opinion of the fathers, indispensable to the safety, freedom, and independence of each section in the Union; and its destruction has illustrated and confirmed the wisdom of their decision.

On this subject, a distinguished Northern writer, in 1860, used the following language:

"At the time of the adoption of the federal Constitution the condition of slaves was very different at the South from what it has since become. At that time there was, as we have shown in a previous chapter, no large branch of industry to engage the blacks, and their future fate was matter of anxiety. The progress of the cotton culture has changed that, and the interests of millions of whites now depend upon the blacks. The opinions of statesmen of that day were formed upon existing facts; could they have seen fifty years into the future their views upon black employment would have undergone an entire change. The blacks were then prospectively a burden; they are now an absolute necessity. They then threatened American civilization; they are now its support. With multiplying numbers they have added to the national wealth. They have become the instruments of political agitation, while they have conferred wealth upon the masses."

From the moment of the formation of the Federal Union there commenced a struggle for political power which has truly not ceased to be directed against the Slave States. The instrument of union, while it provided for the extinction of the slave-trade, which then formed so large a portion of Northern traffic, contained also a provision for black representation in the Southern States, stipulating that that representation should not be changed until 1808, and thereafter only by a vote of three-fourths of all the States. *That provision has been the groundwork of that constant Northern aggression upon Southern interests which has so successfully gained on the federal power until now it imagines the desired three fourths is within its reach, when the South, with its interests, will be at the feet of the abolitionists.* The South has stood steadily on its defence, but while the circle has narrowed in upon it, the North has not ceased to clamor against Southern aggression! Like Jemmy Twitcher, in the farce, who, having robbed a passenger, loses the plunder, and then exclaims, "there must be some dishonest person in the neighborhood!"

The original 13 States that adopted this Constitution were all Slave States with the exception of Massachusetts, which, although it then held no slaves had an interest in continuing the slave trade, in opposition to the wishes of the Slave States. The struggle in the Convention in relation to the discontinuance of the slave-trade, was between the New England States, that desired the traffic, and Virginia and Delaware that wished no more slaves, while those Southern States that had but a few blacks desired to import them without tax. On the vote New Hampshire and Massachusetts voted to continue the trade until 1808, and Virginia and Delaware voted "nay," or for its immediate discontinuance. No sooner had the Constitution been adopted, however, than the annexation of Louisiana became a necessity, in order to give an outlet to the sea for the produce of the West, but, notwithstanding the great advantage which the annexation was to confer upon Massachusetts, she opposed it to the point of threatening to dissolve the Union if it was carried out. That, after the great rebellion of Shay within her borders, was the first disunion threat, and the motive was fear of the political increase of Southern strength. Those fears were like all party pretenses, short-sighted, since that territory has given more Free than Slaves States to the Union. This threat of disunion was made while yet Massachusetts was engaged in the slave-trade, that the State had voted to prolong to 1808. The same cry was renewed in respect of Florida, and again, with greater violence, in the case of Missouri; to be again revived in respect of Texas; and once more, with circumstances of greater atrocity in the case of Kansas. It is remarkable that while Free States come in without any great struggle on the part of the South, the safety of which is threatened by each such accession, the admission of Slave States is the signal of so much strife, and this resistance to a manifest right of the South is denounced as "Southern aggression."

The gradual abolition of slavery in the old Northern States, and the rapidity with which Eastern capital, following migration, has settled the Western States, has given a large preponderance to the free interest in the national councils. Of the 26 senators that sat in the first Congress, all represented a slave interest, more or less; with the States and territories now knocking for admission, there are 72 senators, of whom 32, only represent the slave interest. That interest, from being "a unit" in the Senate, has sunk to a minority of four, and yet the majority do not cease to complain of Southern "aggression." With this rapid decline in the Southern vote in the great "conservative body" of the Senate, the representation in the lower House has fallen to one-third. How long will it be before the desired three-fourths vote, for which a large party yearn, will have been obtained, and, when obtained, what will have become of those Southern rights which are even now denied by party leaders to be any rights at all. In the last 30 years 11 Free States have been prepared for the Union; a similar progress in the next 30 years and the South will have fallen into that constitutional minority which may deprive it of all reserved rights. This circle is closing rapidly in upon it, amid a continually rising cry of abolition, pointed by bloody inroads of armed men. This is called Southern "aggression."[248]

The balance of power was overthrown. The South lost, more and more, her original equality in the Union; and the just design of the fathers was despised and trampled underfoot by the Northern Demos. Every census showed, that her power had diminished, as her dangers had increased; and she no longer found herself in the original Union of equal sections. On the contrary, she found herself in a minority, which the Southern men of 1787 would have shunned as the plague; and threatened by a vast majority as cruel as death, and as inexorable as the grave. This was not the Union of the fathers; but the warped, and perverted Union of unjust rule and domination. The States of New England, never failed to threaten a dissolution of the Union, whenever, in their jealous imaginations, there seemed even a prospect that the balance of power might turn in favor of the South in only one branch of Congress. Yet the more this balance was actually turned in their own favor, and the South, contrary to the design of the fathers, reduced to a hopeless minority, the more imperiously they demanded her implicit submission to Northern rule, and the more fiercely was denounced her every struggle to maintain her original equality and independence as "Southern aggression."

From a table in the work above quoted, it appears that, at each succeeding census, the relative increase of the two sections in the House of Representatives was as follows:

	*	1790	1800	1810	1820	1830	1840	1850
North	35	57	77	104	133	141	135	144
South	30	53	65	79	90	100	88	90
Majority	5	4	12	25	43	41	47	54

* First entry was from before the Census.

Thus, in one branch of the Legislature, the Northern majority, counting Delaware as a Southern State, had increased from a majority of five to a majority of fifty-four representatives. The South, as every reader of American history must know, never would have entered into so unequal a Union with the North; and the North would not have continued in the Union, if she had not always, retained the balance of power in her own hands, and in both branches of Congress.

As the North had so great a majority in the House, it was the more important that the South should, at least, retain her original share of power in the Senate. But even this, she was not allowed to do. In order to gain the complete and uncontrolled ascendency in the Senate, as she had done in the House, the North began to exclude all slave-holding States from the Union. This she attempted in regard to Missouri, and persisted in her unconstitutional attitude, until she was defeated by the votes of a few Northern democrats, who sacrificed themselves to save the Union and their own party. After the restoration of the democratic party, and during its reign, the rights of the States were so clearly vindicated, and so firmly established, that few ventured to claim for Congress the power to exclude a State from the Union, because she held slaves. Hence the Republican party changed its tactics, and endeavored to effect the same unconstitutional design in another way. Not daring to say, as their predecessor had done, that Congress could exclude a slave-holding State from the Union, they determined that no more such States should be formed. For this purpose, they resolved to exclude the South from all the territories of the Union; so that no addition should ever be made to her power, while that of the North was allowed to increase with still greater rapidity. The North resolved, in fact, that every new State formed, and admitted into the Union, should be an accession to her own overgrown power. The South might object and complain; but what could she do? Was she not already in a helpless minority?

If we count Delaware as a Southern State, then the North, instead of a majority one State in the Senate, had a majority of three States, or of six votes, before the first Southern State seceded from the Union. There were eighteen Northern, and only fifteen Southern States, represented in that branch of Congress, which was designed to act as a check on the majority in the House of Representatives. Nor was this all. For there were, at that time, nearly ready to come into the Union, Kansas, Minnesota, Oregon, Washington, Nebraska, Utah, and New Mexico, which would have made the Northern majority as overwhelming in that body, as it was in the other branch of the Federal Legislature.

If the tables had been turned, if the picture had been reversed, the North would have laughed such a Union to scorn. She could not even tolerate, indeed, the bare thought, or imagination, that the South might gain the ascendency in the Senate, in only one branch of the Federal Legislature.

Thus, while the greedy North continued to grow in power, and in a determination to crush the South beneath her feet, she filled the earth with her clamors about "the aggressions of the *slave power,*" appealing to the prejudices and passions of mankind in her unholy crusade against an unknown and despised people. The South simply stood on the defensive. The one struggled for empire, for dominion; the other for independence, for existence. The one struggled to preserve her original equality in the Union; the other to destroy that equality. The one directed all its efforts to uphold the balance of power, established by the authors of the Constitution, and deemed by them the only safeguard of freedom in the Union; the other bent all its energies to break that balance, and grind its fragments to powder.

Hence, the South became extremely sensible of the dangers of her position in the Union. All hope of a "constitutional power of defence" therein, had been wrested from her grasp. That safeguard of her freedom and independence, which the founders of the Republic deemed so essential to both ends of the Union, no longer existed for the South; and she held her rights and interests at the mercy of the North, as it was never intended she should, hold them. She could see, therefore, as clearly as Professor Cairnes, that the extinction of her freedom and independence was, sooner or later, her inevitable destiny in the Union. That dark destiny, however, she beheld with far other eyes than those with which it was contemplated by the Professor of Jurisprudence. Beholding, with fanatical delight, the ultimate ruin of the South in the Union, he denounced secession as treason and rebellion; but it is to be hoped that, in the estimation of mankind, it will not be deemed an unpardonable offence, if she was not entirely devoid of the natural instinct of self-preservation.

Jefferson Davis, in the name of the South, gave utterance to this natural instinct in the Senate of the United States in 1850. "The danger," said he, "is one of our own times, and it is that sectional division of the people which has created the necessity of looking to the question of the balance of power, and which carries with it, when disturbed, the danger of disunion." Such was the treason of Jefferson Davis in 1850! But far bolder language had been used by Northern Statesmen, and by Northern Legislatures, in behalf of the North; not because the North was in a present or real, but only because she was in a future and purely imaginary, minority. The treason of the weak is the patriotism of the strong.

THE RELATIVE DECLINE OF THE SOUTH IN THE NEW UNION

It is a remarkable fact, that from the first settlement of the country, the South continued to increase in population and wealth more rapidly than the North, till the now Union was established. In the Convention of 1787, it was, on all sides, conceded that the South surpassed the North both in population and in wealth. But from that event, from the inauguration of the "more perfect Union," her relative decline began.

This fact has always been ascribed, by the enemies of the South, to the malign influence of the institution of slavery. But slavery existed before the new Union without producing any such effect. Hence, however great the evil influence of slavery may have been, it was not sufficient to counteract the great natural advantages of the South, until the new Union came to its aid. The action of the Federal Government was, in the opinion of many impartial judges, the great cause of this relative decline of the South, in spite of the resources which nature, with a large and liberal hand, had lavished on her teeming soil and beneficent climate.

The influence of this cause is well explained by a devoted friend to the Union. Rice and indigo were, says he, the great staples which, under the protection of the British Crown, had been the sources of the superior wealth of the South before the Revolution. But under the protection, or rather under the contemptuous neglect, of the Federal Government, these great interests languished, and these great staples were finally crushed out of the markets of the world by the hostile legislation of foreign powers. The decline of the South would have been as hopeless as it was rapid, if the cultivation of cotton, in consequence of several well-known improvements and inventions, had not become sufficiently remunerative to stand alone without the aid or support of the Federal Government. This great staple and source of wealth caused the South to revive. It not only arrested the sort of galloping consumption under which she was fast sinking into comparative insignificance, but it also restored her to something of the fulness and the glow of her former prosperity. But the North fixed her eagle eye on the rising prosperity of the South, and soon planted the talons of her tariffs deep in its very vitals.

"The tariff question," says Mr. Ludlow, "may be easily disposed of."[249] He certainly disposes of it with very great ease. A few prudently selected, and carefully trimmed, extracts from Mr. Benton, are among the facile means be employs for the purpose. Let us, then, hear Mr. Benton himself, not in garbled extracts merely, but in the full round utterance of great historic truths. Mr. B. was no friend to the institution of slavery, or to its extension. In regard to this last most exciting question, he was decidedly with the North. But yet, unlike Mr. L. and his school, Mr. Benton could both see and feel that something else beside slavery exerted an evil influence in the United States of America. Accordingly, in 1828, he uttered the following words in the Senate: "I feel for the sad changes which have taken place in the South during the last fifty years. Before the Revolution, it was the seat of wealth as well as of hospitality. Money and all it commanded abounded there. But how now? all this is reversed. Wealth has fled from the South and settled in the regions North of the Potomac; and this in the face of the fact that the South in four staples alone has exported produce since the Revolution, to the value of eight hundred millions of dollars; and the North has exported comparatively nothing. Such an export would indicate unparalleled wealth, but what is the fact? In the place of wealth a universal pressure for money was felt—not enough for current expenses—the price of all property down—the country drooping and languishing—towns and cities decaying—and the frugal habits of the people pushed to the verge of universal self-denial for the preservation of their family estates. Such a result is a strange and wonderful phenomenon. It calls upon statesmen to enquire into the cause." How did slavery produce this wonderful transformation? How did slavery work all this ruin? Slavery, it is well known, existed before the Revolution as well as afterward; and accompanied the South in the palmiest days of her prosperity, as well as in the darkest and most dismal hour of her adversity. Hence it was not, and could not have been, the one cause of so great and so sudden a change. And besides, instead of having ceased to produce, the fair and fruitful South continued to pour forth, in greater abundance than ever, the broad streams of national prosperity and wealth. She was impoverished, not because the fountains of her former supply had been dried up, or even diminished in volume, but because the great streams flowing from them. did not return into her own bosom. Into what region of the earth, then, did these streams empty themselves?

Mr. Benton answers this question, and though his answer is diametrically opposed to the views of the Bright and Cobden school, he is the great authority whom Mr. Ludlow himself has brought upon the stand. Under "Federal legislation," says Mr. Benton, "the exports of the South have been the basis of the Federal revenue . . . *Virginia, the two Carolinas, and Georgia, may be said to defray three fourths of the annual expense of supporting the Federal Government;* and of this great sum annually furnished by them, nothing or next to nothing is returned to them in the shape of Government expenditures. That expenditure flows

in an opposite direction — it flows northwardly in one uniform, unin-
terrupted, and perennial stream. *This is the reason why wealth disappears from the South and rises up in the North. Federal legislation does
all this.* It does it by the simple process of eternally taking from the
South and returning nothing to it. If it returned to the South the whole
or even a good part of what it exacted, the four States south of the
Potomac might stand the action of the system, but the South must be
exhausted of its money and property by a course of legislation which
is forever taking away and never returning anything. Every new tariff
increases the force of this action. No tariff has ever yet included Virginia, the two Carolinas, and Georgia, except to increase the burdens
imposed upon them."

Nor was Mr. Benton alone in this opinion. The political economists
of the North, such as Carey, Elliot, Kettell, and others, who had studied
the sources of national wealth in America, gave precisely the same
explanation of the sudden and wonderful disappearance of wealth
from the South. The North might easily satisfy its own conscience, by
making slavery the scapegoat for its sins; but thinking men, even at the
North, were not so readily deceived. Hence, in an able work entitled
"Southern Wealth and Northern Profits," the author does not hesitate
to tell the people of his own section, that it was gross injustice, if not
hypocrisy, to be always growing rich on the profits of slave-labor; and,
at the same time, to be eternally taunting and insulting the South on
account of slavery. Though it was bitterly denounced as "the sum of
all villainies," it was, nevertheless, the principal factor in Northern
wealth.

In like manner, Professor Elliot, though a Northern man, and an
enemy to slavery; yet, as a political economist, and teacher of the
science in a Northern college, he denied that it had impoverished the
South. On the contrary, he has, in a work styled "Cotton is King,"
shown that slave-labor has been one of the great sources of Northern
wealth. Is it any wonder, then, that the thinking men of the South
should have entertained the same opinion? Is it any wonder, that they
should have agreed with Benton, and Kettell, and Elliot, and other
Northern writers, that it was legislation, and not slavery, which had
impoverished the South? It is certain, that such was the conclusion of
the thinking men of the South, in view of her sad and frightfully altered condition.

"Such a result," says Mr. Benton, "is a strange and wonderful phenomenon. It calls upon *statesmen* to enquire into the cause; and if they enquire upon the theatre of this strange metamorphosis they will receive one universal answer from all ranks and ages, *that it is Federal legislation which has worked this ruin.*" If, under such circumstances or belief, the South had been satisfied with the action of the Federal Government, her people must have been the greatest of all simpletons, or the most patient of all saints. They were neither; they were merely human beings, who had some little regard for their own interests, as well as for those of their neighbors. Consequently, the tariffs of the United States, by which one portion of the people was impoverished for the benefit of another portion of the people, left in the minds of the most influential men of the South a deep and abiding sense of the injustice of Northern legislation.

What less could have been anticipated? All majorities are, in fact, unjust, despotic and oppressive. Hence, in the opinion of the Convention of 1787, if either section should have the majority in both branches of Congress, it would oppress the other. As this opinion was founded on the experience of the past, so it was afterward confirmed by the history of the future. Indeed, if the North, with a majority in both branches of Congress, had not oppressed the South, it would have been unlike every other unchecked power in the history of the world.

There have been, no doubt, lets, hindrances, and pauses in this onward march of the triumphant power of the North. But it has always had its eye fixed on one object of supreme desire, namely, on absolute dominion and control. It had already become absolutely overwhelming in one branch of Congress, with the certainty of soon becoming equally overwhelming in the other. There was not a member of the Convention of 1787, who, if his own section had been in the minority, would not have shrunk from such a Union with horror. He must indeed have been profoundly ignorant of the sentiments of the fathers, as well as of the character of all interested majorities, who could have supposed, for a moment, that the South might have been free, or safe, or happy in such a Union. What! is that freedom which is held at the mercy of another? Is that safety which depends on the will of an interested majority?

What was to have been expected from such a majority, is well described in the speeches of John C. Calhoun; in the "Essay on Liberty" by John Stuart Mill; and in the celebrated work of De Tocqueville on

Democracy in America. Both De Tocqueville and Mill are advocates of democracy; and yet, if possible, they draw more frightful pictures of the tyranny of an unchecked majority, than has John C. Calhoun himself. "The majority in that country," [the United States,] says M. De Tocqueville, "exercise a prodigious actual authority, and a moral influence which is scarcely less preponderant; no obstacles exist which can impede, or so much. as retard its progress, or which can induce it to heed the complaints of those whom it crushes upon its path."[250] How cold, then, and heartless, such a majority! Cruel as death, and inexorable as the grave, it turns a deaf ear to the outcries of those whom it crushes upon its path!

But if such was the unprejudiced conclusion of a great philosophic observer in 1833, what was to have been expected from a sectional majority, growing continually in greatness, in power, and in hatred of the sectional minority? Had the South no reason for her fears? If not, then De Tocqueville, and Mill, and Calhoun, were the veriest simpletons that ever lived. If not, then the founders of the Republic had all read the history of their own times wrong, and wrote libels on the character of unshackled majorities?

M. De Tocqueville has told the exact truth. "This state of things," said he, in 1833, "is fatal in itself, and dangerous for the future. . . If the free institutions of America are ever destroyed, that event may be attributed to the unlimited authority of the majority . . . Anarchy will then might be the result, but it will have been brought about by despotism."[251]

THE FORMATION OF A FACTION

There is a vast difference between a political party and a faction. The one is legitimate, healthful, and conservative; the other is the fatal disease of which nearly all republics have perished. The one is united by principles, or designs, which persons in any part of the Republic may freely adopt and cherish; the other is animated by a "common interest, or passion," which is hostile to other interests of the same community. Now, the great object of the legislation of 1787, was to provide a remedy for the fatal effects of faction.

"Among the numerous advantages," says *The Federalist*, "promised by a well constructed union, none deserves to be more accurately developed than its tendency to break and control the violence of faction. The friend of popular governments, never finds himself so much alarmed for their character and fate, as when he contemplates their propensity to this dangerous vice. He will not fail, therefore, to set a due value on any plan which, without violating the principles to which he is attached, provides a proper cure for it"[252] Mr. Madison, the author of the above words, used still more impressive language on the same subject, in the Virginia Convention of 1788. "On a candid examination of history," he there said, "we shall find that turbulence, violence, and abuse of power, *by the majority trampling on the rights of the minority, have produced factions and commotions, which, in republics, have more frequently than any other cause, produced despotism. If we go over the whole history of ancient and modern republics, we shall find their destruction to have generally resulted from those causes.* If we consider the peculiar situation of the United States, and what are the sources of that diversity of sentiment which pervades its inhabitants, we shall find greater danger to fear, that the same causes may terminate here, in the same fatal effects, which they produced in those republics."[253] Here, then, was the rock on which the new Republic was in the greatest danger of being dashed to pieces. Hence, Mr Madison well adds: "This danger ought to be wisely guarded against." Otherwise, the great Republic must inevitably split on the rock of faction, and go to the bottom, with the republics of the past.

It was, therefore, the great object of the legislation of 1787, to guard the new Republic against the rise, or formation, of a faction. This, as we have already seen, is well stated in *The Federalist*, as follows: "When a majority is included in a faction, the form of popular government, *enables it to sacrifice to its ruling passion, or interest, both the public good and the rights of other citizens. To secure the public good, and private rights, against the danger of such a faction, and at the same time to preserve the spirit and the form of a popular government, is the great object to which our inquiries are directed. Let me add, that it is the great desideratum, by which alone this form of government can be rescued from the opprobrium under which it has so long labored, and be recommended to the esteem and adoption of mankind."[254]*

By what means, then, did the legislators of 1787, hope to remedy the evils of faction; to subdue, if not to eradicate, that fatal disease of republics? Mr. Madison replies: "Perhaps, in the progress of this discussion, it will appear that the only possible remedy for those evils and means of protecting the principles of Republicanism, will be found in that very system which is now exclaimed against as the parent of despotism."[255] That is, in the new Union of 1787.

Now where, and how, did the new Union provide "the only possible remedy" against the evils of faction? According to the view of Mr. Madison, and of the majority of the Convention of 1787, neither the North nor the South would be able to form itself into a dangerous faction; because, as they said, each section will have a majority in one branch of Congress, and thereby hold a constitutional check on the power of the other. But this remedy, as everyone knows, proved a total failure.

The other great remedy against the evils of faction, which, as the legislators of 1787 supposed, existed in the new system; would be found in the great extent of the Union, in the great number and diversity of its interests, which would prevent "any one party being able to outnumber and oppress the rest."[256] This remedy against faction is repeatedly urged by Mr. Madison. Thus, he speaks of the new Union "as the proper antidote for the diseases of faction, which have proved fatal to other popular governments, and of which alarming symptoms have been betrayed by our own,"[257] . . . because "the influence of factious leaders," who "may kindle a flame within their particular States," . . . "will be unable to spread a great conflagration through the other States."[258] Now this great remedy also proved a failure. Factious leaders *did* kindle a conflagration through all the Northern States; and the great North, animated by one "passion, or interest," did form itself into the most terrible faction the world has ever seen, and point all the lightnings of its wrath at the devoted South.

The fact is not denied by many of the great champions of the Northern power. On the contrary, it was made a ground of exultation and boasting, by some of her most eloquent orators. Therefore, it was said "no man has a right to be surprised at this state of things. It is just what we have attempted to bring about. *It is the first sectional party ever organized in this country. It does not know its own face, and calls itself national; but it is not national—it is sectional.* The republican party is a party of the north pledged against the south."[259] *Nothing could have been more true.* Under and in spite of the Constitution designed for the protection of all sections and of all interests alike, the North did form

itself into a faction, and seize all the powers of the Federal Government. This may have been rare sport to the leaders of the faction; it
was the death-knell of the Republic. It was the founders of the Union
themselves being the judges, the fall of the Republic, and the rise of
a despotism.

This faction, it is said, did "not know its own face." Perhaps it was
a little ashamed of its own face. It is certain, that it was very loud in
its professions that all its designs were national and constitutional,
even while it avowed the purpose to "use all constitutional means to
put an end to the institution of slavery." But no such means were
known to the Constitution; which, as the leaders of that faction perfectly well knew, was established and ordained to protect all the institutions of the South, as well as of the North. Use all constitutional
means indeed! Why, the very existence of such a faction, was an outrageous violation of the whole spirit and design of the Constitution of
1787. It was, in one word, the last throe of the mighty Republic, as it
succumbed to the fatal disease of which so many republics had previously perished. Conceived in profound contempt of the wisdom of
Washington, who, in his Farewell Address, had so solemnly warned his
countrymen against the dangers of a sectional party, or faction; it just
marched right onward in the light of its own eyes over broken constitutions, and laws, and oaths, trampling on all alike with imperial scorn
and proud disdain.

The South was advised to "wait for some overt act." But if one finds
himself in company with a strong man armed, who is both able and
willing to crush him, is it wise to "wait for the overt act," or to withdraw from his society as soon as possible? If the strong man armed
should make his withdrawal the occasion of his ruin, that would only
prove, that the companionship was neither safe, nor desirable.

The South, it is true, did not better her condition by her withdrawal
from the North. But is not all history replete with similar instances of
failure in the grand struggle for freedom, safety, and independence?
In the golden words of *The Federalist:* "Justice is the end of government. It is the end of civil society. It ever has been, and it ever will be
pursued, until it be obtained, or until liberty be lost in the pursuit."[260]
It was thus, in the pursuit of justice, that the South lost her liberty. If
she had not engaged in the pursuit, she would have *deserved* to lose her
liberty.

The South, it was said, had nearly always been in the possession of the Government; and it was right, therefore, that the North should take possession of it in her turn. But this is one of the lying fictions of the North. The South never had possession of the Government at all. All the great powers of the Government are, for the most part, lodged in the Congress of the United States, in neither branch of which did the South ever have a majority. She was, indeed, when she entered into the new Union, promised a majority in one branch of Congress; but that promise, like an apple of Sodom, soon turned to dust and ashes in her hands.

Nor had the South as such ever had a President of the United States. The great democratic party generally selected its Presidents from the South. But this did not make them sectional Presidents. Neither Washington, nor Jefferson, nor Madison, nor Monroe, nor Jackson, nor Polk, was a sectional President. On the contrary, so little was there of a sectional nature in their characters, or designs, that each and every one of them was elected to the Presidency of the United States, by a large majority of the Northern votes. Mr. Lincoln, on the other hand, who was a sectional candidate, and put forth on purely sectional grounds, did not receive a single Southern vote. He was, then, the candidate not of a legitimate party, but of the great unconstitutional and anti-republican faction of 1861; that is, the candidate of "the party of the North pledged against the South."

The North, with a majority in both houses of Congress, was perfectly protected against every possible danger of oppression. If, then, a statesman from the South had always filled the office of President, still her situation would have been far more precarious and unprotected than that of the North. The President could introduce no bill into Congress; he could only veto those which he might deem unjust and oppressive. Surely, a most feeble and uncertain protection to the South; since no man stood the least chance for the Presidency, who was not known to favor the wishes and the interests of the mighty North. The North, then in possession of both branches of Congress, and the dazzling prize of the Presidency to influence the leading politicians of the South, was sufficiently secure in the Union, even if all the Presidents had come from the South. But all this did not satisfy the North. On the false plea, that the South had nearly always been in possession of the Government; she determined to take possession of all its departments, the supreme Executive, as well as both branches of the Federal Legislature. Nor is this all. She determined to take and to keep possession of them all in the name of the North, alleging that the South had enjoyed them all long enough; and to wield them all by the terrible faction of "the North pledged against the South." Nor was this all. The great leader, or the great tool, of this faction, declared that he was not bound by the decisions of the Supreme Court of the United States; that he would enforce the Constitution as *he understood it,* and not as it was understood by that high judicial tribunal. Indeed, this mighty faction was got up and organized in direct opposition to, and in open contempt of the decisions of the Supreme Court of the United States; both in the Dred Scott case, and in the case of Prigg vs. the Commonwealth of Pennsylvania. *Its own will was its only law.*

It arose, like some monstrous abortion of night and darkness, from the bottomless depths of a factious contempt for all law and all authority. The decision of the Supreme Court in the case of Prigg, which authorizes the master to seize his fugitive slave *without process* in any State of the Union, was the first object of attack by the great leaders of this faction. The Court was denounced as having been corrupted by pro-slavery sentiments; though this very opinion was delivered by a Northern abolitionist, by Mr. Justice Story himself. Mr. Justice Story could, as we have seen, go great lengths in his advocacy of the Northern cause; but yet, as a Judge of the Supreme Court of the United States, he could not decide in direct and open violation of his oath of office. This instance of his integrity, in which other Northern Judges concurred, brought down the indignation and contempt of the great leaders of the Republican party upon the Court, whose opinion he had delivered. It was then threatened by those factious leaders, that the Supreme Court of the United States should be reorganized, and made to conform to the wishes and sentiments of the North; a purpose which was sure of its fulfilment after the election of Mr. Lincoln, and which would have capped the climax of the lawless designs of the Northern faction "pledged against the South."

Mr. Madison, "the father of the Constitution," believed that such a faction would never arise in the now Union. But he never doubted, for a moment, that if it should arise therein, this would prove that the Federal Government had failed to answer the great end of his creation. For, as we have seen, it was, in his own words, the great object of that

Government, "to secure the public good, and private rights, against the danger of such a faction," by providing against the possibility of its appearance in the bosom of the Republic. This is the great desideratum, which, according to the legislators of 1787, is necessary to remove "the opprobrium under which that form of Government has so long labored," and "to recommend it to the esteem and adoption of mankind," and which they supposed had been supplied by their legislation. But their remedies were too weak. Their practice was not sufficiently *heroic*. Hence the fatal disease of republics, the rise of faction, was not only engendered, but developed into a degree of frightful malignity, which is without a parallel in the history of the world. The design was good; but the execution defective. The fathers, in one word, did not begin to foresee the weakness, the folly, the madness, and the wickedness of their descendants. Hence, their sublime attempt to "establish justice, ensure domestic tranquility, promote the general welfare, and secure the blessings of liberty to their posterity," proved an awful failure. Indeed, if they could only have witnessed the gigantic and terrific faction of 1861, they would have pronounced their own "grand experiment" a disastrous failure. It was so regarded by the South; and, for that reason, the South wished to make an experiment for herself. But, unfortunately, she was already in the horrible clutches of a relentless and a remorseless faction.

Factions have no heart, no conscience, no reason, no consistency, no shame. Would you reason with such a remorseless monster? You might just as well read the riot act to a thunder storm. Would you appease its wrath? Would you soothe its rampant and raging ferocity? Would you appeal to all the tender mercies of our holy religion? You might just as well sing a lullaby to the everlasting roarings of the Pit. The South did not enter into the "new Union" to be governed by any such faction. She entered into the new Union, on the contrary, in order to secure her freedom, her independence, her happiness, her glory; and she lost them all—except her glory.

Even Mr. Madison, with all his devotion to the great work of his own hands, never became so blind an idolater as to resemble that epitome of meanness and climax of servility: "an unconditional Union-man." On the contrary, still breathing the spirit of a freemen, he said: "Were the plan of the Convention adverse to the public happiness, my voice would be, Reject the plan. Were the Union itself inconsistent with the public happiness, it would be, ABOLISH THE UNION."[261] Even as late as 1830, he declared, that "it still remains to be seen whether the Union will answer the ends of its existence or otherwise." If he had lived till 1861, he would have seen that the Union, having failed to prevent the rise and reign of faction, had not answered "the great object" of its creation; and, consequently, no longer deserved to exist. Hence, in 1861, he would either have unveiled the right of secession, or else he would have belied all the great principles, and sentiments, and designs of his life.

SUMMARY OF OTHER CAUSES OF SECESSION

The foregoing grounds or causes of secession are, it seems to me, amply sufficient to justify the South in the exercise of a constitutional right; for which she was amenable to no tribunal on earth, except to the moral sentiments of mankind. But there are still other and powerful causes of secession, which it is unnecessary to discuss in the present work. All the grounds of secession, including those above considered, may be stated as follows:

First, the destruction of the balance of power, which was originally established between the North and the South; and which was deemed by the authors of the Constitution to be essential to the freedom, safety, and happiness of those sections of the Union.

Secondly, the sectional legislation, by which the original poverty of the North was exchanged for the wealth of the South; contrary to the great design of the Constitution, which was to establish the welfare of all sections alike, and not the welfare of one section at the expense of another.

Thirdly, the formation of a faction, or "the party of the North pledged against the South," in direct and open violation of the whole spirit and design of the new Union; involving a failure of the great ends for which the Republic was ordained.

Fourthly, the utter subversion and contemptuous disregard of all the checks of the Constitution, instituted and designed by its authors for the protection of the minority against the majority; and the lawless reign of the Northern Demos.

Fifthly, the unjust treatment of the slavery question, by which the compacts of the Constitution made by the North in favor of the South, were grossly violated by her; while, at the same time, she insisted on the observance of all the compacts made by the South in her own favor.

Sixthly, the sophistry and hypocrisy of the North, by which she attempted to justify her injustice and oppression of the South.

Seventhly, the horrible abuse and slander, heaped on the South, by the writers of the North; in consequence of which she became the most despised people on the face of the globe; whose presence her proud ally felt to be a contamination and a disgrace.

Eighthly, the contemptuous denial of the right of secession; the false statements, and the false logic by which that right was concealed from the people of the North; and the threats of extermination in case the South should dare to exercise that right.

These, it is believed, are the principal causes by which the last hope of freedom for the South in the Union was extinguished; and, consequently, she determined to withdraw from the Union. Bravely and boldly did she strike for Liberty; and, if she fell, it was because, as the London *Times* said, "she had to fight the world."

Chapter XX

The Legislators of 1787 as Political Prophets

"Every particular interest," said Mr. Madison, in the Convention of 1787, "whether in any class of citizens, or any description of States, ought to be secured as far as possible. Wherever there is danger of attack, there ought to be given a constitutional power of defence. But he contended that the States were divided into different interests, not by their difference of size, but from other circumstances; the most material of which resulted partly from climate, but principally from the effects of their having or not having slaves. These two causes concurred in forming the great division of interests in the United States. It did not lie between the large and small States. It lay between the Northern and Southern; and if any defensive power were necessary, it ought to be mutually given to these two interests."[262] In this opinion of the leading member from Virginia, the leading member from Massachusetts fully concurred. For Mr. King "was fully convinced that the question concerning a difference of interest did not lie where it had been hitherto discussed, between the great and the small States, but between the Southern and the Eastern. For this reason he had been willing to yield something, in the proportion of representation, for the security of the Southern."[263] That is, for the protection of the Southern interest, he had, as we have seen, been willing to vote for the fractional representation of slaves. Such was, indeed, the opinion of the Convention.

But while the legislators of 1787 agreed in this opinion, they looked into the future with very different eyes. Considered as political prophets, they may, in fact, be divided into three classes.

At the head of the first class, there stands James Madison, "the father of the Constitution." Seeing, as he did, that the great difficulty before the Convention was to adjust the antagonism between the North and the South, he must have known that the perpetuity of the new Union would depend on the manner in which this difficulty should be settled by their labors. Just before the meeting of the Convention, indeed, this great antagonism had given birth to a tremendous conflict between the North and South, by which the Union was shaken to its foundations. Hence, Mr. Madison had good reason to fear the violence of this antagonism for the future; and he did fear it. For he tells us, that there ought to be given a constitutional power of defence to each of these sections; so that neither could take advantage of the other.

He hoped, he fancied, he predicted that this had been done. The South, he said, will soon have a majority in the House of Representatives, in consequence of the rapid increase of her population; by which she will hold a check on the power of the North. But this adjustment of the great difficulty in question rested on the unstable and fluctuating basis of population. It soon proved to be a foundation of sand. The hope and the prediction of Mr. Madison soon appeared to have been a delusion and a dream. He staked the freedom, the safety, and the happiness of the South, on the happening of a future event, which never came to pass.

Indeed, he did not urge his plan for the adjustment of the formidable antagonism in question; because, as he said, it suggested a difficulty which was too apt to arise of itself. It was, therefore, never adjusted at all, on any solid foundation, or secure principle; and, consequently, did continue to arise of itself, and disturb the new Union with convulsions, from the beginning of its career to the grand explosion of 1861.

Mr. Madison always feared the effects of this great any imperfectly adjusted antagonism between the North and the South. It seems, indeed, as if he wished to hide it from his own eyes, as well as from those of the people. It is a very remarkable fact, that although in the secret Convention of 1787, he pronounced the antagonism between the Northern and the Southern States the greatest of all the difficulties they had to deal with; yet when, in *The Federalist,* he enumerated the difficulties the Convention had to encounter, no allusion whatever is made to this stupendous one. He seems to have imagined, that since it is so apt to arise of itself, the less that is said about it the better. This would, no doubt, have been very wise and prudent, if a great danger might be remedied by simply closing one's eyes upon its existence.

Nothing more easily disturbed his patience, than any allusion to the great danger created by the fearful antagonism in question. In *The Federalist,* — how unlike his usual style! — he pours forth the following strain of lachrymose philanthropy of patriotism: "Hearken not to the

unnatural voice, which tells you that the people of America, knit together as they are by so many chords of affection, can no longer live
together as members of the same family; can no longer continue mutual guardians of their mutual happiness . . . No, my countrymen, shut
your ears against this unhallowed language. Shut your hearts against
the poison which it conveys. The kindred blood which flows in the
veins of American citizens, the mingled blood which they have shed
in the defence of their sacred rights, consecrate their union, and excite
horror at the idea of their becoming aliens, rivals, enemies."[264]

Yet, in spite of all this, Mr. Madison himself must have had serious
misgivings with respect to his beautiful dream of a perpetual peace. For
he knew, as we have seen, that there was danger of a collision between
the North and the South. It is certain, that the voice which he pronounced unnatural, was the voice of truth. For American citizens did
become aliens, rivals, enemies; and mingled their blood far more freely
and fearfully than they ever had done in the defence of their common
rights. But Mr. Madison knew, that in order to secure the adoption of
the new Union, it would be necessary to persuade the people, that the
very first condition of such a Union would always obtain; namely, "a
sufficient amount of sympathy among its populations." Hence, perhaps,
his dream of peace was not all a dream, but partly rhetoric.

The second class of prophets seems to have been without a head.
Indeed it may, perhaps, be doubted, whether they spoke as prophets,
or as diplomatists. It is certain, that they encouraged the notion of Mr.
Madison and other Southern legislators, that the South would certainly
have a majority in the House of Representatives. Several of the most
influential of the Northern legislators seemed quite confident that such
would be the good fortune of the South; and none more so than Mr.
Gouverneur Morris. But were they always sincere in that belief? Or did
they sometimes flatter the false hopes of the South, in order to be able
to drive a better bargain with her? No finite mind can, perhaps, answer
these questions; or tell whether the legislators in question always spoke
as prophets, or sometimes as diplomatists. It is certain, that the expec-
tation held out to the South, that she would be able to control one
branch of Congress, was the promise, the prospect, the bait, by which
she was entrapped into the new Union; into that tremendous dead-fall,
by which, in 1861, she was crushed to the earth. Patrick Henry stood
at the head of the third and last class of prophets.

No man ever more clearly foresaw, or more confidently predicted, the future, than did Patrick Henry the calamities which have fallen on his beloved Virginia. With some of the passages from this class of prophets, I shall conclude this book.

General Pinckney of South Carolina, declared, that "if they [the Southern States,] are to form so considerable a minority, and the regulation of trade is to be given to the General Government, *they will be nothing more than overseers for the Northern States."*

In like manner, Mr. Williamson, of North Carolina, said: "The Southern interest must be extremely endangered by the present arrangement. *The Northern States are to have a majority in the first instance, with the means of perpetuating it."*[265]

George Mason said: "He went on a principle often advanced, and in which he concurred, that a majority, when interested, would oppress the minority. This maxim," [than which none is more just,] "had been verified in the Legislature of Virginia. If we compare the States in this point of view, the eight Northern States have an interest different from the five Southern States; and have, in one branch of the Legislature, thirty-six votes against 29, and in the other in the proportion of eight to three. The Southern States had therefore ample grounds for their suspicions."[266]

Mr. Henry said: "But I am sure, that the dangers of this system are real, when those who have no similar interests with the people of this country, [i.e. Virginia and the South,] are to legislate for us when our dearest interests are to be left in the hands of those whose advantage it will be to infringe them."[267]

In the same Convention, Mr. Grayson, after declaring that it was a struggle between the North and the South for empire, proceeded to say, "Are not all defects and corruptions founded on an inequality of representation and want of responsibility? My greatest objection is, that it will, in its operation, be found unequal, grievous and oppressive. If it have any efficacy at all, it must be by a faction of one part of the Union against another. If it be called into action by a faction of seven States, it will be terrible indeed. We must be at no loss how this combination will be formed. There is a great difference of circumstances between the States. The interests of the carrying States are strikingly different from those of the productive States. I mean not to give offence to any part of America, but mankind are governed by interest.

The carrying States will assuredly unite and our situation will then be wretched indeed. We ought to be wise enough to alertly guard against the abuse of such a government. *Republics, in fact, oppress more than monarchies.*"

"The voice of tradition," said Henry, "I trust will inform posterity of our struggles for freedom. If our descendants be worthy of the name of Americans, they will preserve and hand down to the latest posterity, the transactions of the present times, and though I confess my explanations are not worth the hearing, they will see 'I have done my utmost to preserve their liberty.'" Tyler responded, "I also wish to hand down to posterity my opposition to that system. British tyranny would have been more tolerable."

Notes

1   Federalist No. xliii.
2   The Madison Papers, p. 1184.
3   Commentaries on the Constitution, vol. iii, p. 287, published in 1833.
4   Webster.
5   Rebellion Record, vol. 1, p. 211.
6   The Madison Papers, p. 987.
7   Marshall's Life of Washington, vol. v, chap. 1.
8   The Madison Papers.
9   Article 2.
10 Edward Everett.
11 Mr. Curtis, vol. i., p. 465.
12 The Madison Papers, p. 797.
13 Ibid, p. 1101.
14 Ibid, p. 1103.
15 Elliot's Debates, vol. iii., p. 652.
16 The Madison Papers, p. 1099.
17 Elliot's Debates, vol. iii.
18 Franklin's Works, vol. v., p. 409.
19 The Writings of Washington, vol. ix., p. 280.
20 Vol. v, chap. iii.
21 Book iii, chap. xliii.
22 Rebellion Record, vol. 1, p. 211.
23 Ibid. p. 214.
24 Mr. Webster's Speech of 1830.
25 The Madison Papers, p. 908.
26 The Madison Papers.
27 Ibid, p. 908.
28 Ibid, p. 909.
29 The Madison Papers, p. 908
30 The American Question, by William H. Story. Elliot's Debates. Vol. 1
    p., 42 fl.

31 Mr. Calhoun's speech, Feb. 26, 1833.

32 Speech, Feb. 16, 1833.

33 Madison Papers, p. 1081–2.

34 Madison Papers, p. 1184.

35 The great mind of Mr. Webster was in general more like the ocean in repose than in action; and, as is well known, his habitual indolence often induced him to rely on others for political information. No one who will attentively compare his speech of 1833 with book III., chap. 3, of Story's "Commentaries on the Constitution," can be at any loss to account for the origin of his "new political grammar," his "new rules of syntax," and his "new vocabulary." If he applies these epithets to the doctrines of Morris, and Gerry, and Madison, it is because old things have become new with him, and new things old. The secret of this revolution will be found, as we shall soon prove, in the work of Mr. Justice Story, which work was not written in 1830. Indeed it was not published until 1833; but then the first volume, containing book III , chap. 3, was prepared, it not printed, before the speech of Mr. Webster, with whom the author was on the most intimate terms. It would have been well for the fame of Webster, in the eye of posterity, if he had more carefully examined such a question for himself.

36 Dall. R. p. 419.

37 Elliot's Debates, vol. iii., p. 57.

38 Correspondence. Vol. iv., p. 415.

39 No. xxxix.

40 Hamilton's Works, vol. ii., p. 322.

41 See Paley's Life, attached to his works, p. 13.

42 Commentaries, vol. i., book iii., chap. iii., p. 298.

43 Hamilton's Works, vol. ii., p. 339.

44 Hamilton's Works, vol. ii., p. 445.

45 Madison Papers. Index, cxi., "Convention to revise the Federal Constitution, 587, 617, 619."

46 Vol. i., chap. vi., p. 142.

47 Ibid, p. 143.

48 Vol. i., Book II., chap. i., p. 180; Book III., chap. ii., p. 280.

49 Ibid, Book III., chap. ii., p. 260.

50 Conflict of Laws, p. 307.

51 De Lolme on the Constitution, p. 48.

52 Ibid, p. 287.

53 I say the people, because those who followed the barons at Runnymede demanded and obtained stipulations in favor of the people as well as in favor of their leaders.

54 This is the ground taken, and unanswerably maintained by Hume, in his essay on the "Original Contract." Essays, vol. i., Essay 12. The theory of Rousseau is rejected by M. Comte ("Theorie de Legislation," liv. i. c. 2) on the same ground. Sir William Temple ("Works," vol. ii. pp. 37, 46) had previously rejected the doctrine of the "Social Contract." Kant, the philosopher of Konigsberg, treats it as a frivolous and impractical notion. Heeren ("On Political Theories," p. 239) says that a social contract neither was, nor could have been, actually concluded. Stahl ("Philosophy of Rights," vol. ii., part ii., p. 142) rejects the doctrine as visionary. Godwin, likewise ("Political Justice," book iii., c. 2 and 3) rejects it. The doctrine of the social compact is subjected to an exhaustive analysis by Mr. Austin ("Prov. of Jurisprudence," 331–71) and triumphantly refuted. Jeremy Bentham likewise rejects the same hypothesis as visionary.

55 Story on the Constitution, Book i., chap. iii., p. 37.

56 John Adams's Works, Vol. iv., p. 216.

57 De Tocqueville's "Democracy in America."

58 Life and Writings of Governor Morris, vol. iii., p. 323.

59 Ibid., p. 203.

60 Works, vol. ii., p. 445.

61 Ibid.

62 Madison Papers, p. 693.

63 The resolution was introduced by Mr. Tyler, rather than its author, because, "having never served in Congress," he "had more the ear of the house than those whose services there exposed them to an imputable bias." Madison Papers, p. 696. So great was the jealousy of the Federal Congress in those days.

64 Madison Papers, p. 706. These are the words of the resolution of Virginia; the instructions of the other States were equivalent to these.

65 Ibid, p. 703.

66 Madison Papers, p. 706.

67 The two Websters, Pelatiah and Noah, do show some originality. The one, in 1781, seeing that Congress had not sufficient authority "for the performance of their duties," (though be does not tell us what duties

they had to perform, except to exercise the authority entrusted to them,) suggests the plan of a Continental Convention, for the express purpose, "among other things, of enlarging the duties of their Constitution." The other, in 1784, wished for a Government "which should act, not on States, but directly on individuals." If this idea really originated with Noah Webster, then there are many who will think that his political pamphlet cancelled the obligations which his spelling book conferred on the country. Mr. Webster was also original in his orthography.

68   History of the Constitution of the United States, by Curtis, vol. i, p. 413.

69   Madison Papers, pp. 730–35, etc.

70   Rebellion Record, vol. 1, p. 211.

71   The Madison Papers, p. 783.

72   Art. V.

73   Resolutions which, "by the unanimous order of the Convention" of 1787, was forwarded with the Constitution to Congress.

74   Chapter III.

75   Commentaries on the Constitution, Book iii., chap. ii.

76   We have only said admirable; but, all things considered, Mr. Spence's work is truly a wonderful production.

77   The Madison Papers, p. 1184.

78   Life and Writings of Governor Morris, vol. iii., p. 323.

79   Ibid, vol. iii., p. 193.

80   Life and Writings, vol. iii., p. 193.

81   The Madison Papers, p. 1470.

82   Madison Papers, p. 1177.

83   Ibid, p. 796.

84   Madison Papers, p. 1241.

85   Ibid, p. 1469.

86   Ibid, p. 1470.

87   Speech in Senate, Feb. 16, 1833.

88   Chapter v.

89   Federalist, No. ix.

90   No. xl.

91   No. xxxix.

92   Ibid.

93 See chap. x.

94 No. xxxix.

95 xi.

96 Federalist, No. lxxxv.

97 Ibid.

98 Ibid.

99 Ibid.

100 No. xiii.

101 No. ix.

102 No. xxxvi.

103 No. xl.

104 Hobbes' Works, vol. ii., p. 91.

105 See their Letter.

106 Federalist, No. lxxx.

107 Webster's works, Vol. iii., page 470. Great speech of 1833.

108 Works, Vol. ii, page 334.

109 Chapter IV.

110 See their Letter to Congress.

111 Works, vol. i, p. 331.

112 Works, vol. v, p. 347.

113 Ibid.

114 Madison papers, pp. 732, 734, 761, 861, 1118, 1221, 1225.

115 Works, vol. ii, p. 318. These words are quoted by Mr. Webster, with his expressed approbation.

116 See Articles V. and VI.

117 Works, Vol. v., p. 359.

118 Webster's Works, Vol. v., p. 269.

119 Ibid, Vol. ii., p. 674.

120 Webster's Works, vol. ii., p. 575.

121 Ibid. p. 577.

122 See Chapter II.

123 Works, Vol. vi., page 222.

124 Vol. i., Book iii., chap. iii.

125 Vol. i., Book iii., chap. iii.

126 Indeed, this doctrine, and the very illustration of it, was borrowed by Mr. Lincoln from the celebrated Preacher of Princeton, N. J. Compare Mr. Lincoln's speech with Dr. Hodge on "the State of the Country."

127 Story on the Constitution, vol. i, page 164.

128 Ibid.

129 Story on the Constitution, vol. i, page 163–164.

130 Vol. i., Book xi., chap. i, page 200. Note.

131 Vol. i., Book ii., chap. ii, page 209.

132 Vol. i., Book ii., chap. i., page 197

133 Ibid.

134 Wheaton, page 187.

135 Vol. i., page 323.

136 Vol. i., Book ii., chap. iii., page 323.

137 Vol. i, p. 122.

138 Vol. i, p. 9.

139 Vol. i, p. 9.

140 Vol. i, p. 39.

141 Vol. i, p. 61.

142 Ibid.

143 Vol. i, pp. 39, 40.

144 Vol. i, p. 62.

145 Vol. i, p. 143.

146 Ibid.

147 Vol. i., Book iii., chap. iii., page 296.

148 Appeal from the New to the Old Whigs.

149 Appeal from the New to the Old Whigs.

150 Everett's Orations and Speeches, vol. i., page. 122.

151 Vol. i., page 330.

152 Vol. i., Book ii, p. 198

153 Ibid. p. 194

154 Story's Com. on the Constitution, vol. i, p. 330

155 Vol. i, p. 308.

156 Federalist, No. xxxix.

157 Ibid, No. xl.

158 Federalist No. lxxxii.

159 Federalist No. xxxii.

160 Elliot's Debates, Vol. III., p. 389.

161 Elliot's Debates, Vol. II., p. 180.

162 Ibid. Vol. iii, p. 594.

163 Ibid. Vol. iv, p. 240.

164 Ibid. Vol. ii, p. 503.

165 Federalist, No. xxxii.

166 Webster's Works, vol. iii., p. 322.

167 Federalist.

168 Vattel's Law of Nations, p. 3.

169 See chap. xv.

170 Webster's Works, vol. vi., p. 221.

171 No. xxxviii.

172 Rebellion Record, Vol. I., p. 214.

173 Representative Government, chap. xvii.

174 Anti-Slavery Examiner, Vol. xi, p. 101.

175 Ibid, p. 101.

176 Ibid, p. 118.

177 Ibid, p. 119.

178 Ibid, p. 119.

179 Ibid, p. 104.

180 Anti-Slavery Examiner, Vol. xi, p. 104.

181 Ibid.

182 Ibid. p. 114.

183 Anti-Slavery Examiner, Vol. xi., pp. 111–12.

184 Perhaps that member of his Cabinet knew the design of Mr. Lincoln's administration better than it was then known to Mr. Lincoln himself.

185 Vol. i, Chap. xviii., p. 413.

186 The American Union, p. 201.

187 Vol. iii., chap. xxx., p. 336.

188 Historie Universelle, originally written in Italian, vol. 17, p. 871.

189 European States and Colonies, p. 350–351.

190 Chap. xi.

191 Elliot's Debates, Vol. iii, p. 812.

192 See Virginia Resolutions of 1798; Kentucky Resolutions of 1798 and 1799; the Virginia Report of 1800, &c., &c.

193 The Rev. Dr. Hodge on the State of the Country, p. 24.

194 Ibid. p. 25.

195 Ludlow's History of the United States.

196 Art. VI.

197 Ludlow's History of the United States, pp. 143–4.

198 Story's Commentary on the Constitution. Book iii, ch. iii.

199 Elliott's Debates, vol. 3, pp. 30, 144, 149, 156, 161, 164, 173, 174.
200 Ibid. 530–562.
201 See The Federalist, Nos. xvii, xviii, xix, &c., &c.
202 American Union, p. 245–6.
203 Federalist, No. xxxviii.
204 No. xliii.
205 Chap. iv.
206 Federalist, No. xxii.
207 Vol. i, p. 288.
208 No. xxii.
209 Vol. i, p. 290.
210 Rev. Dr. Hodge on the State of the Country, p. 24.
211 Enlightened by the profound view of his reverend guide, Mr. Lincoln, with a naive originality all his own, might well have asked, what is the difference between a county and a State? Is not a county a little State, and a State a big county? One striking difference must have occurred to him in the course of his reading; the difference, namely, that a State is spelt with a large S, and a county with a small c. He must also have observed that a State is sometimes called "Sovereign." But whether it is called Sovereign because it is spelt with a large S, or spelt with a large S because it is called sovereign, is one of the nice questions in the science of government, which he does not seem to have very fully considered, or positively decided. He had evidently discovered, for he tells us so himself, that a State is usually larger than a county in the extent of its territory; a discovery which, perhaps, led to the profound and original reflection, that the United States have been, and must continue to be, *one State or Nation,* because their territory is *one.* It is to be hoped, indeed, that these sovereign States or counties, as the case may be, shall continue to be united, and that order, tranquility, and happiness shall once more bless their Union. But if so, must not something beside the *one* territory help to produce the happy result? Have not simple confederations existed on the same territories? No, have not some twenty distinct nationalities long existed on the territory of Europe? We may, then, hardly trust the reflection, however profound, that one territory is in itself a sufficiently active and powerful cause to produce one very big State, or county, covering a whole continent.
212 Hodge on the State of the Country, p. 28.

213　No. xxix.

214　No. xl and No. lxxxv.

215　Buchanan's Administration, p 88.

216　Rawle on the Constitution, Chap. xxxii.

217　Elliot's Debates, Vol. 4., p. 563.

218　Ibid, p. 560.

219　Buchanan's Administration, p. 86.

220　Page 5.

221　Page 8.

222　Page 7.

223　Pp. 10–11.

224　P. 21.

225　Proceedings of Hartford Convention, p. 33,

226　Letter of Dec. 30, 1828, in reply to H. Gray Otis and others.

227　Letter of Dec. 30, 1828, in reply to H. Gray Otis and others.

228　Buchanan's Administration, p. 87.

229　Letter of Dec. 30, 1828, to H. Gray Otis, &c.

230　History of United States, by J. M. Ludlow.

231　Ibid.

232　Rebellion Record, Vol. i., p. 20.

233　Jefferson's Works, Vol. vii., p. 229.

234　Ibid Vol. ix., p. 464.

235　Jefferson's Works, Vol. ix., p. 464–5.

236　Elliot's Debates, Vol. iv., p. 571.

237　Jefferson's Works, Vol. iv., p. 305–6.

238　Quoted in Story's Com. vol. 1, p. 288, note.

239　History, by T. M. Ludlow, pp. 44–5.

240　The Slave Power, chap. vi.

241　The Slave Power, p. 164.

242　History, p. 49.

243　No. x.

244　Federalist No. x.

245　Ibid.

246　The American Conflict, p. 46.

247　Ibid, p. 48.

248　Southern Wealth and Northern Profits, p. 139–40.

249　History, p. 306.

250   Democracy in America, Vol. i, p. 801.

251   Ibid, p. 817.

252   No. x.

253   Elliot's Debates, vol. iii, p. 109.

254   No. x.

255   Elliot's Debates, Vol. iii, p. 109.

256   The Federalist, No. xiv.

257   Ibid.

258   Ibid, No. x.

259   Wendell Phillips.

260   No. li.

261   The Federalist, No. xlv.

262   The Madison Papers, p. 1006.

263   Ibid, p. 1067.

264   No. xiv.

265   Ibid, p. 1058

266   Ibid, p. 1387.

267   Elliot's Debates, vol. iii., p. 289.

Index

abolitionists and abolitionism, 112,
114–117, 119, 132, 180
absolute control, 80, 157, 170, 171,
180
account, 24, 36, 39–41, 73, 107, 146,
187
Adams, John, 34, 161
Adams, John Quincy, 20, 21, 108,
148, 152, 153, 162
admission, 12, 30, 83, 85, 153, 177,
181
advantages, in relations, 20, 23, 32,
60, 64, 75, 80, 119, 168, 173, 175,
180, 185, 189, 199, 201
agents, 2, 53, 63, 69, 91, 98, 101,
102, 163
agreement, as legal matter, 23, 30,
72, 75, 91, 92, 94, 95, 112, 113,
117, 119
American Anti-Slavery Society, 114
American Church, 114
American Conflict, 115, 167, 177
American Constitution, 114
American Government, 114
American Independence, 112
American Question, 126, 167
American States, 23, 91
American Union, 82, 109, 113–115,
119, 120, 126, 166
Annapolis Convention, 28, 38, 39
antagonism, 171, 198, 199
anti-slavery, 114
arguments, 22, 36, 44, 45, 93, 96,
125, 125, 134

Articles of Confederation, 1, 6, 7,
25, 27, 42, 45, 46, 74, 86–89, 90,
94, 105–107, 125–127, 136, 169
Articles of Union, 7, 28, 74, 75, 87,
90, 91, 101, 106, 126, 127
assembly, 19, 20, 47, 48, 52, 57, 83,
155
assent, 30, 61, 62, 64, 84, 120
assertions, 5, 6, 9, 10, 13, 22, 41, 42,
56–59, 65–67, 84, 89, 93, 137,
143, 159
association, 12, 58, 109, 120, 127,
141, 145, 155
Attorney General, 145
authorities, 11, 21, 61, 62, 77, 96, 97,
146

Beecher, Henry Ward, 115, 141
benefits, 2, 4, 20, 31, 69, 104, 124,
125, 139, 188
Bentham, Jeremy, 48
Bernard, Professor, 117
Black Republicans, 110
blacks, 116, 168, 171, 174, 179, 180
Blackstone, Justice, 24
blood, 7, 114–117, 131, 144, 200
body of laws, 48
body of people 28, 37, 54, 112, 115,
155
bold assertions, 5, 10, 18, 56–58, 85,
89, 143, 159
Boston, 73, 77, 151, 153
branches, 72, 99, 169–172, 174, 177,
182, 188, 193

British Colonies, 110
British Crown, 82, 89, 185
British Empire, 83, 111
Brougham, Lord, 119, 120
Buchanan, President James, 112,
 117, 118, 145, 148, 152, 153
Burke, Edmund, 92
Butler, Mr., 167

Cairnes, Professor, 168, 172, 184
Calhoun, John C., 12, 45, 142, 148,
 165, 188, 189
cases, 3, 31, 49, 53, 150, 157, 159,
 168, 170
Central Government, 63
Chapman, Maria Weston, 114
circumstances, 38, 48, 77, 90, 148,
 151–153, 155, 156, 180, 198, 201
civil war, 48, 113, 152
class, 116, 125, 171, 198, 200, 201
Clay, Henry, 148
colonies, 82–85, 87–89, 109, 110,
 120
commentaries, 8, 14, 15, 18, 21, 29,
 64, 93
commercial, 38, 39, 74, 83, 148, 149
communities (aggregate of population), 23, 79, 91, 92
compact (theories about):
 between Sovereign States, 41,
  65, 75, 119, 133, 136, 162
 abrogating the old, 23
 articles of, 31
 between the states, 2, 5, 8, 17, 21,
  25, 27, 31, 36, 57, 65, 66, 70,
  77, 78, 95, 107, 128, 131, 137,
  141, 142, 143, 144, 147, 153,
  154, 163, 164

between thirteen sovereign and
 independent states, 143
Constitution and compact are
 twin words, 18
Constitution is a, 5, 8, 17–21, 28,
 76, 119, 128, 133, 136, 144, 145,
 147
Constitution is a compact among
 the states, 2, 25, 27, 31, 36, 57,
 65, 66, 70, 77, 78, 95, 107, 131,
 137, 141, 142, 153, 154, 163, 164
Constitution is compact between
 the society and individual, 23
Constitution is not a compact
 between sovereign States, 133
constitution of England is not a,
 32
explicit and solemn, 19, 21, 23,
 24, 26, 33, 34, 60, 70, 76, 131,
 147
express compact between king
 and people, 32
federative, 162–164
first, 2, 77
implied, 26, 27
language of a, 94
not between individuals, but
 between political societies, 49
not every compact is a Constitution, 22, 24
old Articles of Confederation
 were a, 25
only Government founded in
 real, 21
original, explicit, and solemn
 compact, 23, 26, 33, 34
parties to the compact, 45, 67,
 124, 139

party to a compact has a right to revoke that compact, 136, 137

right to secede from a, 143

should be perpetual, 106

social compact as defined by Hobbes, 69

South no longer bound to keep the compact, 77

theory of the social compact, 24, 33

compromises, 66, 72, 73, 170, 177

conditions and provisions, indispensable, 54, 73, 142, 164, 176–179

confederacy, 10, 15, 29, 39, 40, 56, 58–60, 63, 70, 83, 86, 100, 112, 125, 128, 136, 137, 140, 147, 153, 154, 159

Confederated States, 67, 150

conflict, 1, 72, 77, 87, 89, 115, 130, 131, 160, 167, 169, 177, 199

consent, 5, 12, 20, 26, 27, 30, 31, 47, 59, 60, 64, 75, 88, 94, 105, 107, 109, 112, 117, 138, 140, 141, 171

consent of the people, 59, 60

consequence, 42, 80, 81, 106, 132, 148, 164, 185, 197, 199

consolidation, 53, 62–64, 70, 115, 120, 140, 142

constitution:

abolish the, 80

addresses the language of authority, 94

adoption of a, 87, 108

alter or amend the, 79

authors of, 12, 14, 18, 47, 49, 75, 183, 196

coercion is wrong under the, 117

commentaries on the, 8

is a compact, 5, 17, 18, 28, 36, 49, 58, 66, 67, 70, 76–78, 87, 90, 94, 98–100, 103, 119, 128, 133, 136, 142, 143–147, 154, 159, 177

compromises of the, 72, 73, 170

conflicting theories of the, 119

design of the, 192, 196

draft of the, 34, 45, 54

established not by a federal but by a national act, 44

fathers of the, 11–13, 19, 21, 43, 96, 109, 121, 128, 143, 146, 162, 177

is founded on consent, 30

framers of the, 10, 36, 52, 56, 65, 105, 107, 128

of Great Britain, 25, 32, 119

great expounder of the, 10, 145

historian of the, 10, 39

illustrious architects of the, 57, 66, 143

language of the, 44, 97, 125

of Massachusetts, 23–26, 33, 34

of a national government, 6, 8, 22, 36, 75, 133, 143

nature of the, 17, 46, 50, 51, 61, 66, 162

of a new empire, 24

of New York, 23

Northern theory of the, 45, 46, 50, 82

is not a contract, 30

not promulgated in the name of the States, 41, 42

ordained by the people of the United States, 41, 70

constitution (*continued*)
  palpable infractions of the, 150
  preamble to the, 44, 45, 47, 55,
    64, 122
  ratification of the, 53, 135
  ratifying a new, 21, 24, 26
  rejecting, 63
  seventh Article of the, 63, 65
  Southern theories of the, 165
  States never acceded to the, 5, 12
  stipulations of the, 74
  tenth amendment to the, 98
  terms and articles of the, 31
construction, 51, 86, 106, 113, 121,
  154, 158, 164
contempt, 35, 71, 110, 113, 132, 149,
  151, 158, 192, 194
contest, 84, 99, 165, 169–172
controversy, 5, 5, 8, 45, 99, 136, 138
Convention of 1787, 1, 6, 10–12, 14,
  14, 16, 18–21, 33, 35, 40–42, 45,
  47, 49, 50–55, 57–60, 63, 65,
  69–71, 72, 74, 77, 87, 93, 105,
  106, 127, 128, 130, 134, 137, 138,
  167, 169–171, 175, 176, 179, 184,
  188, 191, 198, 199
Convention of Massachusetts, 21, 27
creed, 104, 105, 141, 148, 161

darkness (as ignorance), 17, 24, 25,
  51, 78, 82, 117, 154, 194
Davis, Jefferson, 4, 184
De Lolme, 32, 119
De Tocqueville, 34, 119, 120, 172,
  188, 189
death, 3, 34, 112, 117, 128, 181, 192
debates, 56, 58, 59, 63, 65, 67, 74,
  121, 166, 167, 176, 177

decisions:
  of the convention, 15, 71, 138,
    168
  Judicial, 34
  of the majority, 62
  of states, 67, 93, 138, 150, 151,
    158
  of the Supreme Court, 194
Declaration of Independence, 6, 79,
  84, 85, 88, 89, 109, 110, 112, 118,
  160, 161, 165
declarations, 2, 6, 14, 37, 57, 70, 71,
  90, 98, 101, 104, 116, 119, 131,
  147–149, 153, 159, 176, 194, 201
defects, 28, 37–39, 106, 201
defence, 84, 124, 150, 169, 171, 175,
  176, 180, 184, 198–200
Delaware, 41, 42, 171, 175, 180, 182,
  183
delegates and delegating power, 10,
  75, 88, 97, 99, 100, 101, 120, 122,
  123, 169
democracy, 6, 34, 53, 119, 172, 175,
  189
Democratic Republic, 34
despotism, 26, 34, 102, 132, 142,
  159, 164, 188
difficulty, 54, 63, 69, 85, 107, 170,
  178, 179, 198, 199
discoveries, 19, 20, 29, 28, 37, 61,
  128, 148, 150, 169
discussion, 9, 38, 46, 52, 86, 99,
  117, 125, 190
dissent, 26
dissolve, 19, 114, 119, 139, 148, 153,
  180
distinguished, 34, 53, 55, 87, 145,
  146, 161, 179

disunion and division, 11, 53, 67, 80, 86, 102, 112, 113, 115, 116, 180, 184, 198

dominion, 109, 140, 157, 170, 171, 177, 183, 188

drafts ,of documents, 30, 33, 34, 45, 54, 89, 157

dreams, 53, 135, 141, 151, 199, 200

duty, 3, 88, 112, 114, 116, 126, 134, 150, 151, 153–155

Eastern States, 19

elections, 52–54, 61, 122, 162, 193

Elliot, Professor, 187

Ellsworth, Oliver, 171

eloquence, 9, 13, 63–65, 121, 123, 141, 142, 148, 150, 165

empire, 24, 59–61, 83, 111, 148, 177, 183, 201

enemies, 59, 62–64, 85, 92, 121, 141, 149, 153, 155, 156, 185, 200

English views, 32, 125–127

error, 15, 51, 70, 145, 146, 161

escape, 27, 102, 112, 119, 121, 127, 130, 132

establishment, 24, 32, 33, 36, 39, 59, 65, 67, 84, 87, 89, 120, 152

Everett, Mr., 8, 20, 57, 132, 156, 158

evil, 76, 123, 148, 150, 159, 175, 185

exercise of power and authority, 31, 35, 75, 80, 89, 91, 92, 99–104, 117, 127, 140, 150, 157, 158, 160, 166, 168, 169, 189, 196, 197

Exeter Hall, 115, 141

expression, 5, 6, 10, 11, 20, 21, 31, 48, 52, 59, 150

extent, 17, 38, 70, 128, 145, 150, 157, 158, 191

extermination, 197

extract, 60, 61, 73, 119, 153, 159, 160

extraordinary, 128, 129, 131, 135

failure, 24, 106, 191, 192, 195, 196

fatal, 63, 64, 118, 189–192, 195

Federal Constitution, 28, 39, 40, 120, 130, 179

Federal Legislature, 72, 170, 177, 183, 193

Federal Party, 152, 163

Federal Union, 1, 2, 6, 7, 25, 97–100, 102, 111, 130, 179

fiction, 27, 33, 34, 82, 89, 151

Florida, 139, 180

foreign, 10, 38, 83, 84, 89, 156, 173, 175, 185

Fortress Monroe, 165

foundation, 13, 24–26, 32, 36, 40–42, 54, 60, 79, 82, 96, 133, 153, 154, 164, 166, 176, 178, 199

framing (political formulation), 6, 25, 28, 41, 42, 76, 105, 128, 131

fraud, 21, 26, 47, 48, 50, 113, 142

free and independent States, 88–90

free choice, 40

Free States, 76, 109, 118, 181

Freeman, Mr., 117

fundamental:
    doctrine, 158
    idea, 112
    law, 2, 6, 23, 27, 28, 30, 47, 62, 131
    principle, 21, 59, 108, 118, 120, 141, 154, 177
    question, 8

Galileo, 120

Garrison, William Lloyd, 112, 113
German Diet, 85
Gerry, Mr., 10, 19
Gorham, Mr., 15
government and politics:
    anarchy, 189
    commonwealth, 98, 104, 157, 194
    democracy, 6, 34, 53, 119, 172,
        175, 182, 189, 193
    elections, 25, 111, 166, 194
    federal government, 11, 20, 21,
        28, 29, 37–40, 46, 57, 69–71,
        74, 75, 88, 96–99, 101, 102,
        109, 117–119, 121–124, 129,
        130, 135, 136, 139, 140, 153,
        159, 160, 163, 169, 185, 186,
        188, 192, 194
    general, 92, 119
    imperialism, 34, 149, 192
    institutions, 93, 119, 134, 189, 192
    politicians, 3, 14, 15, 52, 70, 79,
        86, 92, 98, 122, 142, 193
    rebellion, 3, 8, 46, 76, 77, 85, 114,
        138, 144, 145, 154, 180, 184
    republic, 20, 34, 48, 100, 108,
        111, 115, 144, 169, 171, 175, 189,
        190, 192, 195, 202
    revolution, 20, 32, 88, 105, 116,
        149, 162, 185, 186
    state government, 76, 140
    taxation, 75, 110, 123
    voting, 60, 168
Gray, Harrison, 151
Grayson, Mr., 11, 201
Great Britain, 25, 32, 83–85, 88, 127,
    140, 148, 152, 155
Great League, name for American
    Union of States, 120

Greek States, 108
Greeley, Horace, 108, 115, 167, 178
guilt, 46, 109, 112, 146, 153, 159

Hamilton, Alexander, 23, 28, 29,
    37–39, 58, 60, 61, 63, 66, 70, 134,
    138, 170
Hartford Convention, 146, 149–153,
    155
Hayne, Mr., 149, 151
Henry, Patrick, 11, 52, 53, 63, 64,
    121, 200, 201
Hodge, Dr., 107, 140
honesty, 6, 50, 64, 67, 110, 113
hope, 2, 17, 49, 108, 111, 138, 170,
    184, 190, 197, 199
Hume, Mr., 70

ignorance, 62, 96, 99, 144, 146, 151,
    167, 168
independent States, 6, 61, 62, 67,
    85–90, 96, 98, 100, 127, 143
inference, 105, 107, 122, 136, 137,
    143, 145, 146, 154
inherent, 80, 98, 101–103, 106
injury, 121, 122, 124, 135, 170
injustice, 23, 47, 140, 175, 187, 188,
    197
Innes, Mr., 11
institution, 22, 27, 32, 76, 131, 185,
    192
instrument (political plan), 23–25,
    30, 33, 40–42, 44, 47, 48, 51, 71,
    75, 90, 94, 96, 154, 158, 160, 166,
    179
interpretation, 20, 26, 44–47, 64,
    113, 121–123
Jay, Chief Justice, 20, 83

Jefferson, Thomas, 21, 156, 158, 161, 165
Johnson, President, 115
judges, 124, 150, 151, 158, 161, 185, 192, 194

Kentucky Resolutions, 156–158, 160, 161
King, Rufus, 54, 176

labors, 4, 52, 63, 92, 175, 178, 198
language:
  Constitutional, 18, 36, 44, 70, 97
  of the fathers, 12
  influence of, 13
  new, 18
  unconstitutional, 10, 11, 13, 21
  unequivocal, 24, 43
  varied uses of 9, 12, 27, 82
  of written contracts, 94
league, 5, 23, 27, 28, 84, 86, 87, 120
legal, 9, 91, 108, 117, 118, 136, 137, 145, 154, 166, 172
legislators, 33, 35, 178, 190, 191, 195, 198, 198, 200
legislatures, 2, 24, 28, 29, 37, 39, 40, 52–55, 57, 60, 70, 72, 126, 147, 153, 158, 169–172, 175, 177, 182, 183, 184, 193, 201
lying and deception, 15, 52, 58, 68, 102, 113, 115, 119, 173, 176, 187, 193, 198
Lincoln, Abraham, 109, 110, 115
London Times, 197
Louisiana, 48, 139, 148, 153, 180
Ludlow, Mr., 167, 168, 173, 185, 186

Mackay, Dr., 119

Madison Papers, 15, 51, 105, 166
Madison, James, 1–3, 10, 20, 28, 37–39, 54, 57, 63, 64, 66, 67, 121, 122, 129, 132–136, 161, 169, 171, 175, 190, 191, 194, 195, 198–200
Magna Charta, 32
majority:
  in both branches of Congress, 171, 188
  infuriated, 3
  the North a majority in one branch of the Legislature, 171
  North had a majority in the Senate, 171
  northern, 34, 122, 123, 182, 183
  overbearing, 124, 175
  protect the minority against, 176
  of representatives, 171
  sovereign, 3
  South entrusted her fate to foreign and hostile, 175
  the South had a majority in the House of Representatives, 176
  tyranny of, 171, 175
  will of the majority of the States, 62
  will of the majority of the whole people, 62
Marshall, Chief Justice, 11, 70
Marshall, John, 97
Mason, George, 53, 55, 121, 129, 201
Massachusetts, 10, 19, 21, 23–27, 33, 34, 42, 64, 70, 76, 77, 90, 92, 97, 104, 105, 118, 122, 142, 146–153, 156, 158, 159, 162, 163, 170, 176, 180, 198
Massachusetts Bay, 140
measures, 6, 33, 157–159, 161

Mill, John Stuart, 108, 188

minority, 14, 62, 104, 112, 117, 123, 149, 155, 165, 171, 174, 176, 181–184, 188–190, 196, 201

money, 13, 44, 75, 94, 100, 139, 186, 187

moral issues, 3, 48, 78, 112, 117, 118, 136, 153, 166, 189, 196

Morris, Gouverneur, 19, 33, 47–49, 50, 51, 56, 65, 200

Motley, Mr., 5, 12, 41–43, 107

mutual promises, 31, 72

National Government, 6, 14, 15, 19, 29, 47, 51, 54, 56, 57, 70, 71, 88, 90, 134

necessity, 67, 107, 140, 148, 177, 179, 180, 184

New England, 20, 73, 104, 105, 141, 148, 149, 151–155, 159, 161–165, 180, 181

New Hampshire, 27, 104, 180

New Jersey, 167

New Mexico, 183

New World, 7, 33, 34, 106, 140

New York, 23, 28, 41, 42, 63, 70, 77, 134, 135, 161

Nicholas, Mr., 156

Norman Conquest, 25, 32

North America, 24

North Carolina, 11, 42, 98, 160, 201

Northern Demos, 181, 196

Northern Judges, 194

Northern Legislatures, 184

Northern Profits, 116, 187

Northern School, 14, 16, 52, 86

Northern States, 19, 77, 123, 129, 161–163, 171, 181, 191, 201

Northern Statesmen, 184

objections, 55, 59, 63, 64, 106, 121, 122, 177, 201

obscurity, 154, 156, 169

offices, political, 3, 114, 119, 127, 134, 149, 161, 193, 194

Old World, 25, 33, 69

one nation, 5, 6, 12, 36, 42, 44, 47, 51, 53, 59–62, 65, 70, 79, 82, 84–88, 96, 121, 122

opinions, 1, 6, 47, 66, 67, 72, 78, 119, 132, 134, 137, 179

opportunity, 21, 23, 26, 27, 32, 116

oppression, 121, 122–124, 130, 135, 164, 165, 170, 188, 191, 193, 197, 201, 202

ordinances, 23, 109, 121, 122, 135, 136, 153

Oxford, England, 117

Paley, Dr., 27–29, 164

passion, 1, 3, 99, 108, 120, 126, 127, 144, 189–191

Paterson, Mr., 167

patriotism, 1, 99, 144–146, 165, 184, 199

peace, 4, 37, 75, 84, 89, 108, 109, 111, 120, 129, 152, 155, 200

Pennsylvania, 10, 19, 41, 42, 98, 159, 170, 172, 175, 194

people of America, 5, 6, 36, 40, 46, 47, 49, 51–53, 60–62, 65, 70, 71, 79, 80, 82, 85–87, 91, 93, 95, 96, 121–124, 142, 147, 200

peoples, 52–55, 87, 93, 97, 139, 142

perversion, 52, 60, 122–124, 135, 136, 163, 181

Phillips, Wendell, 114
Pilgrim Fathers, 33, 118, 140, 141
Pinckney, General, 201
Pinckney, C. C., 168, 172
political:
  communities, 7, 41, 44, 46, 51,
    80, 82–91
  creed, 161
  free, sovereign and independent
    political communities, 90
  philosophy, 1, 120, 164
  power, 28, 83, 92, 103, 132, 167,
    173, 174, 179
  prophets, 198, 198
politicians, 3, 14, 15, 52, 70, 79, 86,
  92, 98, 122, 142, 193
poor, 113, 128, 146, 147, 173, 174
popular, 22, 33, 37–39, 79, 82, 162,
  175, 190, 191
possession, 58, 174, 178, 192–194
posterity, 2, 7, 8, 21, 68, 130, 195
power:
  balance of 166, 171, 177–184, 196
  cohesive power of public
    plunder, 142
  of conscription, 150
  a contest for power, not for
    liberty, 170
  of the Constitution, 96, 153, 169,
    175, 176, 196
  of defence, 169, 171, 174, 176,
    177, 184, 198, 199
  delegated, 31, 100, 101, 122, 135,
    136, 139, 157, 169
  despotic, 34, 142
  distribution of, 171, 176
  essential for existence of govern-
    ment, 28

  of Federal government, 6, 20, 21,
    46, 57, 63, 74, 99, 124, 170,
    180, 192
  of legislative repeal, 60
  limitations of 27
  Northern, 35, 41, 77, 188, 191
  of the people, 47, 97, 98
  separate and independent pow-
    ers, 94
  slave 114, 167, 168, 172, 178, 183
  sovereign, 22, 28, 49, 53, 57, 91,
    93, 100 – 106, 135, 166
  of the States, 86, 88, 89, 97
  struggle for, 7, 72, 119, 169, 172
  superior to that of the States, 5,
    44
  States have no power to secede,
    12, 43
powerful:
  aggressions of the, 170
  and determined opponents, 5
  causes of secession, 196
  compacts trampled underfoot by,
    22
practice, 9, 33, 34, 76, 106, 131, 139,
  142, 174, 195
presidents, 193
principles, 7, 10, 13, 21, 30, 58, 79,
  97, 114, 131, 137, 161, 177, 196:
  of the Confederation, 6
  of the Convention of 1787, 176
  abstract metaphysical principles
    of government, 172
  enunciated in the Declaration of
    Independence, 112, 160
  of political communities, 88
  of political philosophy, 1
  of Republicanism, 191

progress, 10, 70, 137, 142, 162, 179, 181, 189, 190

proposition, 17, 36, 50, 70, 96, 135, 143, 171

protection, 124, 132, 140, 150, 171, 175, 176, 185, 191, 193, 196, 198

provisions, 28, 35, 39, 46, 66, 82, 98, 100, 107, 113, 139, 178

pro-slavery sentiments, 194

Puritans, 140

Quincy, Josiah, 153, 154

Randolph, Governor, 11

ratification, 11, 20, 23, 26, 30, 47, 51–55, 60, 61, 65, 121, 122, 134–136, 153

Rawle, William, 145, 154, 164

record, 10, 15, 41, 47, 149, 161

representation:
    basis of, 167, 168, 171–174, 176–178
    effective, 38
    equal, 72
    taxation without, 100
    fractional, 166, 198
    pinciple of 145
    Black or slave, 167, 168, 173, 180

Representatives, 25, 32, 101, 148, 160, 167, 169–172, 176, 178, 182, 183, 199, 200

Republican party, 110–112, 117, 183, 191, 194

resolutions, 10, 18, 20, 42, 46, 53, 57, 75, 77, 114, 147, 150, 153, 156–158, 160–162

restoration, 77, 86, 115, 120, 182, 185

Rhode Island, 11, 40

rights, 6, 32, 33, 49, 53, 55, 63, 69, 70, 72, 82, 96, 98, 99, 102, 104, 113, 139, 142, 149, 150, 155, 156, 159–163, 165, 170, 175, 177, 181, 182, 184, 190, 194, 200

ruin, 4, 77, 78, 179, 184, 186, 188, 192

rule, 44, 117, 132, 159, 168, 175, 177, 181, 182

Russia, 127

safety, 53, 69, 79, 160, 177, 179, 181, 188, 192, 196, 199

Scott, Dred, 194

secession:
    act of, 2, 118
    advocates of, 11
    argument in favor of, 96, 108
    converse of accession is, 9
    doctrine of, 3, 143, 154
    duty of, 112, 114, 116
    furnished a pretext for emancipation of slaves in South, 116
    right of, 1–4, 5, 12, 13, 96, 103, 106–108, 118, 127–129, 131–134, 136, 138, 140, 141, 145, 146, 153–156, 159, 160, 163–165, 166, 196, 197
    as treason and rebellion, 8, 114
    war of, 3

secrets, 45, 82, 110, 117, 149, 152, 155, 199

self-government, 109–112, 118, 160

Senate, 7, 8, 13, 56, 133, 165, 169–172, 176, 181–184, 186

separation, 84–88, 107, 109, 119, 149, 153

Sherman, Roger, 178

Slave States, 74, 76, 112, 179–181
slaves, 111–114, 116, 132, 167, 168,
    172–174, 176, 187, 194
slave-holders, 111, 113, 114, 116
Smith, Sidney, 152
society, 6, 7, 22, 23, 24, 26–28, 50,
    51, 64, 69, 79, 90, 114, 122, 123,
    174, 175, 192
South America, 110
South Carolina, 42, 45, 100, 111, 118,
    138, 148, 149, 151, 164, 168, 172,
    201
Southern Confederacy, 125
Southern States, 124, 182, 183
Southern Wealth, 115, 187
sovereign:
    authority, 79
    body, 59, 61, 62, 65
    nation, 66
    States, 41, 49, 65, 75, 86, 106,
        119, 124, 129, 133, 136, 139,
        141, 150, 162
spectacle, 128–131
Spence, Mr., 45, 119, 131
State Constitutions, 20, 69
State Governments, 25, 89, 92, 97,
    99, 101
State Legislatures, 158
statesman, 21, 73, 106, 156, 175, 193
State-rights, 63, 104, 156, 159, 161,
    162, 165
State-Rights Party, 161
Story, Judge, 31, 85–87, 93–95, 128,
    134, 140, 163
Story, Justice, 5, 6, 8, 11–18, 22, 24,
    26, 29, 33, 44, 51, 64, 66, 74,
    79–81, 82–88, 91–95, 121, 128,
    136–142, 164, 194

struggle, 7, 63, 66, 72, 102, 119,
    179–182, 192, 201
Sumner, Mr., 113
support, 47, 58, 59, 61, 67, 76, 79,
    112, 114, 117, 179, 185
Supreme Court, 20, 85–87, 97, 151,
    194
supreme law, 28, 74, 75, 86, 118,
    126, 138, 147, 166
Supreme Ruler, 21, 23, 26
Swiss Cantons, 85
sympathy, 108, 116, 131, 142, 164,
    200
Syracuse, New York, 77
systems:
    change had been made from a
        confederacy to a different
        system, 56, 58
    grand system of the Federal
        government, 38
    infirmities of the existing federal
        system, 60
    mould the judiciary system, 48
    power of the Federal Govern-
        ment over commerce has
        been called "the cornerstone
        of the whole system", 74
    regular commercial system, 39
    uniform system in their com-
        mercial regulations, 38

Taylor, John, 45
Tennessee, 75
Texas, 74, 75, 132, 139, 180
"three-fifths of all other persons",
    167, 177
transactions, 11, 24, 33, 42, 46, 62,
    69, 174

treason, 3, 77, 85, 114, 125, 130, 184:
  against the sublime authority of
    the people, 46
  dialect of, 143, 144
  the doctrine of the fathers is not,
    144
  of Jefferson Davis, 184
  secession considered as treason
    and rebellion, 8, 143, 154, 184
  secession of 1815 as, 154
  traitors, 4, 58, 104, 105, 116, 130,
    144
  treasonable conduct, 66, 77, 143,
    144, 155, 161, 162
  of the weak is the patriotism of
    the strong, 184
Tucker, Judge, 21
Twitcher, Jemmy, 180
Tyler, Mr., 38
tyranny, 130, 140, 148, 171, 175, 189,
  202

unconstitutional, 10, 11, 13, 21, 70,
  118, 156, 182, 183, 193
United Netherlands, 85
United States Government, 114
universal concepts, 33, 40, 49, 55,
  74, 80, 94, 103, 136, 143, 145
Upshur, Judge, 45

violation, 5, 30, 35, 73, 78, 110, 141,
  150, 192, 194, 196
violence, 28, 29, 44, 113, 149, 175,
  180, 189, 190, 199
Virginia Convention of 1788, 64,
  121–123, 190
Virginia Ordinance, 121, 122, 136
Virginia Resolutions, 20, 57, 147,

  161, 162
Virginia, 37, 41, 64, 98, 121, 123,
  124, 135, 201
voluntary consent, 30, 31

warfare, 114
Washington, George, 11, 12, 135,
  144–146, 192, 193
Washington Cabinet, 110
wealth, 3, 25, 115, 172, 174, 179,
  184–187, 196
Webster, Daniel, 7–22, 26–28, 30,
  31, 36, 39–41, 46, 56–59, 61, 62,
  65–67, 70, 72–74, 76, 81, 94, 99,
  103, 121, 124, 133, 141, 147,
  149–151, 158, 162, 165
Webster, Noah, 39
Webster, Pelatiah, 39, 40
Western States, 181
white population, 3, 168, 171, 173,
  174, 179
William III, 32
will of the people, 79, 101, 145
Wilson, James, 10, 58
Worcester, Massachusetts, 77
       21, 32, 34, 45. 92. 156,
  168, 187, 197